Eloquence and Reason

ROBERT L. TSAI

Eloquence and Reason

CREATING A FIRST AMENDMENT CULTURE

Yale University Press
New Haven &
London

Published with assistance from the Kingsley Trust Association Publication Fund
established by the Scroll and Key Society of Yale College.

Set in Sabon type by Keystone Typesetting, Inc.
Printed in the United States of America.

Library of Congress Cataloging-in-Publication Data
Tsai, Robert L., 1971–
    Eloquence and reason : creating a First Amendment culture / Robert L. Tsai.
        p. cm.
    Includes bibliographical references and index.
    ISBN 978-0-300-11723-3 (cloth : alk. paper)
        1. United States. Constitution. 1st Amendment. 2. Freedom of speech — United
States. I. Title.
KF4770.T73 2008
342.7308'53 — dc22
2008010981

A catalogue record for this book is available from the British Library.

This paper meets the requirements of ANSI/NISO Z39.48-1992 (Permanence of
Paper).
It contains 30 percent postconsumer waste (PCW) and is certified by the Forest
Stewardship Council (FSC).

10 9 8 7 6 5 4 3 2 1

For if the worthiness of eloquence may move us, what worthier thing can there be than with a word to win cities and whole countries.
— *Sir Thomas Wilson, 1553*

Contents

Preface

Many people believe in the promise of the First Amendment before they set eyes on the actual text. Even if they do not know the precise wording of the instrument, they consider the cluster of rights guaranteed by it to be a badge of citizenship. As more Americans came to accept the virtues of expressive liberty during the twentieth century, the First Amendment became synonymous with social progress. Faith in the redemptive power of freedom of expression, in turn, enabled judges to apply constitutional text to encompass a breathtaking range of human functions: thought, emotion, utterance, spirituality, association, deliberation, defiance.

The principal aim of *Eloquence and Reason* is to present a general theory to explain how the words in the Constitution ratified by a distant generation become culturally salient ideas, inscribed in the habits and outlooks of ordinary Americans. This book employs the First Amendment as a case study to illustrate that liberty is not an end state but a state of mind achieved through the formation of a common language and a set of organizing beliefs. Interrogating the structure of the First Amendment as a governing discourse reveals more than the contours of a political belief system. It also uncovers the social and institutional processes through which foundational ideas are generated.

Chapter 1 begins by challenging reigning theories of political community. Such accounts locate the origin of governing ideals in a single (usually, imagined) moment of lawgiving. Instead of fidelity to hypothetically derived rights or to a single text, democratic constitutionalism is better understood as a project to cultivate faith in the rule of law and to build a political vocabulary for the elaboration of governing ideals. According to this account, a written constitution provides the key terms for determining a society's organizing beliefs, but they are not the only terms that matter. Instead of obedient subjects who conform to legal meanings dictated by text, autonomous citizens use canonical texts creatively in civic debate.

Central to this conception of constitutionalism is the idea of rhetorical freedom — a citizenry's right to reimagine the past and to determine grammatical arrangements. This idea preserves the moral agency of the individual and ensures that popular sovereignty is not simply a mystical phrase but one that can be realized in the social world. One's rhetorical freedom is not boundless but subject to the "precepts of eloquence" — the customs governing acceptable forms and procedures for engaging in public debate. The rest of the chapter evaluates the structure of First Amendment law. It does so by identifying three necessary features of any legal opinion that articulates and applies First Amendment ideas: rules of decision for resolving disputes, the political beliefs upon which those rules depend, and the popular language employed to explain constitutional ideas.

Chapters 2 through 5 analyze the First Amendment as a distinctive governing discourse, or, to borrow Quentin Skinner's words, one of "the changing political languages in which societies talk to themselves." While it assuredly was not the only discourse of power in twentieth-century America, First Amendment rhetoric became a force to be reckoned with during this period, encouraging support for judicial articulation of rights and affecting the development of other legal discourses. To the extent that judges and public officials present coherent visions of the rule of law with a plural audience in mind and citizens, in response, choose to manipulate these constructions for their own ends, investigating their rhetorical preferences can yield insights into Americans' enduring values and practices.

One of the most persistent but controversial features of First Amendment debate is metaphor. Chapter 2 defends a place for metaphor within democratic theory notwithstanding considerable criticism of its legitimacy. This mainstay of popular constitutional language helps to make legal principles cognizable by the average citizen; promotes linguistic affinity; lends law the appearance of stability; and eases transitions to new governing regimes. Although there are many methods of fostering social support for the law, metaphors — and the popular sayings that have capitalized on the most vivid of metaphors — have been instrumental to the advancement of free speech norms.

Chapter 3 turns to the task of identifying the social and institutional processes that produce and sustain constitutional meaning. The challenge for any
theory of legal transformation is to confront the demands of historicity and
predictability. A model must account for order as well as resistance. It must
explain the creativity of past constitutional outcomes and identify the source
of constraints on such behavior. To these ends, a people's discursive strategies
can be understood to behave within "linguistic regimes," a relatively stable
union of rhetorical practice, political tenets, and legal rules over time. Searching for noticeable continuities and discontinuities can be profitable even
though the existence of rhetorical freedom means that ideas and the words
available to convey those ideas are always, at some level, contested. Shifts
from one regime to another can entail changes to the rules judges use to decide
disputes, as well as changes to the active terminology at a historical moment.
To illustrate these insights, this chapter examines two popular tropes — "the
marketplace of ideas" metaphor and the rhetoric of fire — as evidence of the
social constraints on rhetorical innovation. It also examines the organization
of these metaphors and the historical patterns in lawyers' use of such devices.

Chapter 4 compares the experiences of two social movements that succeeded in transforming prevailing constitutional understandings: the civil
rights movement's expansion of the right to protest and social conservatives'
reformation of the Religion Clauses. Each coalition of activists and lawyers
utilized a First Amendment metaphor to rally supporters, focus public attention on a set of pressing social issues, and challenge dominant readings of
canonical text. In the 1960s, civil rights protestors armed themselves with the
meeting metaphor and, while resisting official control of their agenda, secured
lasting changes to free speech vernacular. In the years following the 1962
Supreme Court decision banning state-sponsored school prayer, social conservatives attacked, eroded, and eventually dislodged a reigning construct of
liberal ideology: the wall of separation between church and state. Each of
these movements engaged the life cycle of a linguistic regime by controlling the
political pathways through which governing language is created.

Popular movements are not the only methods of influencing syntax or grammar, nor do they comprise the only vehicles for generating countertraditions.
Intense rhetorical interactions between the branches of the national government have also altered the meaning of the First Amendment. Chapter 5 inves-
tigates how a president can impact the content of juridic discourse and the
pace of its development by appealing to popular sovereignty. It also illustrates
how complex the interactions between text and the spoken word can be.
Critical rhetorical interventions in public debate by Franklin D. Roosevelt in
the early 1940s gave a distinctly anti-authoritarian cast to governing language.

After the Supreme Court, in 1940, denied First Amendment protection to school-age Jehovah's Witnesses who refused to salute the flag, FDR gave a number of speeches extolling the rights of expression and religion. Apparently sensing the lack of institutional support for their parsimonious reading of the Constitution, the Justices reversed themselves three years later. In this sequence of events, orality and text interacted in such a way that judicial text lost its persuasive force and demanded rewriting. Over time, exchanges between Americans and their governing institutions produced a language of rights profoundly influenced by perceptions of the Good War.

Americans' experiences with the First Amendment suggest that judges have a crucial task: monitoring the aesthetic qualities of constitutional language to ensure its vitality in each generation. Chapter 6 defends a facilitative model of adjudication, rejecting the translation model of adjudication, in which a jurist's primary duty is to discern an earlier generation's original intentions or expectations. Besides settling disputes, a jurist must attend to the management of governing discourses. In endorsing, ignoring, or suppressing such discourses, judges help to determine the rhetorical strategies that might be active and useful in public debate. Adjudication as facilitation calls for attention to the social plausibility of readings of text and the accuracy with which the constitutional system is portrayed. Far from being anachronistic, this model of judging is elaborated in the Framers' writings on judicial power. It also accords with their hope that the Bill of Rights would become not just a "parchment barrier" but also a cluster of ideas that are both well known and widely respected.

The search for theoretical foundations organizes this study. Its efforts to bring questions of social process into sharper focus are based on one last premise: before one can make wise decisions about the proper scope of the First Amendment, it is a good idea to have a sound theory to explain the present.

Acknowledgments

I am blessed with colleagues whose criticisms have enriched this work. Bruce Ackerman, Nestor Davidson, Garrett Epps, Alan Howard, Bill Marshall, Michelle McKinley, James O'Fallon, Neil Richards, David Skover, Tammy Sun, and anonymous reviewers for Yale University Press provided detailed comments on the manuscript. Conversations with John Brigham, Barry Friedman, Joe Lowndes, Michael O'Malley, Jeff Powell, Nelson Tebbe, and Mark Weiner about the project proved endlessly stimulating. John Arsenault, Kaitlan Monroe, Margaret Otzel, and John Shuford provided valuable editorial assistance. Draft chapters were presented at the University of Alabama, Chicago-Kent College of Law (Illinois Institute of Technology), University of Oregon, Saint Louis University, Washington University in St. Louis, Seattle University, and University of Washington. The generosity of my deans, Laird Kirkpatrick and Margie Paris, permitted me to finish the book.

My interest in the concept of community as a faith system was nurtured early on by S. Scott Bartchy. He showed me how the words of a committed group can intimate its members' closely held traditions, their darkest fears, and their most transcendent aspirations. Finally, my investigation of these themes in the pages that follow would not have been possible without Tammy, Graeme, and Nora, who make up my dearest community.

Freedom as a Matter of Faith

Mostly ignored by the United States Supreme Court for the first hundred years after its reduction to parchment, the First Amendment played a central role in a transformation of American political identity during the twentieth century. During this period, the rights to speech and religion became defining features of citizenship in the nation-state and the enforcement of rights the primary responsibility of the courts. In turn, the reach and intricacy of judge-made law developed well beyond what the gentlemen of 1789 could have foreseen. First Amendment law today defines and demarcates an impressive amount of social life. No longer limited to the right to speak or publish, the "First Freedoms" extend to unconventional strategies of protest, artistic creations and scientific discoveries, and matters of the intellect, self-definition, and spirituality.[1]

An underlying order belies the unruliness on the surface of First Amendment law, but it is not maintained by reason alone. To appreciate freedom of speech as a distinctive way of life, it may be fruitful to conceptualize the law as a sophisticated system of devotional practices, rather than as merely a set of conflict-resolving protocols or commands backed by threats.[2]

This orientation promises greater descriptive accuracy for three related reasons. First, it goes some distance toward explaining the intensity of feeling that the populace has for the right to speak, assemble, and petition. Opinion polls and learned treatises consistently locate free speech at the center of democratic constitutionalism. As Kent Greenawalt explains: "[n]o one doubts that freedom of speech and of the press is a cornerstone of liberal democracy."[3] Some theorists posit that political community is, or ought to be, grounded in neutral principles of governance. However, it is exceedingly difficult to imagine that a promise of procedural fairness or disinterested decision making alone could generate this depth of support for substantive values.

Faith in the rule of law permits the people to be remarkably tolerant of the ragged patterns that First Amendment doctrine actually assumes relative to a society's professed ideals; accepting of the interpretive discretion of jurists and public officials; and forgiving of occasional mistakes of logic and lapses of judgment in securing its guarantees. Moreover, that Americans can continue to envision a unitary First Amendment while permitting a multiplicity of actors and subnational communities to regulate expressive life with significant variation attests to the deep wellspring of support for these foundational ideals.[4]

Second, the devotional perspective better accounts for the breadth of societal commitment to First Amendment values, particularly among individuals who enjoy no legal expertise or who have intermittent contact with the formal instruments of state power. Even as experts concern themselves with whether doctrine is coherent and predictable, ordinary people have rarely wavered in their dedication to its ideals. The chasm between the concerns of elites and the daily lives of the population is bridged by the political imagination. In such a faith community based on rule of law values, interdependent people are constituted by such values and modes of relating to one another.

Third, to treat constitutionalism as a close cousin of religious observance is to perceive the pathological aspects of historical practice as lucidly as the salutary ones — the tendency of free speech ideology to exclude competing structures of thought and valuation, a practitioner's willingness to cabin critical judgment within dominant categories, the danger of democratic ritual replacing rather than accompanying public deliberation. Once free speech is understood as a social legacy, such facets of constitutional existence can be treated as ever-present risks to be managed, rather than as the enemies of rationality that can be defeated once and for all.

While the people today adore the First Amendment, their faith was not always so robust. Even at midcentury, Zechariah Chafee remarked: "the First Amendment had no hold on the people's minds."[5] As the Judiciary awakened to its own role, provocative but isolated dissents were converted into soaring declarations of liberty; the fragile words of freedom emerged as a dialect spoken by the mighty and powerless alike. It is worth studying the rhetorical practices of those living with (and within) the First Amendment because citizens' speech-about-speech is the best evidence of what the polity as a whole believes, what it plans to do over time, and whether liberty may be worth the social costs. Not everyone, of course, has the power to make his interests known. To discern the First Amendment's social structure, we cannot stop at reasoned solutions but must get beyond jurists' carefully crafted representations of law.

It is one thing to claim that belief in the rule of law — particularly a conception of higher law grounded in freedom of expression — represents the basis of American political community.[6] It is quite another to arrive at the essence of the joint enterprise. Examining a society's monuments can provide a sense of its ideals, but the impression is likely to be vague and unsatisfactory; generalized as such dedications always are, they sacrifice texture for bland concreteness.

More promising are analyses of a people's vocabulary — their living memorials to the world. As Foucault tells us in *The Order of Things*: "Languages, though imperfect knowledge themselves, are the faithful memory of the progress of knowledge toward perfection. They lead into error, but they record what has been learned."[7] Foucault goes on to observe that "[w]hat civilizations and peoples leave us as the monuments of their thought is not so much their texts as their vocabularies, their syntaxes, the sounds of their languages rather than the words they spoke." His anthropological skepticism of text arises from a sense that "what is written . . . is always of less value as evidence than are the words themselves," illuminating a group's collective knowledge and self-understandings. Each society strives to "control the production of discourses" by enforcing "rules of exclusion" to determine what can be said, who can say it, and according to what terms.[8] In thus creating "speaking subjects," governing discourses discipline those who are described by or must resort to such modalities. For Foucault, studying history as "ensembles of discursive events" unveils the ideological and authority-producing aspects of a common language.

Now this is a historiographical principle worth bearing in mind: the contradictions of a people can be discerned from their communicative practices. Whether or not Foucault intended it, the implication that seems to follow proves equally useful: even if the visible representations of social control can tell only part of a people's story, social knowledge and discursive tendencies together may be sufficient to constitute a people unto themselves. As simple as it sounds, and as ancient as the idea may be, the very notion contradicts reigning accounts of political self-organization.

Instead of arising in the material world or inhabiting a particular place or time, Western theories of the state arise from an imaginary primitive society.

Hobbes envisions a world of every man for himself at the beginning of time; the state is said to arise from a mutual desire to escape this selfish and violence-filled state of nature. Locke's version emphasizes human agency over historical process, hypothesizing a shining moment when a society's inhabitants reach a meeting of the minds with the goal of taking their scheme of government beyond rudimentary rules of conduct. The moral philosophies of Robert Nozick and John Rawls build upon this prepolitical model to elaborate the just society. Taking the Lockean state of nature as his point of departure, Nozick argues that the "minimal" night-watchman state is morally justified— "[a]ny more extensive state violates people's rights."[9] Rawlsian justice requires us to imagine an individual in the original position, stripped of knowledge of many of his life circumstances, yet somehow prepared to bargain for himself and his fellow citizens. The principles derived from the prepolitical position both legitimate the state and represent the ties that bind individuals to each other.

Because these accounts do not arise from the world as we know it but instead are derived from thought experiments, they share a great deal with the creation myths of earlier peoples. Their assumptions are front-loaded and unverifiable; a great deal must be taken for granted if either theory is to describe democratic life in the here and now. To accept Nozick's articulation of social cooperation, we must agree not only as to the substance of a bundle of prepolitical rights but also that these rights apply as side constraints to a wide array of collective decisions after the state has been formed. Rawls contends that the individual, enshrouded in a "veil of ignorance," would select two principles for self-governance: first, equality in the assignment of basic rights and duties, or what he calls "equal basic liberties"; second, inequality of wealth and social standing as a just outcome "only if they result in compensating benefits for everyone, and in particular for the least advantaged members of society."[10]

Yet, it is far from obvious why the state should be theorized from such a deracinated starting point; nor is it apparent that any actual state has ever been founded by the risk averse. It makes far more sense—both in terms of paying due respect to the achievements of past generations and in arriving at deeper insights as to the constitutional system in action—if one starts from a position in which persons are equipped with the full range of human faculties and the knowledge of the challenges they face. As these precommitment strategies themselves suggest, the critical faculties for engaging each other about the good life are reason, voice, and imagination. Moreover, the most profitable theories of the state draw from historical experience, rather than from hypothesis.

There is another reason to eschew precommitment as a strategy for self-rule.

Such accounts provide too thin a foundation for community—certainly the kind of committed, risk-taking fellowship envisioned by the Framers of the Constitution. To see the weaknesses of prepolitical liberty, recall Nozick, for whom the grounding for civic attachments is the fear of one's neighbors as potential aggressors. The state, on this view, is little more than the extension of a neighbor's selfish ambitions—the aggregation of every neighbor's unfiltered desires. If anything, the state's monopoly on force makes it a constant threat to freedom, as others' preferences can be honed into instruments of oppression.

Where proponents of prepolitical liberty stress apprehension of violence as the basis of communal relationships, members of the Revolutionary generation set their sights on a more ambitious undertaking, one they believed "has no parallel in the annals of human society." Colonists believed that they had broken from the "political bands which have connected them with one another" not merely to establish a national protective association or to bring greater efficiency to governmental affairs but for the grander purpose of forging "the many bonds of affection" that would help society to transcend man's "reason and his self-love."[11] Many colonists expressed hope for a moral regeneration achieved through "patriotism and love of justice." Civic leaders spoke of a constitutionalism of "comprehensive benevolence" that would produce a "change of mind" and an antidote to ethical decay. The Framers' pragmatism in implementing their democratic designs was leavened with idealism about their aims, their secular vocabulary of governance infused with notions of radical reciprocity from the covenantal tradition.

Despite the simple beauty of the precommitment model of governance, it can neither account for the modern state nor ensure its survival.[12] A project to derive ageless principles from an imaginary starting point is not only doomed to overlook the actual practice of self-governance but also encourages another, more debilitating mistake: treating rights as end states to be preserved rather than as the terms for debating values and priorities. The suggestion that substantive values have been finally determined has a mystifying effect, implying that rights are fixed rather than contested and inviting abdication of the autonomy necessary to self-governance. The precommitment model, moreover, lacks a convincing theory of transmission, an explication of the continuation of the state. Even if deathless principles actually made up the idée fixe of self-rule, how would each successive generation know this to be true? What vehicles will its members employ to keep the revolutionary project from unraveling with the passing of their brethren?

What today's citizens have most in common with those of yesterday and tomorrow is not a compact or a bundle of primordial fears. It is not even a shared territory. Rather, it is a set of political beliefs and a governing vocabulary for the elaboration and internalization of those beliefs over time. A common tongue serves as a repository of collective aspirations, as well as the principal means by which a people's faith is manifest in the social world.

A language-based theory of constitutional democracy avoids the trap of the universal by insisting upon local knowledge.[13] In lieu of undeviating rules of engagement derived from thought experiments, it depends upon a people's historical practices in pursuit of a civic enterprise. Instead of preserving a priori conceptions of individuality separate and apart from the state, the approach treats individual self-image and democratic mission as intricately enmeshed. Constitutional language is the primary means by which the state reproduces itself over time. In the mind of every citizen lives an image of the Republic.

To the extent that tales of political genesis retain their vitality in American discourse, they are not dependable memories of actual events but vestiges of political imaginations from the past. Even if they fail as theories of self-governance, they remain part of the material used by the living to reconstruct their mutual commitments.

Text as One Aspect of a People's Vocabulary

If political faith is expressed primarily through language, and if — to borrow Jefferson Powell's elegant phrasing — America is a community built on words,[14] which words count? To put it another way, given that America is a nation organized according to a Constitution, what is the relationship between the words committed to writing and those committed to collective memory?

Those who reify text insist that where text is ambiguous or open-ended, the discursive habits of leading citizens who founded a society matter, not a prepolitical need for survival. Proponents of this position invoke a tradition that links Hugo Black to Antonin Scalia. But their mistake is to show little patience for what Clifford Geertz calls "the informal logic of actual life";[15] they profess an altogether impressive faith that there is one true reading of any text. Or, if they do not themselves believe this, they find value in projecting what they do not entirely believe for the sake of good order. For all of its defects, the text-bound vision of social life remains attractive because of its simplicity, the romantic aura of sturdy commitment. To profess to applying text strictly is to suggest, powerfully, that one's word is one's bond.

The difficulty is that no one living today wrote those words or forged those bonds — not even the commitment to freedom of expression. More than a minor blemish, this is the fatal defect of a text-bound vision of self-rule. Why should an autonomous person live according to another's word? The answer cannot rely on acquiescence, which is a negation of moral agency, a denial of constitutionalism itself.

Nor does a complete solution to the problem of agency come from the original inscriptive act. Jed Rubenfeld, who has launched one of the more comprehensive attacks against speech-modeled theories of government, contends that dialogue is incompatible with written constitutionalism. He argues that voice-based models are "presentist," constituting persons who seek merely to "live in the moment."[16] According to the logic of a sharp dichotomy between writing and speaking, Rubenfeld insists that it is text alone that can appeal to more than individual self-interest and survive beyond the conflict at hand.

Writing is an essential modality, but by no means the exclusive method, by which political aspirations are realized. The inscription of text tried to displace, but did not entirely eclipse, older folkways. Nor could it halt changes in cultural processes through which text is comprehended and contested. Despite the fact that legal texts saturate everyday existence, the practice of oral advocacy — ritualized verbal sparring over the meaning of governing texts — serves as a constant reminder that writings do not dictate outcomes. Rather, citizens use text to make practical knowledge out of political traditions.

The general will of the people is expressed over time, and it can be understood to exist — if it is to exist at all — only in terms that average citizens can comprehend and call into existence. Treating political faith as the generative force of constitutionalism dissolves the dichotomy between writing and talking, just as it unravels any hard and fast distinction between the present oriented and the temporally extended.

A decision maker should certainly privilege written text over vernacular where the two are irreconcilably opposed. That much is inherent to written constitutionalism. But, short of this scenario, it is difficult to say that text is superior to vernacular in the exposition of political faith. The moment facially ludicrous glosses are put aside, one must confront the reality that most of the time one is deciding among plausible constructions of text. The readings of text by presently constituted people are no substitute for original text if and only if social support for the two can be meaningfully distinguished. But little proof exists that extratextual grammar is inherently unstable or that words in the Constitution enjoy unwavering obedience. Indeed, there is substantial evidence to the contrary: the nontextual notions of "academic freedom," "freedom of association," and "freedom of thought" have become entrenched in important sectors of society; meanwhile, once dominant and codified modes of constitutional debate — such as labeling rights as "privileges" — have lost popular credence.[17]

In fact, introducing time (t) into a people's exercise of rhetorical freedom proves to be the undoing of writing's jealous claim of priority over speaking. Constitutional vernacular demonstrates its dominance over time; text becomes less dispositive as successive political struggles and social interactions fill a people's vocabulary. Suppose that at $t = \iota$, a mobilized citizenry enacts the First Amendment's guarantees. The official record of debate is sparse; imagine, too, that the leading men who draft the document and the citizens who ratify it are motivated by a diverse set of personal experiences under colonial rule. They deliberately select open-textured words, with an eye toward allowing the precise contours of expressive liberty to unfold through concrete applications.

Now assume that at $t = 1$ a decision maker must determine whether the text protects an individual who is arrested for failing to obtain a permit before preaching in Boston Common, a park operated by the city of Boston and made available for public enjoyment. Every reading of text is a function of accepted rhetorical forms, past readings of text, interpretive ingenuity, and relevant contexts. Observe how the vocabulary that is authorized by judges through actual usage changes along with context and meaning. Appearing before a tribunal, the street preacher argues that "Boston Common is the property of the inhabitants of the city of Boston, and dedicated to the use of the people of that city and the public in many ways; and the preaching of the gospel there has been, from time immemorial to a recent period, one of these ways." The judge consults the scant historical record and finds little of value, but still he must decide the question. Ultimately, the jurist refuses to recognize a First Amendment right to use the park. His rationale: "For the legislature absolutely or conditionally to forbid public speaking in a highway or public park is no more an infringement of the rights of a member of the public than for the owner of a private house to forbid it in his house."[18]

This statement comes from an actual case decided in 1897: *Davis v. Commonwealth of Massachusetts*. Already, the people living at $t = 1$ are instrumentally reshaping available rhetorical forms to create new meaning, rather than "enforcing" self-evident understandings of text. The decision maker selects the metaphor of the government-as-landowner from existing vernacular and reuses it in the context of late nineteenth century valuations of the commons. The choice of terminology is not altogether surprising, given the dominance of property rights rhetoric in the discourse of the age.[19] Legal rhetoric here initiates anthropomorphosis, depicting the state as "the owner of a private house," causing its apparent dignitary interests to assume epic proportions, and extinguishing any reciprocal obligations that might be said to exist in "his house." The stakes in the matter thus characterized, the scope of the First Amendment pivots around the state's asserted power to "absolutely control" territory and "absolutely exclude" unwanted guests from the sidewalk; the citizen enjoys "no particular right . . . to the use of the common." Having subjugated the right of speech to the right of property so completely, the only constraint upon the state's untrammeled power to exclude would be a competing property claim: "When no proprietary rights interfere, the legislature may end the right of the public to enter upon the public place by putting an end to the dedication to public uses."

As to the individual's further argument that the law invests in the mayor arbitrary and unreasonable discretion over speech rights, the jurist reasons from an expansive starting point that "[t]he right to absolutely exclude all right to use necessarily includes the authority to determine under what circumstances such use may be availed of, as the greater power contains the lesser." In other words, the language of property excludes the competing legal language of rationality. The state-as-property-owner can deny access to anyone, for an arbitrary reason or no reason at all. Choices made among the discourses on liberty rendered freedom the exclusive provenance of the state, rather than something retained or shared in by individuals.

It is, of course, child's play to fault this reading of text as unwisely constrained by the reader's own habitus and to demand that one instead employ a more generous reading of the phrase "freedom of speech." But it would be a mistake to insist there is a true reading of text or to expect an arid reading of law devoid of extratextual resources. Law can never be read out of context, for there is no intrinsic meaning to text; textual significance is always an irreducible product of the writer's and reader's social milieus.

At $t = 2$, when a similar question arises a generation later, subtext and context achieve their superiority to text. The 1939 decision of *Hague v. Committee for Industrial Organization* concerns whether a locality may repeatedly, and without a strong justification, refuse permission to a workers' rights organization to hold gatherings in the open air and at public places. The group asserts that "the ordinances are unconstitutional and void, or are being enforced . . . in an unconstitutional and discriminatory way."

On this occasion, First Amendment text is read generously so as to protect the planned activity. Jurists deploy an alternative metaphor in the hope that it will resonate with Americans who have recently experienced years of progressive politics, union organizing, and activism in the streets. It is that of the government-as-trustee charged with an "ancient" obligation to preserve expressive sites for the people's benefit: "Wherever the title of streets and parks may rest, they have immemorially been held in trust for the use of the public and, time out of mind, have been used for purposes of assembly, communicating thoughts between citizens, and discussing public questions. Such use of the streets and public places has, from ancient times, been a part of the privileges, immunities, rights, and liberties of citizens."[20]

The language of "trusteeship" has its origins in a legal specialty as well as in the political vernacular of the Founding era, evoking the notion of a temporary charge obligated to act to execute what is in the best interests of the beneficiaries of the trust.[21] Without breaking completely from the earlier model of ownership, the activated metaphor nevertheless facilitates an evasion of the earlier linguistic framework of "absolute" state power. Accordingly, the Justices conclude: "it is clear that the right peaceably to assemble and to discuss these topics, and to communicate respecting them, whether orally or in writing, is a privilege inherent in citizenship of the United States." Although the First Amendment right, like the state's regulatory power, is not "absolute," the law now ensures that "it must not, in the guise of regulation, be abridged or denied."

If one peers beyond the law's appeal to an unbroken tradition, it should be obvious that a new discourse has gradually emerged from the old, not displacing it entirely but presenting itself as an alternative way of portraying the state's role in securing expressive freedom. The word-picture suits well a New Deal Court that had broken the spell of *Lochner v. New York* at last, rendered in an environment in which "communication of views on national questions" had recently led to major changes in foundational values. According to this emerging popular orientation toward government, the benevolent state has both powers over and responsibilities to the people.[22] The government can retain the trust of the people if it takes care to act "in trust" of the sites dedicated to the exercise of their most precious rights. Applying these techniques to the matter at hand, the Justices determine both that the sidewalks and streets are to be treated as public forums and that the law in question must be invalidated because it can be made "the instrument of arbitrary suppression of free expression of views."

The interactions between text and extratextual modalities become more complicated over time, increasing the potential permutations in form that the law might take. As t gets exponentially larger, the evocative saying "time out of mind" and its related public trust concepts stimulate myriad elaborations of text resulting in the invalidation of antinoise laws, the protection of mass demonstrations, and other practices constraining the management of government property.[23]

Putting text in its rightful place reveals a deeper truth about the nature of constitutional discourse. It is impossible to commune with political ancestors; one can only act in their name. To absorb this simple truth is to understand that it is futile to search for a single, accurate channeling of the Founding generation's preferences. One is instead choosing among plausible visions of law. More than doing justice to a distant generation's choice of words, democratic constitutionalism involves justifying our actions to ourselves. Text is but one aspect of a people's vocabulary for this never-ending task.

The original act of inscription represented the dawn of a new age, not the consecration of the last one.[24] Text-bound visions of community are finally revealed to be not simply descriptively inaccurate but also dangerous. Collapsing vocabulary into text would obliterate the law's capacity to generate a feeling of ownership in the process of self-rule. The space between the written and the spoken must be protected as if our political lives depended on it. Rhetorical freedom — each citizen's authority to re-imagine the political past — fills this space between text and voice, comprising a necessary ingredient of authorship. It is a right corollary to and deriving from popular sovereignty, which is "a power existing in the people at large, at any time, for any cause, or for no cause, but their own sovereign pleasure, to alter or annihilate both the mode and essence of any former government, and adopt a new one in its stead."[25] Recognizing discretion to revisit the past and recompose constitutional language does justice to the human subject that text-based and precommitment models do not, treating the citizen as an autonomous actor endowed with human faculties and essential knowledge of civic life. In the absence of rhetorical freedom, individual consent and the general will are elusive fictions. Without the capacity to actualize sovereignty and translate aspirations into action, there can be no authentic destiny; there is only the unbearable past to be replayed endlessly.

Make no mistake: parchment matters.[26] That momentous break from the past, culminating in a written instrument, carried with it the imperative that certain words should not be forgotten by successive generations. But even its writtenness provides no guarantee of fidelity; social memory remains dependent upon opportunities for instruments to become tested and, in the testing, for text to have consequence in a given era. Nor does the fact of writing ensure any particular arrangement of the various promises committed to text. It is the priorities of a presently constituted people striving to live up to textual commitments that reveal how a society synthesizes the written and the spoken and determines what is remembered and what is forgotten.

Of all the foundational aspirations Americans have chosen to live by, the First Amendment has arguably ventured the farthest from its English and colonial origins. Whereas the nation's intellectual forefathers were most troubled by the coercive force of prior restraints, today freedom of expression extends to all manner of postpublication actions taken by the state that might unduly impede the free flow of information. The common law's disdain for prior restraints itself has undergone a dramatic evolution: no longer concerned solely with the constabulary seizure of printing equipment or the licensing of the press, the concept has proven capacious enough to encompass judicial injunctions against speech, predemonstration permit regimes, and other ex ante measures that inhibit individual or group expression.[27] The distance between the law's halting beginnings and the richness of contemporary constitutional discourse does not mean that society's commitment to free speech is unstable or illegitimate. Quite the contrary: it is evidence that law has successfully colonized the political imagination.

The Precepts of Eloquence and Reason

If mythological beginnings cannot bind the living, procedural rules are no match for a people's ingenuity, and text can tell us only where to begin, is there no limit to innovation? Does rhetorical freedom reduce constitutionalism to ceaseless wordplay? The short answer is that governing language behaves according to informal rules of intelligibility and legitimacy, and constitutional actors engage public debate in such a manner that observes these customs out of respect and a desire to communicate effectively.

For instruction on how a society creates and enforces such self-regulating language rules, it is useful to consult a treatise that explicates the interplay between rhetoric and statecraft. Published in 1553, *The Arte of Rhetorique* was authored by Sir Thomas Wilson and "one of the most successful books of its kind" of the English renaissance.[28] Wilson, who hailed from a modest family in Lincolnshire, studied Greek at Cambridge and civil law in Italy. Through hard work and good fortune, he rose to serve the Crown in a number of important governmental and diplomatic capacities.

In *The Arte of Rhetorique*, Wilson describes three ends for every oration: to "teach," to "delight," and to "persuade." He treats text in oral-aural terms, not as text to be read silently and absorbed but as literature to be performed openly. Wilson understands rhetoric as "an artificial declaration of the mind in the handling of any cause called in contention that may through reason largely be discussed." Part of the same scholastic tradition as dialectics, rhetoric— with its emphasis upon artistry and knowledge of persuasive form—nevertheless permits a wider range of appeals to logic, emotion, and experience. "[S]uch is the power of eloquence and reason," Wilson asserts, "that most men are forced even to yield in that which most standeth against their will."

Rhetoric's place in statecraft, Wilson claims, became secured through historical precedent: it was told that Pyrrhus, King of the Epirotes, frequently called upon the orator and scholar Cineas to convince entire towns and peoples to end their resistance to his armies. So successful was this strategy when a town would not yield to military might that "Cineas, through the eloquence of his tongue won more cities unto him than ever [Pyrrhus] should else have been able by force to subdue." According to Wilson, whether one represents the interests of the state or a citizen, the duty of every orator is to learn first the rules of logic and then the "precepts of eloquence." He then proceeded to identify systematically the necessary parts of every oration (he believed there were seven) and the types of oration (three: demonstrative, declarative, and judicial).

Wilson's general approach, which envisions rhetoric as "an artificial declaration of the mind," offers a useful organizing device for identifying the constraints on modern legal discourse once a structural turn is made. It is possible to understand the precepts of eloquence that regulate constitutional debate to consist of the customs identifying the grammar deemed acceptable for a particular inquiry; the conventions regulating the actual usage of such terminology; and the overarching purposes of governing language to elucidate, illustrate, and perpetuate. These precepts, in turn, are bounded by what is culturally feasible.

Social attitudes act upon the precepts of eloquence in three main ways: (1) causing some modalities to be active, and therefore persuasive, at a particular historical moment, while rendering other rhetorical forms dormant or unusable; (2) shaping the range of socially plausible readings of text in a given dispute; and (3) driving the expectations for the roles played by participants to a public conversation.

With this initial rough cut at identifying linguistic constraints, one can begin to solve the puzzles of agency and responsibility in the elaboration of public reason. First is the relationship between individual and group action. One person may voice objections to certain understandings of the Constitution, while another might feel obligated by group norms to obey settled interpretations. The source of such norms may be an institution, the nation-state, a local community, a civic group, or the family; invariably, constraints on rhetorical freedom arise from some combination of these norms-generating entities. Rhetorical discretion must therefore exist and be preserved at several levels, enabling critical judgment on a human scale while holding out the prospect of reflective action. There remains, at all times, a certain tension between the idea of individual voice and group action, with the latter dependent upon, yet forever at the mercy of, undisciplined exercise of the former.

Creative license turns on a number of factors, including one's investment in a prevailing regime of governance, the relative priority accorded to one's various group memberships, the formal or informal leadership roles one might play within a social group or institution, and other experiences that might bear on the disposition and objectives of a constitutional actor. Recognizing linguistic diversity and the socially grounded nature of language rules accords with Foucault's insight that a language exerts incomplete control over the human subject. At the same time, doing so incorporates the observations of analysts of constitutional language who stress that the patterns of actual usage acquire sufficient force that those who wish to move others to action feel compelled to operate within established forms.[29]

Identifying the precepts of eloquence as the primary source of constraint on rhetorical innovation leads to a second principle: skepticism toward claims of specialization or exclusivity in constitutional debate. Working in this tradition, Keith Whittington seeks to find a distinctive role for each of the three branches of national government. Although Whittington rejects the claim of judicial supremacy, institutional specialty remains a theme in his work that organizes bureaucratic actors, makes each distinctive within his own sphere of action, and prescribes what each participant to a debate is permitted to do and say.[30] Whittington's model of constitutional discourse insists that such distinctions are important, although it is not apparent to what extent they can be self-regulating or must be enforced by others. By contrast, constitutionalism according to the precepts of eloquence depends upon no firm distinctions between "interpreting" the text and "constructing" it — each involves, in the most basic sense, a public appeal to foundational ideas. For Wilson, judicial context presents differences in the consequences of rhetoric, not in the conventions that dictate the legitimacy or efficacy of one's presentation. The central factor in constitutional legitimacy is therefore not who speaks or even what one's end-goal might be but whether a speaker's representation of the Constitution conforms to the expectations of listeners.

A third implication, once it is acknowledged that the integrity of legal language is protected by differently constituted persons over time, is that the precepts of eloquence themselves cannot remain static. Incorporating the factor of time into the model arguably departs from Wilson's sixteenth century approach, which evidenced variation in an orator's purposes and audience but not in historical practice, but doing so greatly enhances one's grasp of language rules in action. Certain terms cycle forever out of the constitutional lexicon, even as others acquire such troublesome connotations as to render them no longer effective. The rules of exclusion that determine the sphere of rhetorical freedom necessarily change as the social conditions under which that discretion is exercised change. An actor's instrumental reasons for using constitutional rhetoric drive linguistic innovation even as they produce subtleties in public meaning. The key to descriptive accuracy for theory, as much as success in litigation or politics, is to identify and maximize the active terminology of particular moments.[31]

Rhetorical freedom, then, is not the absence of constraint. It is, instead, the engagement with past forms by the living to arrive at compromises over the practical value of traditions. In this endeavor, the mores that govern a people's discursive interactions, the memory of past historical events, and the prevailing ethos all provide overlapping constraints on rhetorical experimentation. Whether a presentation of law successfully instructs, stimulates, or convinces one's fellow citizens can be answered only in part by resorting to expectations of how debate should proceed. The rest of the answer must be found in how receptive others are to the message and whether their sympathies, in turn, are translated into word and deed.

The Structure of First Amendment Language

Now that a preliminary set of analytical terms has been defined, it is time to apply them in tracing the contours of First Amendment law. Contrary to Thomas Emerson's influential view, grounded in a theory of the modern bureaucratic state, the system of freedom of expression at its core does not contain "a group of rights assured to individual members of the society."[32] Rather, an identifiable set of political beliefs constitutes the core of free speech; rights flow from these foundational beliefs.

Core beliefs are logically and historically prior to any conception of rights; they are made concrete in the articulation, contest, and enforcement of rights. Legal rights do not naturally occur; they are a creation of society to identify, particularize, and perpetuate interests deemed valuable to political self-understanding. In the absence of a culture of respect for such rights, they are worth no more than the paper they are printed on.

Rather than mutually exclusive faculties, reason and faith are synergistic phenomena. Public reason can be engaged only by reference to widely shared assumptions about political existence. By the same token, constitutional attachments could not endure if they did not take shape in the material world. Freedom of expression today is a social commitment built upon several precepts:

1. The First Amendment is preservative of other rights.
2. Maximizing the quantity of speech perfects deliberative democracy.
3. A free society is measured by its tolerance of dissent.
4. Freedom of speech aids the pursuit of knowledge and truth.

5. Expressive liberty aids the perfection of the human.
6. Government should be agnostic toward one's perspective.
7. The right to speak is meaningless unless it includes some capacity to formulate an idea and deliver it with a reasonable opportunity for success.
8. A speaker should not be permitted to set all of the terms under which expression occurs.
9. Freedom of expression is worth the social costs.
10. Courts are suited to the articulation and defense of expressive liberty.

Each of these sincerely held political beliefs rests on a network of associated assumptions, rather than on scientific proofs; the expectation is that none of these root beliefs has been or need be subjected to empirical testing. As a people, we take the beliefs as we find them. Contested as these organizing ideas may be in certain circles, so long as they find favor among a critical mass of institutional actors and average Americans, the system may be said to persist.

Although Emerson argues that the right of freedom of belief "lies at the heart of a democratic society," it is more accurate to say that "freedom of conscience" has emerged as a politico–cultural value over time and that the corresponding legal right has followed. Similarly, when Alexander Meiklejohn confidently asserts that "[n]o one can doubt that, in any well-governed society, the legislature has both the right and the duty to prohibit certain forms of speech," his statement reflects that acceptance of the state's regulatory control over speech had, by midcentury, become equally entrenched.[33] That these opposing statements can be readily asserted as incontrovertible facts — often in the same breath — underscores the accuracy of treating expressive liberty in devotional terms.

Some free speech tenets have taken hold of the imagination in recent times; others have survived periods of upheaval. Recognizing that political thought lies at the center of legal thought is not the same as claiming that these beliefs have existed since the earliest days of the Republic or that they should be frozen for all time. It is only to accept that, in the ordinary course of things, law arises from politics and that the language of rights is a species of political discourse.

A foundational commitment may be expressed in governing text, juridic statements, official pronouncements, or the mobilized slogans of constitutional politics. But these manifestations of belief in the rule of law are always partial; they must be painstakingly pieced together before patterns of pooled learning may be discerned. Not only is a legal right the culmination of collective faith expressed at a particular moment in time; a right exists insofar as it is sustained by a continuing set of political beliefs.

Every article of faith is officially maintained through preferred categories

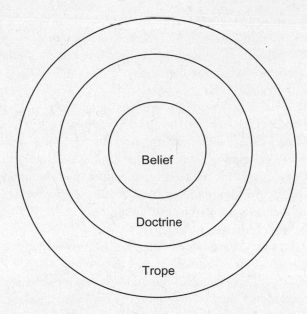

Figure 1

and rules and popularized through an associated set of rhetorical strategies. These tropes include memorable catchphrases, narratives, metaphors, and prototypes. Popular language "triggers" deeply held political beliefs. If doctrinal architecture is a manifestation of political commitment, then every poetic flourish contains traces of both doctrine and collective faith (fig. 1).

One of the most venerable root beliefs is that freedom of expression enhances deliberative democracy. It drives the work of theorists such as Meiklejohn, who argues that "[t]he principle of the freedom of speech springs from the necessities of the program of self-government," and John Hart Ely, who insists that the rights implied in the First Amendment's text are "critical to the functioning of an open and effective democratic process."[34] In the elaboration of this article of faith, courts have crafted rules such as the one that treasures political speech by requiring the most compelling rationale and a close fit between the state's ends and means before political debate may be impeded.[35]

Major precepts operate in interlocking fashion. For instance, the root belief that some types of expression are intrinsically valuable and, hence, deserving of legal protection presupposes that (1) a variety of social phenomena can be dissected, measured, and classified; (2) reasonably useful criteria exist by which to accomplish these tasks; and (3) lawyers are sufficiently competent and trusted to participate in an enforcement regime.

Each core precept operates less as an ironclad rule than as a social expectation; adherence to that article of faith by the average person, no less than the individual in a position of authority, serves as a baseline condition of citizenship. In this respect, a people's underlying political faith is richer than societal "acceptance of a rule." H. L. A. Hart conceptualizes law as a "union of primary and secondary rules" establishing duties and powers — with compliance as the touchstone. Hart posits two minimal conditions for law to exist: "obedience by ordinary citizens and . . . acceptance by officials of secondary rules as critical common standards of official behavior." The centrality of acquiescence to Hart's theory leads him to extreme outcomes: "The society in which this was so might be deplorably sheeplike; the sheep might end in the slaughterhouse. But there is little reason for thinking that it could not exist or for denying it the title of a legal system."[36]

Whereas Hart treats "the ordinary citizen" as a "relatively passive" receptor of law, Americans' faith in the rule of law can better be described as inspirational, sophisticated, and dynamic. Core beliefs are supplemented by a series of derived beliefs, distinguished by tolerance of a greater degree of deviation from these maxims. Inconsistency in adhering to these minor precepts apparently does not undermine our basic agreement to abide by the political-legal order or assault our political self. These minor beliefs, too, are part of a network of doctrinal rules and popular phrases. Take the derived belief that the state lacks the expertise or requisite sensitivity to make distinctions based on the subject matter of one's expression. That belief is represented in the strict scrutiny test implemented by judges, which subjects content-based distinctions to an exacting ends-means analysis. A pithy catchphrase — "one man's vulgarity is another's lyric" — reinforces the naturalness and timelessness of this supplementary belief and publicizes it for the common man. In linking a charge of blasphemy with a recognition of musicality, the aphorism popularizes the idea described by Fred Schauer as "the principle of non-judgment."[37]

Other unions of the technical and the popular proliferate in free speech thought. Today, Americans live with a collective sense that tolerance of controversial speech aids public deliberation, regardless of the truth of the claim. This precept is manifested as a legal rule according to which strict scrutiny is triggered by a law whose operation turns on the effect of speech on the listener. In turn, a general toleration of dissent is inculcated by a related popular saying that reminds citizens that they have no right to exercise a "heckler's veto." Similarly, governmental actors are instructed that a certain amount of precision is required in the drafting of laws in the hope that attention to statutory language reduces the risk of deterring worthwhile expression. This presumption is enforced through a rule that speech-inhibiting laws should be neither overbroad in scope nor vaguely worded. And, once again, the average person is given a modality for describing the deleterious consequences of the state's actions: such a law has a "chilling effect."

First Amendment beliefs operate in no way like rules, though their presence makes rules possible. The core tenets of free speech ideology may be stable at any given historical moment, yet they are invoked to design a multiplicity of doctrinal standards, which in turn may be utilized to reach divergent outcomes. Instead of dictating particular outcomes, political beliefs invite creativity within a range of possible behaviors; rather than eliciting blind obedience, they tend to inspire engagement and contest.

To illustrate the exercise of rhetorical freedom at the level of the individual and as a matter of collective action, consider the famous Pentagon Papers controversy, which entailed a claim of governmental secrecy and a countervailing assertion of the public's right to know. The dispute produced a fractured set of rulings, laying bare the various strands of thought, emotion, and belief that are ordinarily tied in a more fetching bundle. Lawyers for the United States sought an affirmative injunction to prevent the *New York Times* and the *Washington Post* from publishing a set of classified documents that studied the process of American foreign policy-making in Vietnam. The only rationale around which the Justices could achieve consensus was that "[a]ny system of prior restraints of expression comes to this Court bearing a heavy presumption against its constitutional validity" and that the Government failed to meet that burden.[38] From that single point of agreement, opinions spilled in every direction.

Each jurist appealed to widespread adherence to the ideal of robust debate but emphasized a slightly different aspect of that tradition. Ever the textualist, Hugo Black saw in the words of the First Amendment the Framers' intent "to outlaw [prior restraints] in this Nation for all time." Writing separately, Justice Black insisted that only such a bright-line doctrinal rule could do justice to our collective belief in an "informed representative government." In sweeping terms, he interpreted the introductory clause "Congress shall make no law" to mean that the "Government's power to censor the press was abolished so that the press would remain forever free to censure the Government." Given this starting point, it was obvious to Justice Black that "every moment's continuance of the injunctions against these newspapers amounts to a flagrant, indefensible, and continuing violation of the First Amendment."

Justice Black's concurring opinion exhibited a willful blindness toward the interpretive consequences of the moment; indeed, no serious engagement with the state's national security concerns could be discovered. He was sublimely confident that every calculus of costs was made at the moment of inscribing original text. His construction of the First Amendment bore all of the hall-marks of text-bound logic: an appeal to nonderogable rights inscribed in stone "for all time," a preference for one-size-fits-all solutions, and an abiding confidence in the efficacy of law-oriented corrections to the "abuses" of politics and "deception in government."[39]

The remaining expositions displayed greater nuance in the application of abstract ideals to the matter at hand. Keeping faith with the ideal of robust debate but parting ways with Justice Black on doctrinal particularities, Justice William Brennan conceded that prior restraints could be constitutionally obtained in a time of war. However, he treated this as a "single, extremely narrow" exception. For Justice Brennan, the best hope for reconciling free speech and the survival of the Republic lay not in a broad reading of the text but in demanding rich context. Before an injunction could issue, he would require government lawyers to come forward with evidence demonstrating that disclosure of state secrets would "inevitably, directly, and immediately" imperil specific war plans in the field. Whether or not his stringent legal test offered a realistic framework, Justice Brennan's vision of free speech tolerated no judicial restraints "predicated upon surmise or conjecture that untoward consequences may result."

For his part, Justice Potter Stewart paid homage to one of the basic expectations of a society organized under the First Amendment: "without an informed and free press there cannot be an enlightened people." At the same time, he advanced a line of argument based on institutional specialty: if the executive branch had issued regulations pursuant to its inherent and "largely unshared power" to conduct foreign affairs and tend to the national defense, it might be a different case entirely—a possibility that Justice Douglas rejected out of hand. In the absence of such representations of law over claims of political expediency Justice Stewart, like Justice Brennan, was unwilling to say that disclosure of the classified study would result in "direct, immediate, and irreparable damage to our Nation or its people."

Justice Byron White proved to be the voice of pragmatism. He expressed "confidence" that "revelation of these documents will do substantial damage to public interests." Nevertheless, he abided by the principle of prior restraint, a doctrine that actualizes a collective faith in the idea that the circulation of even terribly damaging ideas can be beneficial for democracy in the long run. Although he was unwilling to sign on to Justice Brennan's generous pro-speech formulation, his fidelity to the tenets of expressive liberty did not cloud his judgment either for the Government or for the would-be publisher; nor did it blind him to the real-world consequences of construing text.

The separate opinions of Chief Justice Warren Burger and Justice John

Marshall Harlan stood as bookends to Justice Black's unqualified acceptance of judicial competence. Pointing to holes in the factual record, they decried the "irresponsibly feverish" pace at which important questions were decided. Still, as criticisms of the circumstances under which the Judiciary's interpretive prerogative was exercised, they nevertheless confirmed social acceptance of the power of judicial review.

The Pentagon Papers controversy was just one contest, but it exemplified the basic contours of expressive liberty as a regime of perception and faith. Despite the deep disagreements that the case engendered, the Justices rallied around a central set of pro-liberty values. Inasmuch as constitutional vocabulary fashions and maintains a community based on ideas, a spirit of radical inclusiveness — exemplified by agnosticism toward the substance of one's expression — can be said to pervade our contemporary existence.

This spirit of nonjudgment entails some curious attributes. Despite a professed neutrality toward the content of ideas, in practice it has not meant that no distinctions can be made; rather, it has meant only that no idea should be excluded from the public square simply because the idea is silly, profane, or politically charged. Meiklejohn describes this widely shared ethic: "To be afraid of ideas, any idea, is to be unfit for self-government."[40]

At the same time, the ideal of radical inclusiveness exists alongside a penchant for exclusivity. Within the symbolic community of ideas, there remains a strong tendency to prioritize certain types of expression as valuable in a democracy: antigovernment expression, print media, artistic and scientific expositions. Ideas labeled low-value speech — such as the obscene, the violence-producing, and the defamatory — may be categorically excluded from the public sphere not simply because of the harms allegedly caused by their dissemination but also because they are traditionally unprotected types of expression. As the High Court has explained, "there are certain . . . classes of speech, the prevention and punishment of which have never been thought to raise any Constitutional problem."[41] Indeed, but for a largely unexamined adherence to custom, proscription of these types of expression would otherwise transgress vital secondary precepts: the first disfavors speech-based regimes that only indirectly combat social ills, and the second demands governmental agnosticism toward a speaker's perspective. With each of these unprotected types of expression, the chain of causation from an utterance to the alleged harm to be avoided is exceedingly attenuated (obscenity, libel), or the harm to be avoided arises directly from its effect of the speech on the listener (fighting words). Nevertheless, decision makers routinely violate both rules of inclusion when they confront a set of historically excludable words.

The coexistence of these polar principles of inclusiveness and exclusiveness within the public mind is best understood within a complex system of political belief. Citizens can apparently hold fast to both precepts without experiencing prolonged discomfort. Any dissonance is ameliorated through resort to special sociolegal categories, otherwise disfavored rationales, and assurances that the people have done it a certain way for as long as anyone can remember.

All of this underscores a more general point: no community can long exist without borders both real and imagined. As rare as it has been lately, the very act of defining something as not-speech but as conduct, or of refusing legal protection to obvious message-bearing activity, is to deny it status and space to flourish and to mark its speaker for separation. All of these acts of boundary maintenance reflect the necessity of ritual exclusion, even if it is only to confirm a people's existence and their ideals. Max Black cogently observes: "if a common language provides a universe of shared meanings for its speakers, it also separates them poignantly from the others."[42]

A white supremacist who sets fire to a cross for the purpose of terrorizing a black family has, at a basic level, forfeited his entitlement to participate in the widest zone of expressive freedom; he soon finds his liberty circumscribed in ways both large and small. A revolutionary who crosses over from abstract advocacy of regime change into exhortation of imminent illegality has invited official containment. In either situation, little sympathy is wrung from the fact that a socially valuable idea might be entwined with the individual's purpose to harm others or to sow general disorder.[43]

The degree of the state's legitimate response in any particular situation varies according to the nature of the expression, the strength of the state's countervailing interests, and the state's regulatory strategy of choice. In resolving a dispute, a jurist may sound as if the answer is obvious or commanded by the text of the Constitution or past practice. There is, however, no escaping the consequences of judgment backed by faith: a community has determined that these speech-acts go too far and that the coercive authority of the state may be deployed — in the name of the people — to penalize such behavior. Even faith has its limits.

Metaphor and Community

Evocative metaphors abound in First Amendment thought. Some are fashioned to remind citizens of cherished ideals; others are calculated to stoke their deepest fears of democratic excess. Expressive liberty means "free trade in ideas," Oliver Wendell Holmes pronounced in the 1919 decision *Abrams v. United States*, creating the imagery of an integrated and efficient economy to promote a legal order in which ideas move easily from willing creators to interested recipients. When a party proposes a more restrictive reading of text, he might caution, as Holmes did in another case decided the same year, that expression should not be tolerated "in quarters where a little breath would be enough to kindle a flame."[1]

More substantial than a flourish, metaphor remains a pervasive and puzzling feature of constitutional language. To its critics from within legal liberalism, metaphor is distracting, seductive, or, worse, antithetical to the aims of public reason. For many, its appearance in the law is a "pestilence" that must be contained and the tendency to resort to figurative modalities resisted at all costs.[2]

The strategy of those who have taken up the challenge of justifying metaphor has been to argue that it is ineradicable. This characterizes Steven Winter's defense of legal metaphor. Applying George Lakoff and Mark Johnson's research on the cognitive dimensions of metaphoric reasoning to the law,

Winter argues that metaphor is an element of ordinary language that is essential to the comprehension of ideas. For Winter, the ubiquity and utility of the device are sufficient to justify its presence in legal discourse. Because "metaphor is an essential aspect of human rationality, there can be no difference in kind between the 'rigors' of reason and the demands of poetry."[3]

Even if it is true, however, that the figurative can never be totally banished from the law, this linguistic reality can provide only a partial basis for tolerating metaphor. For if not all metaphors are alike in form or function, the ineradicability defense begins to unravel. Once the category mistake is identified, it then becomes possible to separate indispensable metaphors from nonessential ones. At that point, the absence of a more robust theoretical grounding for metaphor allows the extirpating instinct to return with renewed vigor.

Winter's refusal to distinguish between art and reason confuses the imperatives of the state with the necessities of private existence. Equating ordinary discourse with governing discourse threatens to leave the state at the mercy of popular culture and to render art unable to resist the demands of the state. If public reason serves functions even occasionally at odds with the objectives of poetry, then it is not enough to prove that metaphor is an act of human ingenuity. Something more must be said on metaphor's behalf from within democratic theory.

What are the functions of this small-scale art? Aristotle celebrated metaphor as a witty analogy that "produces understanding and recognition through . . . generic similarity."[4] For Aristotle, metaphor is merely one among many techniques used to persuade and achieve catharsis, relegated to the realm of rhetoric and poetics but not epistemology or ontology. Others have stressed the emotion-producing dimension of the device, its power to make one feel a sense of communion with a natural order.

More recently, Lakoff and Johnson make metaphor the centerpiece of their theory of linguistic understanding. Drawing upon the cognitive sciences, they contend that metaphor serves as the great building block of human interaction, activating an "experiential gestalt" that allows words to be decoded by those who share a common language. Consider two metaphors—the container and travel—used to illustrate Lakoff and Johnson's thesis:

> The meaning is right there *in* the words.
> Your ideas *came through* to us.[5]

Each metaphor fuses knowledge from two conceptual domains; new meaning is produced through the juxtaposition of these incongruous chains of connotation. As these sentences suggest, human beings organize ideas *in* mental containers of all shapes and sizes; they also send ideas *in motion* to persuade others. These linguistic structures provide content and coherence to ordinary language. Researchers in language acquisition have discovered that our capacity to engage in imaginative thinking arises from our earliest interactions with the human body and the world. Manipulating language creatively, a speaker maps knowledge from a heuristic with proven utility onto an unknown object or concept to illuminate the second idea. Further metaphorical innovations become increasingly abstract and sophisticated, building on existing linguistic models.

Taking the cognitive foundations of ordinary language as a starting point, a thicker defense of metaphor can be made by situating it in constitutional design and historical practice. Beyond its potential to elicit emotional responses, and beyond even its capacity to engage our analogic faculties, metaphor's virtues lie in its potential to elucidate and proliferate visions of the democratic order. In particular, these units of language play a role in the establishment and maintenance of constitutional norms by creating or destroying the narrative structure of the law and by relocating the sites of state authority.

It is essential at the outset to distinguish between basic-level metaphor and its specialized variety. Basic or first-order metaphors are fundamental features of communication itself. Thus, when Lakoff and Johnson explicate the container metaphor and the travel metaphor,[6] they describe two linguistic structures that are to the formation of ideas what air and water are to basic survival. One cannot avoid using such facets of ordinary language without giving up on the possibility of intelligibility. It is impossible to do without basic-level metaphors in everyday discourse, just as it is impossible to do without them in legal discourse.

The same cannot be said of constitutional metaphors. First Amendment metaphors such as the "bulwark of liberty" or the "revolutionary spark"[7] are not indispensable in the sense that legal utterances would be incomprehensible without them. Rather, these specialized terms are valuable in that they elaborate and psychologically legitimate a set of foundational ethics and frameworks for governance. By fulfilling a highly particularized set of state functions, they assist in the construction of democratic self-governance as a social practice that is lived, valued, contested, and perpetuated. One can certainly choose to expend significant energy avoiding such word-tools entirely, but something important would still be lost in the translation of constitutional ideas between public officials and the ordinary people who authorize their actions.

Call these second-order metaphors. This term signifies qualitative differences in category and function, as well as in importance to the dynamics of political self-understanding. These rhetorical compositions are more special-ized in function than are first-order metaphors, and they require more inten-tionality in their usage. Many are created in one doctrinal setting and become closely associated with a particular set of political and legal ideas, only to be appropriated for entirely different social domains. Second-order metaphors engage the political imagination in a more extended fashion and with greater ideological potency than first-order metaphors, enjoying a special capacity to cultivate belief in the rule of law. All manner of metaphor appear in the law, but only certain ones acquire regime-building significance.

Discerning the peculiarities of second-order metaphor does not diminish its value to the law but instead locates it more solidly within institutional dy-namics. Doing so also observes an elementary distinction between popular culture (the domain of everyday utterances, privately generated ideas) and legal culture (a realm in which even informal practices make claims of author-ity). The processes of constitutional language and ordinary language interface at crucial points, but their domains are not coterminous.

Every specialized metaphor constructs a portable vision of American de-mocracy. It projects an attractive and accessible image of the constitutional order, thereby helping to sustain an interpretive community. In appealing to this community bounded by the imagination, metaphor conveys a set of pre-ferred institutional arrangements, values, and sensibilities, with the goal of legitimizing or challenging an exercise of state authority.

As one prominent example of metaphor as a microsystem of political thought, take Justice Antonin Scalia's "culture war" metaphor, unleashed first in *Romer v. Evans* and later recycled to great effect in *Lawrence v. Texas*. In 1992, the people of the State of Colorado approved an amendment to the state constitution that barred the extension of legal protections to individuals on the basis of sexual orientation. The *Romer* Court overturned the measure as a violation of the equality principle that prevents the creation of a class of permanent outcasts. In a withering dissent, Scalia wrote: "I think it no business of the courts (as opposed to the political branches) to take sides in this culture war. . . . When the Court takes sides in the culture wars, it tends to be with the knights rather than the villeins — and more specifically with the Templars, reflecting the views and values of the lawyer class from which the Court's Members are drawn."[8]

In *Lawrence,* the High Court invalidated a Texas law that banned only same-sex sodomy, reasoning that it unjustifiably encroached upon the right to liberty. Justice Scalia's dissent elaborated upon the image-schema in which politics = war: "It is clear from this that the Court has taken sides in the culture war, departing from its role of assuring, as neutral observer, that the democratic rules of engagement are observed." Those who would take Scalia to task for the bitterness of his prose often miss the deeper point.[9] His terminology is effective and eminently quotable precisely because it cuts to the quick. According to the "gestalt" or "frame of understanding" activated by the metaphor, politics is a bloody affair, especially when controversial social questions are involved. The framing of the legal dispute in these terms implicitly treats homosexuality not as a personal trait but rather as a "cultural" choice subject to social control. If ordinary politics is akin to armed conflict, then we must learn to live with the fact that there will be casualties in the struggle over the manner of such social control. Underscoring the systematicity of metaphor, the frame also suggests that in such instances, the authority of federal courts is limited to enforcing certain procedural "rules of engagement."

Notice that the gestalt treats sexual minorities not as potential victims of the political process but as full participants; the presentation is designed to endorse a general policy of noninterventionism on the part of the Supreme Court. According to the vision of self-governance encapsulated in Justice Scalia's martial imagery, the people are better off — or at least have no cause to complain — when left to their own devices. Faced with a full-blown "culture war," courts are more likely to supplant collective moral preferences with poor shadows of their own when they "take sides." Judicial involvement in a matter characterized in such terms is not only deeply undemocratic but is also likely to lead to the rejection of widely held communal values. All second-order metaphors make populist appeals; Scalia's rendition of politics-as-war is simply more provocative than most.

One might react to this vision of law in any number of ways that reflect embedded theories of constitutionalism. First, one could adopt the perspective of the technician, whose primary concerns revolve around fidelity to doctrinal form, notice of rights and duties, and administrability of rules. From this perspective, it is tempting to say that courts should stay out of cultural conflicts, but it is more challenging to distinguish such phenomena from other highly fraught matters on a principled basis. Before one can accept Justice Scalia's binary characterization of the stakes, it is necessary to interrogate whether logical and efficacious standards can be formulated to justify even occasional judicial nonaction.

Second, one might sharply disagree with Scalia's ode to judicial passivity. The politics-as-war metaphor takes at its baseline the so-called countermajoritarian difficulty — the persistent notion that the judge is an aberrant feature of the democratic order because judicial review entails the power to strike down a popularly enacted law. Not only does Justice Scalia oversimplify the fast-moving political dynamics by suggesting that social contests are fair fights; he also denies that democratic values might call for the taking of sides. War is not invariably engaged by hosts of equal strength, and judges themselves are not to be confined to stalking the edges of the arena of conflict. This rights-privileging critique is most frequently made by the interventionist, who see the courts' business as primarily to curb majoritarian excesses. Cardozo's militaristic rendering of the judicial function serves as a nice counterpoint to Scalia's imagery that sidelines the judge to a position of neutral observer; the court's tools are part of an "armory," he writes, "capable of furnishing a weapon for the fight and of hewing a path to justice."[10] According to Cardozo, the judge's rightful place is on the front lines in the defense of liberal democracy.

A third possibility — reflected in an account of constitutionalism within the precepts of eloquence — is that elite values are unavoidable in governing language, but they are not monolithic. Justice Scalia presents an irreconcilable opposition between hegemony by intellectual elites (a risk posed by judicial decision making) and popular preferences (facilitated through judicial inaction), yet this is surely a false choice. Constitutional language always represents an amalgamation of elite and majoritarian conceptions of politics. Seen in this light, Scalia's hard objection to judicial participation falls away. A policy of nonintervention does nothing to alter the basic fact that governing discourse must be filtered through institutions populated by social elites. Conversely, judges' involvement in the production of constitutional vernacular may very well enhance popular self-rule. To borrow Cardozo's words, the judge is not the only one who has access to the legal armory, and, separate and apart from actual outcomes, the judge can hone rhetorical weapons that prove useful for others in the pursuit of their constitutional causes.

When the occasion suited him, Holmes proved willing to reverse the polarity of connotations in the fire metaphor in order to remind the populace that "eloquence may set fire to reason." On such occasions, his implication was this: not only can speech instruct, but provocative expression can stimulate rational discussion. It should be increasingly apparent that eloquence does far more than set fire to reason. Figurative language, in particular, aids democratic institution building in several respects that go beyond the reinforcement of legal propositions. Constitutional actors deploy metaphors to teach lessons about the possibilities and limits of freedom, ritually establish the boundaries of the relevant interpretive world, and ease social transitions. Specifically, figurative language:

- Constitutes a political community and fosters bonds of fellowship;
- Converts constitutional ideals into terms accessible to and usable by members of the community;

- Legitimates institutional relationships and role themes; and
- Repairs rifts in the political imagination posed by changed social norms, changes in governing personnel, and political realignments.

Each function of popular constitutional language addresses a facet of civic myth-making. The term "myth" is used here nonpejoratively to describe the synthetic processes through which belief in the existence of a nation-state and its organizing values are cultivated over time.

Promoting Fellowship

The challenge for statesmen of every age is to form a lasting and more just society. Built by human hands, a constitutional democracy must nevertheless transcend human frailties. If and only if the new order survives its birthmoment can a people begin to fulfill its dream of a "more perfect union."[11] Unless a founding generation's energy and public-spiritedness are captured so as to inspire its heirs, its greatest achievements will pass away with the age.

It is no secret that the Framers' solution emphasized institutional design writ large: a division of formal authority vertically (federalism) and horizontally (separation of powers). Although the precise relationship between political culture and ruling institutions was left undertheorized, their necessary interconnections are evidenced by plentiful colonial descriptions of Americans as "a people descended from the same ancestors, speaking the same language, professing the same religion, attached to the same principles of government, very similar in their manners and customs."[12]

As a product of the political culture, metaphor can be understood as an element of democratic design writ small, a method of presenting a community's governing precepts so as to maximize popular consumption. To the extent its vividness stimulates reflection, such a composition facilitates the internalization of foundational principles and guards against erosion of the political order from within. Although classical theorists concentrated on curricular programs to inculcate virtue, democratic idioms arguably do as much work to spread and sustain governing ideals.

Plato slyly admits as much in *The Republic*. Foreseeing the need to engage in storytelling in order to forge "the courage of the citizen,"[13] he choreographs this exchange between the figure of Socrates and his companions:

> But still, hear the rest of the myth: "All of you in the city are brothers," we'll tell them, "but the most precious are the ones fit to rule, because when the god formed you at birth he mixed gold into them, silver into the auxiliaries, and iron and bronze into the farmers and craftsmen." . . . And we'll pretend there's

an oracle that predicts the downfall of the city when she's guarded by the guardian of iron or bronze. Can you think of a scheme to make them believe this tale, Glaucon?

"Not them," he replied, "But their sons and descendants and all later peoples."[14]

For Plato, the myth of the ideal city's origins extends the state from a brick-and-mortar institution to a realm ruled by the senses. According to Plato's metaphoric reasoning, a well-ordered society consists of political equals (accomplished through resort to familial descriptors) whose different talents are maximized (the complicating deployment of varying metals and skill sets). Civic storytelling negotiates the tension between organizing ideals and the practicalities of governance while simultaneously joining past, present, and future subjects of the law into a single temporal community — the paradigm-smashing founders along with their "sons, and descendants, and all later peoples." Plato's political mythology is enabled by an extended metaphor of a society populated by persons born of different metals, as well as the metonymic identification of each citizen-type with a particular social function. This entire social order is derived from an external source of law — the "oracle."

As his turn to the figurative implies, practical considerations preclude workaday governance by too large a group — hence the necessity of cultivating the virtuous among the many without relinquishing the idea of civic equality. Elsewhere, Plato selects a revealing metaphor to describe the process of political acculturation as "a scheme to persuade [the guardians-to-be] to take our laws like a beautiful dye."[15] Thus, despite his consistent claim that there is a difference between direct accounts of reality and those that depend on likenesses and secondary images, Plato's own choice of words presumes the existence of a linguistic process for making sense of the polity's ideals.

To be sure, practitioners of classical republicanism failed to appreciate any incongruity between the promise of civic equality and the exclusion of women, slaves, and other social outcasts from public life. Moreover, their reliance on specialization and social status ran the risk of reproducing vertical hierarchy without eliciting broad horizontal participation. Nevertheless, a valuable insight — one that can be recovered from the debris of the past — is that metaphor imposes order on human existence to give it shared identity and destiny. It is not necessary to ally oneself with the most extreme abuses of rhetorical power to recognize that figurative language is not only a proper implement of statecraft but also one of the principal means for a democratic society to reproduce itself. Face-to-face interactions may be more difficult in the modern republic, but the underlying cultural strategy for inculcating civic ideals remains the same.

In *The Republic,* a well-timed shift to figurative language draws listeners and readers into the very ideal state that Plato describes; the characters' verbal exchanges constitute the community by populating and ordering the city. Moreover, Plato himself models the behavior expected of every citizen in a democracy: an ability to deploy popular language in order to interact with others, a willingness to experiment with political forms, the desire to enter into a lasting fellowship. Writing in another era, Sir Thomas Wilson expressed similar optimism that metaphor could be domesticated by the state, deeming an oration "wonderfully enriched when apt metaphors are got and applied to the matter."[16] Wilson, like Plato and Aristotle before him, saw value in harnessing the potential of the figurative: "Neither can any one persuade effectuously, and win men by weight of his oration without the help of words altered and translated."

The capacity of popular language to constitute a people is confirmed in more recent studies. In *Imagined Communities*,[17] Benedict Anderson argues that the rise of vernacular and print capitalism tied the people of early modern Europe together such that nationalism could become possible. These changes ended the dominance of Latin as a governing discourse, reduced the power of religiously inspired time, and lent a greater sense of permanence to the idea of a people. Anderson posits that emerging rhetorical forms — which he called "languages of power" — made possible the recalibration of the connections among fraternity, sovereignty, and time. In analogous fashion, it may be possible to say that political idioms bind Americans in such a way that "in the minds of each lives the image of their community."[18] Common linguistic modes of governance unite the populace even though it may be divided by substantive goals and backgrounds. These distinctive languages of power are the vehicles through which foundational text becomes inscribed upon the political psyche.

It is possible to understand the crafting of judicial text, and the use of metaphor in doing so, as the enterprising use of popular language to enforce the idea of a nation. Consider the spectacular vision of political fraternity on display in the flag salute controversy of 1943. Initially disposed to grant school boards the authority to punish school-age Jehovah's Witnesses who refused to pay homage to this emblem of nationhood, the Supreme Court suddenly reversed course to hold such a practice abhorrent to the First Amendment. Robert Jackson's landmark ruling, *West Virginia State Board of Education v. Barnette*, pursued a two-track strategy of persuasion. On one level, the Justices and the parties before them battled over the applicability of precedent (including whether to overrule a prior decision), the intentions of school officials in demanding observance of the flag, and the significance of operative facts — all matters bearing upon what Philip Bobbitt has helpfully described as the six "modalities of constitutional argument."[19] But, for all his efforts at defining rhetorical forms, Bobbitt goes too far in drawing the line at the literal: "There is no constitutional legal argument outside these modalities. Outside these forms, a proposition about the U.S. constitution can be a fact, or be elegant, or be amusing or even poetic, and although such assessments exist as legal statements in some possible legal world, they are not actualized in our legal world."

For, on another plane, in *Barnette,* illustrative metaphors created competing visions of democratic existence — the stuff of popular constitutional meaning-making. If the first set of rhetorical forms were aimed at convincing lawyers and policymakers of the wisdom of the decision, the second set helped to draw for ordinary Americans the symbolic contours of political community and the values that constitute the community. "If there is any fixed star in our constitutional constellation," Justice Jackson explained, "it is that no official, high or petty, can prescribe what shall be orthodox . . . or force citizens to confess by word or act their faith therein." This quotable maxim — devoid of jargon, full of populist brio — would become an influential tool in the construction of a political community in which belief in expressive liberty is a defining feature.[20] The phrase treats that temporal community as a given, existing prior to any particular conflict and outliving the crisis of the moment.

The celestial metaphor rings in this revelation: political elites cannot demand lock-step obedience from the people, any more than they can seat a permanent ruling class. If democracy is to thrive in the minds of the citizenry, it must be secured through the word and the spirit, rather than the sword. This is the central article of faith of the normative community fashioned through judicial exposition of text. Like Plato's own appeal to an oracle as the source for the civic myth, the *Barnette* Court formally objectifies and externalizes the source of law in a constitutional text; resort to the existence of a "constitutional constellation" evokes and reinforces the claim of an external authority.

By introducing a new image into the dispute over the social significance of the American flag — a "fixed star" — and juxtaposing the two symbols, the opinion fashions an iconographic hierarchy in which the star supplants the flag in legal significance without diminishing its political radiance. In so doing, the Justices subtly turn a discrete dispute over patriotism (flag) into a never-ending debate over higher principles (constellation), thereby subordinating the first set of state interests to the second, more enduring set of concerns. The message: as soaring as the flag might be, one's affection for a national treasure should not be equated with, much less be allowed to preempt, fidelity to constitutional ideals. A people might be moved by flags, but it must be guided by stars.

The High Court's pair of controversial rulings shielding flag burning as a type of symbolic expression paints similarly resplendent word-pictures of public life. Aware that the ultimate fate of any conception of political community lies with the people, jurists couch their arguments in strikingly populist terms. What the Justices themselves refer to as a "joust of principles"[21] transpires on two planes at once: the literal and the symbolic. Juridic language facilitates interplay between doctrine and iconography, knowledge and faith, the mundane and the infinite.

Subtly characterizing the government as a diligent owner of intellectual property, some of the Justices in dissent argue that the flag is "an important national asset" and that the state is within its rights to restrain others from "tarnish[ing] its value" in the marketplace. Deterring a flag burner, John Paul Stevens suggests, is no different from punishing someone for leaving "graffiti on the Washington Monument" or "spray paint[ing] . . . his message of dissatisfaction on the façade of the Lincoln Memorial."[22]

In response, Justice Brennan's opinion for the Supreme Court in *Texas v. Johnson* asserts that if there is a finite resource at stake, it is liberty, and incarcerating the flag burner "dilute[s] the freedom that this cherished symbol represents."[23] The ruling goes on to generate momentum for the unassailable logic of expressive liberty with a flurry of evocative second-order metaphors. There are other "virtually sacred" principles such as racial equality, he points out, but the First Amendment does not shield them so they might remain "unquestioned in the marketplace of ideas."[24] In this manner, the Court counteracts the flag-as-property metaphor with its mirror image: the antidesecration law as an unfair measure to restrain trade.

The ruling closes by capturing the "persuasive power of the flag itself" in a plea for the people to seek common ground. The flag is reconceived and "immortalized" as a metonym for the people's most noble instincts: "the Nation's resilience," its citizenry's courage and self-reliance.[25] Have no fear, the Court suggests, the flag will remain intact for as long as the people subscribe to its principles; the flag's symbolism is timeless, untouchable. Expelling the misfit from their midst will do more harm than good to the bonds of fellowship, the move implies, defiling the organizing principles for which the flag stands.

Notice that this rhetorical strategy momentarily invites citizens to separate their belief in America's ideals (spirit) from physical representations of that belief (symbol). This method of decoupling creates the necessary mental space for observers to accept the fact that a flag burner will go unpunished, while affirming their devotion to the rule of law. Constitutional rhetoric exploits the people's belief in a distinction between higher law and ordinary law in order to bridge antagonistic voices in the community.

There is a unifying message communicated once again in poetic terms: the "fixed star" of the American political order, its "bedrock principle," its "life-blood," is none other than the First Amendment. The Justices' metaphors of choice impart the seeming stability, vibrancy, and unassailability of the principle that toleration of antigovernment expression should be an organizing ideal of the nation's long-term enterprise.[26] If the nation itself was conceived in a disrespectful act of revolt, then the practice of dissent must be enshrined as an "article of faith" in the democratic system.

It is now possible to discern the contours of the imagined community partially inscribed by metaphor: it is constituted by tolerance of ideas, regardless of how disturbing. The fates of the proponent and the opponent of an idea are inseparably linked by a single tradition. The instigator and the corruptor may still be banished from our midst, but only under stringent conditions; the hate-monger, the blasphemer, the fool, and the ingrate must be suffered, one and all.

Leveling the Constitution

Locke, who theorized a contract-based origin for civil society, also explicated a philosophy of knowledge. *An Essay Concerning Human Understanding* is a broad-ranging treatment of the origins and nature of human knowledge, its relation to the divine and the material world, and the methods by which knowledge is shared. In his analysis of words as signifiers of ideas, Locke is singularly dismissive of figurative modalities. Hoping to banish these devices from reason's empire, he calls them "cheats," which "in all discourses that pretend to inform or instruct, [are] wholly to be avoided." His rationale: "the artificial and figurative application of words . . . are for nothing else but to insinuate wrong ideas, move the passions, and thereby mislead the judgment."[27] Although Locke begins in promising fashion by situating language in human experience and describing it as "the great instrument and common tie of society," he abruptly goes astray. He treats language as wholly "subservient to instruction and knowledge" in the search for preexisting truths. For Locke, the chief ends of language are to "make known one man's thoughts or ideas to another"; "to do it with as much ease and quickness as possible"; and "thereby to convey the knowledge of things." Because of the "great reputation" of the rhetorical tradition, he stops short of calling figurative speech and allusion "an imperfection or abuse" of language. Locke relies on a distinction between "harangues and popular addresses" and "all discourses that pretend to inform or instruct" in order to isolate metaphor, but it is obvious that, unlike Wilson, he dismissively relegates rhetorics to the "arts of deceiving."

To dissolve the Lockean premise of incompatibility, the most profitable starting point is a proposition borne out in cognitive science: virtually anyone can construct a metaphor or disassemble one. No special tutelage is necessary to participate in this exercise; a neophyte could do it. In fact, the lasting insight of empiricists who study language acquisition is that these skills are second nature, one part hard-wiring and one part cultural know-how.[28] Studies show that children display ingenuity, playfulness, and diligence as they construct their worlds of meaning through trial and error. An early awakening to metaphorical experimentation is followed by a more literal stage of linguistic development, but the vast majority of adults retain the imaginative capacity to shape social experience in symbolic and relational ways.

Metaphors are culled from a reservoir of shared life experiences radiating outward from our physical interactions with our environment — this is what Mark Johnson means when he considers metaphor to be "embodied."[29] Consider Felix Frankfurter's comment in *Butler v. Michigan* that reducing the scope of permissible reading material to that which is fit only for children amounts to "burning down the house to roast the pig."[30] Butler challenged his conviction for selling obscene literature that "manifestly tend[ed] to the corruption of the morals of youth." Citing the First Amendment and dispatching this legal saying, the Court reversed his conviction and ordered his release.

The house-on-fire metaphor hones a delicacy, the home, and an all-too-common disaster into a finely wrought instrument to serve pro-speech norms. As almost anyone with a rudimentary knowledge of the law can grasp, the act of roasting a pig stands for the well-intentioned act of the government, while the metaphorical house signifies our constitutional order. The combination of these representations creates new meaning. As Justice Frankfurter articulates the embedded principle elsewhere: "the law respects the wisdom of not burning even part of a house" in pursuit of laudable goals.[31] The composition enlists the bodily sensations of pain, fear, and sympathy to teach lessons about the rule of law. An aphorism that warns against unnecessary risk-taking to satisfy private urges is converted into a reminder that public values may be eroded in the name of popular aims.

A number of additional observations can be made as to the salutary qualities of nonliteral modalities. Metaphor can be showy or subtle, and it is easily manipulated. It is but a fragment of constitutional thought, necessarily unfinished. Nevertheless, each of the traits Locke disparages can, on balance, be said to add value to civic debate. In fact, even under Locke's own standards as to the proper ends of language — efficient instruction of another and the diffusion of knowledge — it is possible to appreciate not only why the state resorts to the figurative but also why the state should encourage citizens' facility with the technique. The leveling characteristics of such political vernacular can be traced along four trajectories: instantiation, access, portability, and differentiation.

A specialized metaphor fuses high-minded abstraction and gritty experience. It relies heavily on bodily understandings: a need for nourishment, covetousness of rare things, a desire for bodily integrity and shelter, a fear of incursions. Note that a referenced event need not have been actually experienced by a reader or listener for the modality to work (*e.g.*, caught in a fire); one need only be able to have sensory reactions and expect certain reactions to flow from particular events (*e.g.*, pain and unease from the presence of fire).

In mapping governing principles onto day-to-day events, the composition instantiates technical and abstract ideas. Acquiring physical form through association with bodily ideas and common objects renders governing principles salient to a citizen's daily life. The concretizing force of metaphor, in turn, has two salutary consequences: first, the communicative technique extends the audience beyond the immediate participants in a dispute to others who may viscerally identify with the parties or their respective agendas; second, metaphor engages strangers to a conversation in a manner that increases the chances that they will feel a personal stake in the outcome.

Instantiation and open texture are mutually reinforcing. Metaphor's unification of daily event and official program renders governing principles accessible to laypersons. Individuals unschooled in the fine points of doctrinal argumentation can appreciate the gist of the typical second-order metaphor. The capaciousness of the modality makes taking advantage of it a fairly simple matter. Rudimentary knowledge of how figurative language operates is all that is required for a turn at rhetorical innovation. So long as citizens who possess the innate human ability to have emotionally differentiating responses to visual or aural stimuli and to categorize social experiences exist in sufficient numbers, the material of daily existence can be drawn upon to convey constitutional meaning.

Thus, the risk that any particular metaphor will mystify or mislead is ameliorated in part by its malleability, the ease with which an individual can reinvent the form and challenge its intended message. Although figurative rhetoric is by its nature incomplete, it is not significantly less complete than features of legal argumentation that provoke comparatively less outcry: allusions, slippery slopes, and analogies. These other features of language, too, may be abused on occasion, but few would go so far as to enjoin their use in all instances.

Comprehension and usage of popular language breed both facility with form and fidelity to a set of ideas. This likely results from the interconnectedness of governing precepts and the words used to convey them. Exposure to one necessitates exposure to the other. Intelligible usage of a people's vocabulary forces confrontation with substance as well as form. An individual who contends that judges should stay out of "culture wars" or declares in legal filings that toleration of dissent is "the cornerstone of our democracy," simultaneously claims the rhetorical birthright that citizenship affords and demonstrates loyalty to the polity.[32] In this sense, usage of established rhetorical forms is not the reflection of a strategic choice alone. It also signals to listeners that the creator of a metaphor respects indigenous political heritage and is willing to abide by the conventions of public debate.

On reconsideration, metaphor serves not as the repository of a "faded mythology,"[33] as some have claimed, but as a utensil for the care of the political imagination here and now. In this respect, Max Black's theory of "interactivity" between two semantic domains and Paul Ricouer's insistence upon metaphor's capacity to generate "new congruence" along cognitive dimensions should be synthesized. It is best not to treat these accounts of linguistic process (semantic versus cognitive) as mutually exclusive. Instead, it is more accurate to treat them as representing different facets of a single process that produces civic meaning. The interaction of different domains of knowledge creates a particular set of connotations and, therefore, new points of contact between sources of knowledge that did not previously exist. It is also true that the composition imparts information by encouraging a person to interiorize the ideas presented.

The aural-visual-relational features of language merge into a participatory dimension. Instead of merely substituting one set of ideas for another, metaphor stages a clash of meanings that invites a bystander to participate in political fellowship. The juxtaposition is jarring, puzzling, arresting, a contradiction imparting a previously unknown chain of connotations. This observation builds upon Ted Cohen's conception of metaphor as an efficacious modality for "cultivating intimacy" between speaker and listener. As Cohen explains this sense of linguistic affinity: "There is a unique way in which the maker and the appreciator of a metaphor are drawn closer to one another. Three aspects are involved: (1) the speaker issues a kind of concealed invitation; (2) the hearer expends a special effort to accept the invitation; and (3) this transaction constitutes the acknowledgment of a community."[34]

Strategically placed in an oration or text, a second-order metaphor beckons, teasing the curiosity like a miniature puzzle. It invites the citizen first to reconcile the incongruities inherent in its message; then, it encourages that individual, having resolved the incompatibility (or at least made peace with its nested meanings), to internalize and repeat it. One might say that working with forms that are both mysterious and familiar during public debate is, in this additional sense, an affiliative act: by reworking the idioms of self-rule, members of the polity bring themselves into close contact as they labor to perfect their democratic society.

A constitution achieves its legitimacy in part by ensuring a measure of revisability. As Louis Seidman argues, "unsettlement" of the text's meaning preserves the possibility of constitutional renewal. The knowledge that a text's meaning can be discerned but should never be allowed to calcify promotes civic engagement while reducing political alienation. Whether this lesson should be derived from the generality of original text, the flexibility of governing superstructure, or the weight of historical practice, the basic thrust of the claim is that substantive ideals should remain, at some level, contestable.[35] The claim of linguistic creativity is an adjacent one: the structure of constitutional language itself signals the Constitution's unsettled nature, while familiarity with its basic forms encourages dissent through recomposition. Just as the Constitution countenances no permanent class of political losers, so, too, one searches in vain for a single formula for elaborating a nation's values over time. Often, there is agreement only as to form.

During a debate over foundational commitments, advocates strive for the organizing theme or turn of phrase that might capture the stakes involved. Even as metaphor fulfills what Locke described as the need for efficient communication, its terse provocation tends to elicit a rejoinder. Far from disabling the power of reason, figurative discourse instead stimulates creative and logical building of countermetaphors and alternative story lines.[36] In deliberations over the constitutionality of regulating such matters as sexual expression or hate speech, lawyers on all sides of an issue have been known to frame their presentations in the rhetoric of fire. Similarly, in the debate over campaign financing, advocates have sparred over whether the "marketplace of ideas" should be realized through a self-regulating system or one that permits targeted interventions by the state to prevent well-funded individuals from skewing electoral discussions. In each of these situations, the propensity to confront the popular terminology of one's adversary and to place one's own position in a more convincing arrangement suggests the democracy-enhancing nature of these devices.

There is a certain tension in the fact that metaphor's naturalizing power exists alongside its capacity to accentuate. Although every rhetorical composition dramatizes some features of communal life and occludes others, its artificiality remains undeniable. The aesthetics of metaphor serve as a reminder that all societies are fabrications. Even as a particular device solicits adherents to a particular model of governance, its existence hints at a democratic formulation yet to be imagined.

Another salient attribute of metaphor is its portability — that is, the ease with which the device travels from one social domain to another, gathering and shedding information along the way. In spite of its incompleteness, a tidy metaphor can, under the right circumstances, convey constitutional knowledge in ways that can transcend the control of institutions, political parties, and social groups.[37] If a popular device gains traction in one social domain, it can acquire authority in another domain through modeling, adoption, or imitation, influencing tactics and finding its own composition altered in the process.

A metaphor's quotable and compact nature enhances its diffusion through society. It is a sensory-literary creation that lends itself to be reused to introduce or organize such a report. Take the Supreme Court's landmark decision holding that First Amendment principles restrain the government's regulatory authority over the Internet. Enacted in 1996, the Communications Decency Act prohibited the transmission of obscene or indecent material to persons under the age of eighteen. Striking down the statute, John Paul Stevens delivered this adaptation of the fire metaphor: "In *Sable*, we remarked that the speech restriction at issue there amounted to 'burn[ing] the house to roast the pig.' The CDA, casting a far darker shadow over free speech, threatens to torch a large segment of the Internet community."[38]

In the days and weeks following *Reno v. American Civil Liberties Union*, it was the rare reporter who failed to seize on this statement as the Supreme Court's encapsulation of the stakes involved or as the theme around which to organize the reporter's own secondhand analysis. The media labeled this passage of the opinion "quotable"; the words appeared in a synopsis of the ruling written by the Associated Press and, once they were picked up on the wires, circulated in newspapers across the country. With commentators and advocacy groups lining up to laud or lament the Justices' collective act of "extinguishing the CDA fire," the extended metaphor quickly became shorthand for the decision itself.[39] From the standpoint of democratic theory, metaphor's compactness and resilience should be counted as advantageous in an information-saturated society. The composition can be deployed by state actors or citizens to harness the dynamics of popular culture in the service of democratic goals.

Cultivating popular language generally and encouraging the use of metaphor specifically may aid the project of pluralism, with only a minor modification of pluralism to encompass linguistic variety.[40] For such a trope not only facilitates the diffusion of political knowledge among different sectors of society but does so by differentiating the methods for construing text. In its fusion of doctrine and vernacular, a metaphor joins the two without destroying either element; its preservation of semantic difference models respect for linguistic variety. Citizens are empowered and inspired by a multiplicity of idioms for appreciating the Constitution that appeal to a variety of faculties and sources: logic or emotion, theory or history, the literal or the transcendent.

Local participation in the creation of civic meaning is difficult to deny as a historical fact, despite the Supreme Court's many pronouncements on the need for uniform readings of the law. The complexity of multiple jurisdictions and the organizational overlap in the American system of government suggest that a diversity of constitutional understandings is not only tolerated but also desirable. So long as institutions remain empowered to give authoritative voice to governing principles when it counts, a pluralism of meanings and styles should be welcomed rather than feared.

To this point, the argument has proceeded by evaluating how popular language can enhance control of textual meaning by subnational communities. Under normal conditions, the converse should also be true: the decentralization of political authority can foster linguistic development in arenas that are most likely to generate reflective action. Parochial habits and policy priorities mix with democratic idioms during constitutional conflicts to produce variations in dialect that resonate with the populace. The intensity of local stakes and the repetition of these encounters with the Constitution can converge to spur greater facility with political grammar. And the more one is immersed in such discursive events and becomes proficient in the American languages of power, the closer the polity approaches the republican ideal.

Legitimating Institutional Arrangements

Beyond articulating grand visions of political life and popularizing core principles, metaphor has the psychological power to fortify or destabilize ruling institutions — once we see that the state is maintained not only by brick-and-mortar plans but also by complicated strategies of perception. The intricacies of metaphorical discourse can be identified in a single controversy, but what is even more important is the impact over time of such discourse.

Every specialized metaphor engages a set of performative dynamics by instantiating the full force of institutional authority and by moving the citizenry to think in certain ways about constitutional actors' places in their lives. Legal language invites readers or listeners to perceive an official act as justified or not, a cause for celebration or a point of outrage, an inevitable or unnatural course of action.

There are a rhythm and a structure to metaphorical discourse, just as there are conventions to be observed when it comes to formal argumentation. Ritual theory illuminates the relation of linguistic content to process. According to Victor Turner, social dramas unfold in four stages. During the opening act, a social breach is initiated and revealed. In the second stage, crisis seizes the entire arena as the stakes of conflict are articulated. The third stage is characterized by the marshaling and expenditure of social energy to redress the breach. In the fourth and concluding stage, either the party responsible for the breach is reintegrated into the community or the breach itself is ritualistically legitimized.[41]

Although a judicial opinion is rendered during the later stages of a public contest, the elements of ritual inhere in the organization of constitutional language. If judicially created text stages a grand performance, then even its smallest unit can initiate a script, replete with roles, cues, and scene blocking. Consider *Gitlow v. New York*, an early First Amendment decision involving the suppression of socialist propaganda during World War I. Authorities pursued Benjamin Gitlow under a criminal anarchy statute for disseminating revolutionary literature. The Court affirmed his conviction on appeal, concluding that the state is within its police power to curb propaganda that "threaten[s] breaches of the peace and ultimate revolution."[42] Over Justice Holmes's dissent, a majority of the Supreme Court raised this fantastic image of doom: "A single revolutionary spark may kindle a fire that, smouldering for a time, may burst into a sweeping and destructive conflagration. It cannot be said that the State is acting arbitrarily or unreasonably when in the exercise of its judgment as to the measures necessary to public peace and safety, it seeks to extinguish the spark without waiting until it has enkindled the flame or blazed into the conflagration."[43]

The Justices unleashed the fire metaphor in order to strip the orator's actions of any public value and to fortify the highly deferential "bad tendency" rule: "a State in the exercise of its police power may punish those who abuse this freedom by utterances . . . tending to corrupt public morals, incite to crime, or disturb the public peace."

As *Gitlow* illustrates, each specialized metaphor initiates a script, that is, a "structure that describes appropriate sequences of events in a particular context."[44] According to research in the cognitive sciences, a script is a heuristic upon which a narrative is built. Every social context contains such stock scripts, which imply chronology, order, and progression. Because scripts arise from a people's canonical experiences, once a script is activated through word choice, one expects certain facts to have occurred, even if they are not explicitly mentioned. Accordingly, a script facilitates the comprehension and internalization of legal norms through shortcuts. These linguistic structures, which are plentiful in any healthy constitutional culture, play a critical role in the normalization of official acts.

The recurring script or scenario[45] initiated by the speech-as-fire metaphor can be charted in the following four stages:

> An arsonist-speaker's words threaten the legal order → A political actor extinguishes the metaphorical fire through isolation of the speaker → The Supreme Court endorses the political action → Constitutional equilibrium is restored.

The ethical lessons vary from presentation to presentation, just as the narrative details diverge, but the underlying conversational structure remains largely intact. As the opinion-reader is taken through each step, the elements of danger, crisis, tragedy, redemption, and denouement are forecast and allowed to unfold. The unruly and dangerous aspects of social life are dramatized, then ritually confronted, and ultimately tamed by the soothing tones of constitutional rhetoric. Crafted just so, the speech-as-fire metaphor engages a particularly dire story line: the citizen is asked to contemplate the very destruction of democratic institutions. Psychologically, the narrative engages one's instinct for self-preservation and then redirects that sentiment on behalf of the public order.

Each script legitimates a set of roles within the legal order. Just as Plato's civic myth prescribed ideal models of status and function, so, too, modern constitutional vernacular populates the political imagination with a cast of recurring characters. The "role themes" assigned to each constitutional actor by a rhetorical composition convey the scope of one's authority; through such assignments, the device implies the naturalness of the political functions and relationships so described. The speech-as-fire metaphor validates not only a particular doctrinal rule (*e.g.*, the "bad tendency" test) but also the primacy of the state actors who aim to stamp out the "revolutionary spark" before irreparable damage is done. The judge, by contrast, is portrayed as an enabler, whose proper place is to aid—not lead—the defense of the constitutional order. In the least privileged position is the individual speaker, derided as the figurative arsonist, stamped as morally and legally worthy of isolation.

Now consider the clever bit of role reversal that occurred in *Reno v. American Civil Liberties Union*. Because of the seemingly broad reach of the Communications Decency Act and the absence of technology that could be used to confirm the age of viewers who might be exposed to online speech, the High Court deemed the law unduly restrictive of protected expression. Justice Stevens's opinion described the Internet as a "new marketplace of ideas," a medium of boundless social utility, where the goods in trade are as "diverse as human thought."[46] His words portrayed the Internet as a vibrant bazaar where persons transact business on relatively equal footing, rather than as a shadowy place where dangers to the child lurk in every corner. In an ominous passage emphasizing the threat to expressive values posed by the statute, Justice Stevens stated: "The CDA, casting a far darker shadow over free speech, threatens to torch a large segment of the Internet community."

Although the fire metaphor makes a return engagement to public discourse, the underlying script has been completely rewritten. The device still invokes a community's negative experiences with fire as a phenomenon, but its scenes have a new organization and a fresh set of role themes:

A regulation-as-fire threatens the democratic order → Conflict arises between the Supreme Court and another constitutional actor → Judicial authority is dispensed to meet the threat → Invalidating the state action repairs the breach.

Each part in the performance of legal authority has been ingeniously recast. Previously, the extended metaphor cast the State as the heroic figure, authorized to interdict the "hotheaded speech on the street corner." Now, it is the Supreme Court that is authorized by legal language to intervene in order to prevent the government from "torching the Internet." The feelings of welcome and gratitude the citizen was urged to feel for the State in *Gitlow* have been replaced by an abiding distrust of the State-turned-arsonist. Concomitantly, the warm sentiments for the State have been transferred to the Court, which should be trusted to have the people's interests at heart. Like Cardozo's vision of judges "hewing a path to justice," the house-afire saying rhetorically positions the court on the frontlines in the fight to save liberal democracy from its own excesses — in this instance, from abuses of the right to free speech.

Initially formulated as shorthand for judicial deference, this incendiary metaphor has been transformed into an instrument by which to reinforce the practice of judicial review — not only the power to assess the constitutionality of political acts but, arguably, also a monopoly on final review. Originally crafted to bolster state action, the composition has acquired the cognitive power to unsettle support for the state's regulatory schemes.

Each party to a constitutional debate — the politician, the judge, and the individual — claims to have the people's interests at heart. The elected official points to the fact of his election by a presently constituted electorate; the individual speaker claims that his interests are congruent with those of the people at large; the judge invokes the authority to interpret the law so as to safeguard the long-term interests of the citizenry. The "virtual" representation of this jockeying can be diagrammed (figs. 2–3).

A second-order metaphor replicates a privileged alliance either between the state and the judge (fig. 2) or between the judge and the speaker (fig. 3). When the speech-as-fire metaphor is utilized, the first arrangement is set against, and ultimately delegitimates, the individual's claim to speak on behalf of the people (fig. 2); when the regulation-as-fire metaphor is deployed, the second configuration elevates the status of the speaker while short-circuiting the claim of authority by political actors (fig. 3).

In any given contest, a rhetorically forged alliance momentarily weakens the position of the subjugated constitutional actor (or the losing party). The simple schema itself is reproduced in the minds of the populace. Over time, second-order metaphors can play a part in the ongoing struggle for status and

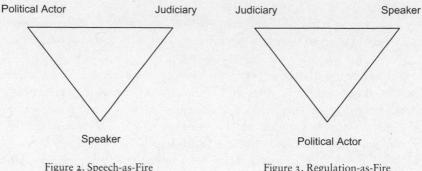

Figure 2. Speech-as-Fire   Figure 3. Regulation-as-Fire

advantage among constitutional actors. As they gain prominence through usage and a track record of success, they are employed to preserve existing spheres of political influence or to make the case for new prerogatives. Indeed, as the next two chapters elaborate, repetition of these rhetorical constructions has simultaneously reflected popular acceptance of judicial constitutionalism and enabled its continued development. This has been the case even if the ascendance of the ideal of judicial participation in the production of foundational norms has not entirely displaced the tradition of popular sovereignty.

Repairing Rifts

In addition to helping create political community and open access, metaphor can ease disjunctions introduced through the passage of time. Law prefers to be internal and invisible to the workings of political life, its public appearances routine and predictable. A constant threat to law's reign is the impression that social forces have overtaken the law, rendering it anachronistic; another is the sense that shifts in personnel or individual preference can alter the trajectory of the law. In such circumstances, constitutional language must address social change, at least implicitly, or risk a spread of the crisis of faith. When one feels alienated from the law, when it no longer exerts a gravitational pull on one's behavior, the instinct is to express that sense of loss metaphorically; a jurist might say that the law's foundations have become "unmoored" or "eroded."[47]

The capacity of language to solve deficits in the law's legitimacy is its reparative function. Principled behavior by stewards of the law, including adherence to stare decisis, certainly plays a role in projecting a sense of equilibrium.[48] But, as important as these tasks are, ensuring strict fidelity to past decisions and maintaining the logical integrity of judicial reasoning can do only so much to engender collective belief in the rule of law. The nuances of precedent and interpretive methodology may hold the attention of elites, but their intricacies are lost on the average citizen, especially during moments of transition.

To fill the gap between what the law is and what it will become, constitutional vernacular operates as an additional mediating and stabilizing device. Transformations in legal doctrine and society as a whole can be simultaneously facilitated and masked by established tropes. Because of its adaptive nature, metaphor can be deployed to absorb social change and to facilitate the ritual reestablishment of legal boundaries. Through selective use of such fragments, even the most significant changes to the polity can be made familiar, reasonable, and ultimately palatable.

It is possible to detect the reparative function of language at work as jurists grappled with the evolution of cultural tastes in the second half of the twentieth century. Take the classic obscenity case *Stanley v. Georgia*, which stands at the intersection of the Fourth Amendment and the First Amendment. Suspecting Robert Stanley of illegal bookmaking, police officers entered Stanley's home to execute a warrant and came upon a cache of sexually explicit materials. He was duly charged with possession of "obscene matter" in violation of state law. On appeal, Stanley conceded that the seized films were legally obscene, yet boldly argued that constitutional principles nevertheless shielded him from prosecution. In a decision published in 1969, Justice Thurgood Marshall agreed: "the First and Fourteenth Amendments prohibit making mere private possession of obscene material a crime."[49]

To those who prefer strict adherence to precedent or the imputed expectations of the men who wrote the Constitution, the outcome is difficult to explain. Despite the nascent right to obtain and use contraception sketched four years earlier in *Griswold v. Connecticut*, a decision grounded in marriage and procreative destiny, *Stanley* could hardly have been foreshadowed in existing precedent. The law of obscenity had in the years leading up to *Stanley* consistently confirmed the authority of the state to proscribe obscenity as a traditionally unprotected material.[50] The original rationale for regulating obscenity is moral corruption of the soul, and if this justification still is to be met with a straight face, the concern is stronger, not weaker, when it comes to acquisition and perusal of material in the home; the ruling obviously made it more difficult to reduce the demand for obscenity.[51] The Fourth Amendment has never prevented the police from physically entering the home; it merely sets the conditions for "reasonable" search and seizure. Yet, what the Court fashioned in *Stanley* was not a prophylactic rule but a categorical one that forbade criminalization of possession or the use of obscenity in the home altogether.

It is by perceiving changes in legal customs through interactions with exogenous events that some preliminary answers can be reached. Any national moral consensus that might have existed had been breaking down for decades; the sexual revolution then under way represented only one of the more visible manifestations of the deep changes in Americans' postwar consumption patterns. As standards of public morality became more fluid in response to changes in popular culture, so the morality of obscenity law became contestable. The people's waning faith in the project of criminalizing sexual expression was mirrored in the Supreme Court's heightened interest in redrawing legal rules in this area, as well as in the institution's increasingly fractured rationales in discrete controversies.[52]

Notwithstanding such dramatic shifts, the law could not freely admit these social changes without facing charges of illegitimacy. Instead of openly acknowledging their desire to be culturally responsive, the Justices refashioned doctrinal rules into increasingly cumbersome tests to account for social change. They also refined older rhetorical vehicles to re-present a coherent vision of the First Amendment. Antitotalitarianism emerged as the language of choice as the political legacy of the last just war was distilled into an evocative metaphor: "If the First Amendment means anything, it means that a State has no business telling a man, sitting alone in his own house, what books he may read or what films he may watch. Our whole constitutional heritage rebels at the thought of giving government the power to control men's minds."[53]

Accordingly, the High Court equated the state's prosecution of Stanley for possessing obscenity with an attempt at "controlling a person's private thoughts."[54] In doing so, it erected a metaphorical bulwark against official efforts to prescribe "the moral content" of ideas. Years after World War II, the antitotalitarian legacy of that generational experience remained a formidable language of power. Having saved the nation's political institutions from Nazism and Fascism, leaders now turned their reconstructive project to the human intellect. *Stanley* reflects this crucial turn in the development of our popular First Amendment vocabulary. Disfavored regulations of speech are today routinely ridiculed as "thought control."[55]

In truth, figurative language had been used to ease transitions in public morality long before *Stanley*. As early as 1957, in the companion cases *Roth v. United States* and *Alberts v. California*,[56] the Supreme Court began to distinguish more carefully between protected works of sexuality and unprotected presentations of obscenity in both literal and symbolic terms. There, the Justices rejected the *Hicklin* test, which would have allowed the state to outlaw sexually explicit literature if isolated portions of a work offended members of the community especially vulnerable to the corrupting power of obscenity. Instead, the Justices urged a formula that permitted regulatory action only when an average person, applying "contemporary community standards," could find that "the dominant theme" of an entire work "appeals to the prurient interest." They would later refine the formula by requiring a higher degree of moral outrage — that the work be "patently offensive" — and by protecting material that has "serious literary, artistic, political, or scientific value."

Justice Brennan depicted the Constitution as an impregnable fortress to accompany the Supreme Court's heightened interest in rule making: "The door barring federal and state intrusion into this area cannot be left ajar; it must be kept tightly closed and opened only the slightest crack necessary to prevent encroachment upon more important interests."[57] This coordinated effort to draw upon popular attitudes about the sanctity of the home and the permanence of the Bill of Rights encouraged acceptance of the outcome and the notion of judicially enforced rights. Protecting one, the juxtaposition suggested, served to protect the other. "Ceaseless vigilance," Justice Brennan argued, was necessary to prevent "their erosion by Congress or by the States."

This identical scene in which the Justices portray themselves standing guard over the Constitution and the home or the intellect — with its metaphor intact — would be reenacted in a series of disputes that followed.[58] *Smith v. California*, for instance, concerned a state law that imposed strict liability on any bookstore found to have an obscene work on its shelves. Justice William Brennan, writing for the Court, concluded: "This ordinance opens that door too far. The existence of the State's power to prevent the distribution of obscene matter does not mean that there can be no constitutional barrier to any form of practical exercise of that power." *Stanley* itself may have arisen from a highly contingent series of occurrences, but the imagery that made expressive liberty possible would not be confined to the home.

The barrier metaphor, so plentiful in other areas, had gained a foothold on the First Amendment imagination. Seen in this light, *Stanley* represents the culmination of institutional and linguistic dynamics a long time in the making. The Justices did not simply recycle the Bill of Rights-as-bulwark aphorism mechanically but rather imaginatively extended the trope to safeguard the processes of the human mind. Henceforth, it would become commonplace for Americans to warn against the state "intrud[ing] on free speech rights," as if it were invading a home or breaching a sacred sphere, even when no physical intrusion of any type was involved.[59] Despite its inherent contradictions, *Stanley* remains an illustration of the power of popular tropes to account for social change and project the stability of the law.

Synthesis

A few final points follow from the realization that figurative rhetoric plays a part in the construction of the political imagination. First, analytically, it may be useful to separate the micro-operations of language, but in actuality the functions are mutually interacting. Metaphor's open and nomadic qualities can be enlisted to foster a sense of affinity among citizens who disagree about the good life. This potential for political intimacy enables the normalization of bureaucratic configurations. The regenerative power of popular language depends in part on its capacity to level and legitimate the law.

Second, if metaphor can be counted among the most visible and moving features of constitutional language, one should not be surprised to discover that it is relatively more likely to be publicized in secondary media than are dry recitations of ancient maxims. Its wider dissemination, in turn, increases the chances that it will be appropriated by others. All of this suggests that one should pay careful attention to dicta, for it is in the so-called nonessential portions of judicial rulings, legal memoranda, and policy statements that such direct appeals to the populace are to be found.

Third, recognition of metaphor's contributions to political culture does not preclude the possibility of criticizing the wisdom of specific arrangements or the patterns of their actual usage in democratic life. It is wise to accept that metaphor is an enduring feature of constitutional practice, but it would be a mistake to assume that every composition maximizes a nation's substantive commitments or satisfies the precepts of eloquence. Recognizing that law operates as a system of discursive practices complicates normative inquiry, but it should not disable those concerned about democratic design from theorizing the appropriate relationship between political culture and institutional practices.

Fourth, giving credence to popular representations of the Constitution raises a distinctive set of challenges. It uncovers, rather than suppresses, the possibility of tension between what elites believe and what average citizens may perceive. While a certain degree of departure is inevitable and even socially valuable, something more must be said about how divergent constructions of text should be handled. Does securing a place for metaphor in adjudicative discourse lead to an intolerable degree of instability in the law? How should institutions respond when activists and lawyers press for the endorsement of new formulations? In fact, constitutional law does enjoy a measure of stability over time, but the constraints are not found where one might expect. To appreciate the creativity and banality inherent to rhetorical freedom, it is necessary to evaluate the practices of the people when they have sought to reclaim the First Amendment as their own.

3

Linguistic Transformation

Every faith tradition has its creation stories; the First Amendment is no exception. As lawyers learn, the civic myth that recounts the birth of the right to speak one's mind in America begins with the missed opportunities of the World War I decisions, and the "end of the story" is the 1969 decision *Brandenburg v. Ohio*, in which the promise of expressive liberty is ultimately realized.[1] Despite the proliferation of First Amendment rules for nearly every occasion, it is this overarching narrative of institutional awakening that "lies close to the heart of the American free speech tradition." Even though the precedent cannot be counted among the best known of the Supreme Court's rulings, the themes articulated in the precedent accord with a popular belief in the progress of the law, expansive notions of individualism, and a close connection between the First Amendment and self-governance.

Creation stories present a political tradition as a coherent and progressive whole, thereby playing an important part in the continuation of the rule of law, but they occlude the naturally complicated currents of linguistic development. An inordinate focus on the refinement of rules may lead one to overlook the contradictions, discontinuities, and reversals in the construction of the political imagination. As a result, the tale about the perfection of First Amendment law necessarily misses the heuristics and vocabulary that arose to make sense of historical events. Within these vehicles of constitutional transformation can be found not only the pooled learning of a people, but also loss and gain, convergence and dissensus, control and resistance.

The circumstances giving rise to the doctrinal apogee were straightforward: Clarence Brandenburg, a local Klan leader, gave a brief, hate-filled tirade at a rather poorly attended rally. Standing before twelve hooded figures and a burning cross, he urged the ragtag group to "bury the niggers" and "send the Jews back to Israel" and warned "that there might have to be some revengeance taken" if political conditions did not improve to the Klan's liking. Without ever commenting directly upon Brandenburg's rant, the Justices overturned his criminal syndicalism conviction because of the statute's failure to distinguish between "mere advocacy" and "incitement to imminent lawless action." While the latter may be freely punished, they reasoned, the former would henceforth be "immunized from governmental control" so as to protect a panoramic range of controversial, disturbing — and even silencing — types of speech and assembly.[2]

Yet *Brandenburg* is considerably more than what Harry Kalven once described as an instance in which "the law and the tradition worked themselves pure." The controversy has become "one of the blessings of our liberty" — a general representation of society's willingness to make sacrifices for the First Amendment's glory. For better or for worse, the precedent evokes the deeply held political belief that expressive liberty demands tolerance of the "misguided, even hurtful" speech of the citizenry.[3]

It is possible to read the case as a reflection of a historical moment and as significant primarily for its coordination of particular rhetorical trends. Recall that the judicial attitude toward the First Amendment initially manifested itself in concerns about "inflammatory" speech conditions and irresponsible individuals "falsely shouting 'fire' in a crowded theater." Barely a generation later, in a conflict involving burning crosses and racially provocative invective, the language of fire was nowhere to be found. The temptation to underscore the threat presented by a radical's words had apparently subsided; jurists duly avoided the repressive language of fire in *Brandenburg* and decisions that followed from it.

With the ascendance of the ideals of expressive liberty in postwar America, the rhetoric of fire in its original form proved to be a disfavored strategy for framing the stakes of a First Amendment conflict. When such a statement or trope appeared, it usually served as a foil, a convenient point of departure. Justice Douglas's concurring opinion in *Brandenburg* illustrates this point. While he agreed with the disposition of the matter in favor of the Klansman, he was moved to argue separately that the "clear and present danger" test, conceived during a declared war, should have no power to dictate outcomes "in days of peace." Unable to ignore the incendiary rhetoric of the past like his brethren, Justice Douglas invoked it for the purpose of reducing its influence: "The example usually given by those who would punish speech is the case of one who falsely shouts fire in a crowded theatre. This is, however, a classic case where speech is brigaded with action."[4]

Eschewing what many elites now considered the primitive rhetoric of an earlier time, the *Brandenburg* Court employed an alternative set of conceptual tools and popular sayings surrounding the right to assembly, which had, by the mid-1960s, emerged as a preferred method of characterizing and extending the reach of the First Amendment. The State of Ohio's criminal syndicalism statute, the Justices stated, "forbid[s], on pain of criminal punishment, assembly with others merely to advocate the described type of action."

In a telling footnote, the Court quoted Chief Justice Charles Evans Hughes's statement in *DeJonge v. Oregon* that "the right of peaceable assembly is a right cognate to those of free speech and free press and is equally fundamental."[5] *DeJonge* concerned a successful challenge brought by socialists to a state criminal syndicalism act and was the watershed moment when the Court applied the First Amendment to the states by way of the Fourteenth Amendment's Due Process Clause. In ringing terms, Justice Hughes had then declared that the "holding of meetings for political action cannot be proscribed."

The choice to couch the facts of *Brandenburg* in republican idioms rather than fire-based vernacular had a dramatic effect. Deserved or not, Brandenburg's gathering was cast as a meeting of a civic organization by the soothing cadence of this ascendant discursive strategy. The Klan's illiberal and historically violent agenda benefited from its association with the glorious tradition of the American people meeting out-of-doors to resolve the nation's most pressing social ills. This legal fiction repels regulation, the Court stated, unless it can be demonstrated that a speaker's utterance is likely to produce "imminent lawless action." No one pretended that the group's message had intrinsic value or tried to demonstrate how its racist rallies might contribute to public reason; yet this was precisely the point. The structure of First Amendment discourse pushed this question to the periphery. According to the logic of radical inclusiveness that now governed the state's attitude toward ideas, the more extreme the speech, the greater a test it poses to First Amendment ideals.

These fragments of constitutional thought that have proved so crucial to the construction of our civic mythology teach several lessons about the challenges of foundational discourse. At any moment in time, governing language contains remnants of past political struggles and the accommodation of elite and popular understandings of law. Layered one upon another, these multiple constructions provide durability to and accountability for foundational commitments. Juridic discourse, then, always contains traces of self-rule.

Moreover, these delicate fusions of reason and artistry invite further originality. Whether it takes the form of a majority opinion's deliberate blurring of an issue, a concurring statement's attempt to limit or expand the majority's rationale, or a dissent that castigates prevailing understandings of text, each composition points a way toward reformation. Judicial constructions themselves present the tools for engaging future debate, whether it is an alternative construction, a turn of phrase, or the articulation of a budding article of faith not yet validated by the law.

Seeing beyond the civic myth that *Brandenburg* perpetuates requires examination of a number of interrelated themes articulated during other contests. This chapter and the next will evaluate four significant developments in First Amendment thought: the free market reformation of the postwar imagination; the reversal of the rhetoric of fire during the same period; African Americans' reinvention of assembly-based forms during their struggle for equal rights; and the religious revival that destabilized the wall of separation as a governing construct. The first two experiences predate *Brandenburg;* the last two transpired in its wake. Untangling these discursive trends reveals that linguistic transformation is a genus of constitutional revolution. These patterns of reconstitution, in turn, challenge prevailing models of legal change.

The Fire Next Time

To contemplate these descriptive principles in action, consider the emergence, resurgence, and transformation of the rhetoric of fire in historical time. This popular construct developed in patterns traceable to significant historical events but also entailed innovation when no major crisis loomed. For analytical purposes, it may be useful to divide the career of the fire metaphor into three epochs: (1) 1919 to the Second World War; (2) a transitional decade after the global conflict; and (3) the late 1950s to the present day.

Each of these periods is characterized by a linguistic regime, defined as a stable union of political beliefs, governing rules, and popular language over time. A regime provides the social structure within which rules are rationally formulated and implemented, and identifies the subset of "active" terms in a people's vocabulary. Besides determining the range of plausible readings of the Constitution, a regime also limits the possible number of configurations that constitutional language might theoretically take. The linguistic regime thus represents the operation of the precepts of eloquence in historical time.

A regime is not totalizing in the sense that its existence prevents alternative constructions entirely from coming into fruition. Social consensus of this sort does not obliterate the space for autonomy and creativity. Instead, a linguistic regime shapes the range of possibilities that constitutional actors believe to be both textually plausible and strategically desirable.

During the first epoch, constitutional actors utilized the fire metaphor to conceptualize individual expression in parsimonious terms, fortify the "bad tendency" test, and maximize the authority of the state to interdict the negative consequences of speech before they actually materialized. During the interregnum, two overlapping patterns took hold as First Amendment traditions clashed: the first, a synchronic pattern of speech-restrictive usages in reaction to new exigencies; the second, a diachronic pattern in which earlier rhetorical forms demonstrated their resilience as they found themselves increasingly deployed for pro-speech purposes. In the third era, the pro-speech version of the metaphor demonstrated its dominance. Originally associated with a single doctrine — the law of incitement — it became an all-purpose instrument for the advancement of expressive norms.

The fire motif appeared in judicial discourse at a time when war angst seized the entire field of action. In 1919, Charles Schenck and Elizabeth Baer appealed their convictions under the Espionage Act to the United States Supreme Court. Their overt acts consisted of mailing circulars that deplored conscription laws as despotic. Rejecting their First Amendment defense in *Schenck v. United States*, Justice Holmes likened the defendants' actions to "falsely shouting fire in a crowded theater." Just as raising a false alarm would cause widespread panic and inflict injury on an untold number of persons, so the Justices claimed that the mailing of the antidraft circulars might prompt a wave of draft dodging that would impede the war effort.

Holmes cited no particular source for his turn of phrase, though some have speculated that he might have been "touched by fire" through his Civil War service, had a peculiar fascination with firefighting, or was influenced by the rash of destructive theater fires that swept cities during that era.[6] Whatever his inspiration may have been, the legal saying served as an early prototype for unprotected expression. The notion of a reckless individual issuing a false alarm would, over time, develop into a trusted implement of legal authority as decision makers reenacted the scenario to warn of the limits of freedom.

A few days later, the Justices published an opinion resolving the appeal of Jacob Frohwerk. Federal authorities had charged Frohwerk under the Espionage Act for conspiracy to obstruct the draft. A series of articles published by Frohwerk drew the attention of censors. These articles claimed that the American army had been raised illegally, attributed the war to the economic self-interests of a cabal of leading men, and lauded the spirit of the German people.

When Frohwerk defended against the prosecution on free speech grounds, the Justices of the Supreme Court proved unsympathetic. Holmes's ruling began with a literal statement of legal principle and ended with a metaphorical plea to respect the exigencies of the times:

It may be that all this might be said or written even in time of war in circumstances that would not make it a crime. We do not lose our right to condemn either measures or men because the country is at war. . . . But we must take the case on the record as it is, and on that record it is impossible to say that it might not have been found that the circulation of the paper was in quarters where a little breath would be enough to kindle a flame and that the fact was known and relied upon by those who sent the paper out.[7]

Frohwerk v. United States treated a set of expressive acts — here, the preparation and distribution of reading material — as the equivalent of "kindl[ing] a flame." Moreover, its suggestion that the social environment was combustible, easily sparked by "a little breath," worked against Justice Holmes's introductory remarks insisting that one's rights cannot be extinguished because of war. Despite his initial gesture to the contrary, Holmes's metaphoric presentation indicated that the context for one's utterances would make all the difference in the world. The negative consequences attributable to Frohwerk's revolutionary tracts could be avoided by approving the authorities' choice to arrest the would-be fire starter.

By the time the Justices had stoked a single "flame" into "a sweeping and destructive conflagration" in *Gitlow v. New York*, a compelling network of word relationships had been firmly established:

discuss: inflame::
reflection: reaction::
reason: passion::
order: disorder::
democracy: socialism

Along one set of homologies, legal language invited citizens to make the following associations when the exercise of a First Amendment right appeared to be compatible with the legal order: discuss — reflection — reason — order — democracy. When the speech-as-fire metaphor was unleashed, however, an observer faced an opposing chain of negative resonances: inflame — reaction — passion — disorder — socialism.

His colleagues went too far for Holmes in *Gitlow*, and he dissented from their decision to affirm the conviction of an individual who did little more than arrange for the printing and circulation of a socialist manifesto. "[W]hatever may be thought of the redundant discourse before us," he reasoned from the circumstances, the socialist's words "had no chance of starting a present conflagration." In defeat, Holmes offered an elegant reminder: "Eloquence may set fire to reason."

For the next decade, the state frequently imitated and elaborated the speech-as-fire metaphor to curb undesirable utterances, even as countervailing trends could be detected. In this respect, *Schenck* and *Frohwerk*, both decided in 1919, might be explained as juridic statements rendered at a time when the outcome of the global conflict remained in doubt. *Gitlow*, handed down in 1925, cannot be so easily brushed aside as a product of war anxiety. The exigencies necessitating heightened security had passed; an armistice had long since been signed. This curiosity requires a different explanation. Once the rhetorical reconstruction of the legal order is understood as an extension of the physical rebuilding of a society's governing institutions, an answer becomes possible. Although hostilities had long since ended by the time of *Gitlow*, for many persons, including certain members of the Supreme Court, speech-restrictive discourse proved valuable for preserving the gains of war. This popular construction of the law equated programs to suppress foreign ideologies and domestic fanaticism with "measures to protect the public peace and safety." For those who perceived a need to protect the populace from foreign ideas and social unrest, the language of fire remained attractive. Creations under extraordinary times now held ominous ramifications for ordinary affairs.

An analogous pattern of definition and suppression thus emerged in the immediate aftermath of the Second World War. Ritual reestablishment of the rule of law through identical rhetorical forms made judicial resolutions during the interregnum appear eerily like replays of earlier events. *Dennis v. United States*, decided in 1951, was heard against the backdrop of communist ideology as the ascendant threat to political self-understanding at home. The majority opinion affirming the convictions of several Communists for conspiracy to overthrow the government once again erupted in fire, stressing the "inflammable nature of world conditions." Figurative modalities facilitated the predictive mind-set expected of decision makers faced with such an issue. "If the ingredients of the reaction are present," the Justices concluded, "we cannot bind the Government to wait until the catalyst is added."[8] In this way, legal language licensed governing institutions to repel intruding ideologies.

This shared discourse tempted even those who disagreed with the substance of the ruling. Justice Jackson, for his part, would have gone further than the majority. He argued that the clear and present danger test could be helpful when a situation involves "a hot-headed speech on the street corner, or circulation of a few incendiary pamphlets" but that the approach, which had been drafted during peacetime, had reached its breaking point. Accordingly, he proposed putting aside the clear and present danger test and affording the state greater latitude to combat insidious forms of totalitarianism on the home front.

Not to be outdone, Justice Douglas resisted the speech-as-fire metaphor by limiting its historical reach and repeating a speech-protective version created by Louis Brandeis. Douglas began his dissenting opinion by acknowledging that "[s]peech innocuous one year may at another time fan such destructive flames that it must be halted in the interests of the safety of the Republic." He followed with Justice Brandeis's evocative concurrence in *Whitney v. California* that "Men feared witches and burnt women. It is the function of speech to free men from the bondage of irrational fears." Douglas's implication: in punishing the defendants for teaching Communism, the Court had succumbed to a most regressive impulse.

Beauharnais v. Illinois, decided in 1952, tracked the structure of First Amendment grammar during the interregnum. At issue was an Illinois law that prohibited the publication of any work that portrayed "depravity, criminality, unchastity, or lack of virtue of a class of citizens . . . [or] exposes the citizens of any race, color, creed, or religion to contempt, derision, or obloquy." Citing the statute, the State prosecuted Joseph Beauharnais for distributing leaflets that accused African Americans of engaging in general aggressions and various specific crimes and implored local officials to take action.

Turning aside Beauharnais's invocation of the First Amendment, the Supreme Court upheld the group libel statute by stretching the notion of libel as a category of unprotected expression. In support of this interpretive move, the Justices painted a "scene of exacerbated tension between races, often flaring into violence and destruction."[9] As a result, the Justices authorized the state to take action against "inflammatory" falsehoods that "promote strife and tend powerfully to obstruct the manifold adjustments required for free, ordered life in a metropolitan, polyglot community."

Although the circumstances may have been different, jurists again asked citizens to envision individual expression as an incendiary device, setting off a predictable chain of propositional and nonpropositional connotations. Justice Jackson, who dissented from the majority's complete insulation of the law, preferred an approach that would have made the state's power to quash group libel fact-specific. He insisted that "[o]ne of the merits of the clear and present danger test is that the triers of fact would take into account the realities of race relations and any smouldering fires to be fanned into holocausts."

Despite the apparent strength of the speech-as-fire metaphor's hold upon the political imagination during the interregnum, equally powerful variations on the theme began to appear, culminating in an emerging counterdiscourse that emphasized the virtues of expressive liberty and minimized the risks of advocating extreme ideas. By the late 1950s, the political imagination began to undergo a profound transformation, eventually resulting in a corresponding alteration to the dominant linguistic regime. Rhetorical maintenance of the public mind in response to social disjunction called for alternating mind-sets focused on preservation and reconstruction. When a sense of crisis appeared the most acute, institutions tended to favor highly context-based readings of text that facilitated the power of the state to discipline the would-be speaker. As the sense of urgency receded, jurists exhibited an increased willingness to elaborate more general principles enabling cultural dissent.

The speech-restrictive form of the rhetoric of fire eventually ceded ground to its speech-protective counterpart during the interregnum. Why the revolutionary change in First Amendment language? The sociolegal dynamics are complicated, but the most plausible explanation is twofold: (1) the most visceral external threat necessitating the preservationist mind-set had subsided, with the Cold War settling into a kind of stasis; and (2) as the nation transitioned from the phase of psychological self-defense to rebuilding, public relations supplanted raw military strength in the struggle to extend democratic ideals on a global scale. These factors collectively gave rise to what Victor Turner calls a "liminal moment" between paradigms, or a "state of being in between successive participations in social milieux dominated by social structural considerations."[10]

The social disjunction created space for experimentation, and the trial-and-error in Americans' exercise of rhetorical freedom irrevocably altered the grammatical structure of the law. The postwar mind-set led to a relaxation of the metaphorical field that gave rise to early juridic notions of the First Amendment but also prompted a search for a more diverse array of methods to articulate a burgeoning confidence in the social utility of individual expression. Just as the more repressive First Amendment language appeared in a burst of incendiary rhetoric, so, too, the nascent language of expressive liberty had to be sculpted from prevailing forms. Justice Holmes's reminder that "eloquence may set fire to reason," along with Justice Brandeis's witch-burning mantra, would be rediscovered by a new generation of advocates. At the same time, proregulatory discourse began to lose institutional support.

Few metaphors would have more impact in bridging historical epochs than the one contained in Frankfurter's pig roast mantra. Unveiled for the first time in a 1946 case testing the right to a jury trial, Justice Frankfurter cautioned against "burning down the barn to roast a pig." A year later, in an antitrust matter, he shrewdly converted the barn into a house, no doubt a more appealing image with the rise of home ownership and the decline of the agrarian economy. Because these artifacts of ordinary language appeared in concurring opinions rather than texts that garnered majority assent, they did not instigate widespread copying by other jurists. Instead, the full Court's usage of this aphorism in the 1957 case *Butler v. Michigan* would secure its place in the constitutional lexicon for decades to come.[11]

Butler presented the question of whether an obscenity law could be squared with the First Amendment. The statute under review enjoined the publication or distribution of materials "manifestly tending to the corruption of the morals of youth." After some preliminary remarks, the High Court came to its main point: "The State insists that, by thus quarantining the general reading public against books not too rugged for grown men and women in order to shield juvenile innocence, it is exercising its power to promote the general welfare. Surely, this is to burn the house to roast the pig."

Employing ordinary language to stir feelings of outrage toward the speaker during the first epoch, constitutional actors recalibrated fire-based rhetoric in the third epoch to highlight the deliberative value of controversial speech and to chide state officials for overreacting to social ills by sacrificing basic rights.[12] The popular saying dramatized the *Butler* Court's doctrinal conclusion that the legislation at issue was "not reasonably restricted to the evil with which it is said to deal." Beyond reinforcing a particular rule and a set of institutional arrangements that facilitated judicial enforcement of that rule, the regulation-as-fire metaphor drew a visual and aural linkage among the following terms: state — torch — overbroad — tyranny.

In ensuing decades, jurists took turns reinventing the house-on-fire adage while adhering to its speech-friendly structure. By the 1980s, the pro-speech rendition of the fire metaphor had become an entrenched feature of Americans' expressive existence. In *R.A.V. v. City of St. Paul*, the Supreme Court invalidated a local antibias ordinance that prohibited the display of any symbol, including a burning cross or swastika, "which one knows or has reasonable grounds to know arouses anger, alarm or resentment in others on the basis of race, color, creed, religion, or gender." The City Council enacted the law to deter what is known colloquially as "hate speech." Justice Scalia's opinion for the Court determined that the law — which had already been narrowed by the Minnesota Supreme Court to apply only to unprotected "fighting words" — nevertheless violated two relevant maxims: the preference against content-based regulation of expression and the more stringent ban on viewpoint-based discrimination. The first rule is grounded in a fear that discretion to distinguish between types of speech inevitably draws officials into making inappropriate value judgments about the utility of such expression; the second rule deems it inappropriate for the state to be motivated by a desire to disfavor a particular perspective on a topic of debate.

Having explained how the enactment transgressed these principles, Justice Scalia added: "Let there be no mistake about our belief that burning a cross in someone's front yard is reprehensible. But St. Paul has sufficient means at its disposal to prevent such behavior without adding the First Amendment to the fire."[13] Justice Scalia's startling gambit juxtaposed an actual occurrence with an entirely conjectural one: the destruction of a treasured foundational commitment. Initiating a full sensory experience, the technique simultaneously (1) raised the stakes of the controversy exponentially; (2) transferred one's repugnance for the cross burner to the would-be constitution burner, whose regulatory actions should be understood as imminently more dangerous; and (3) signaled that any other outcome would endanger parties not before the Court who might be nonetheless caught up in the raging "fire."[14]

R.A.V. serves as a reminder that the inability of a popular construct to command a majority can be just as telling as the success of one that wins the day. Justice Stevens authored a concurring opinion in which he found the ordinance to be constitutionally overbroad but not defective on the grounds given by the majority. Unlike other Justices, who found troubling the law's singling out of some "fighting words" over others, Justice Stevens would have allowed public officials to create subcategories of unprotected expression — including one that singled out racially intimidating speech-acts for special sanction. He began his review of the statute by pointing out: "Conduct that creates special risks or causes special harms may be prohibited by special rules. Lighting a fire near an ammunition dump or a gasoline storage tank is especially dangerous; such behavior may be punished more severely than burning trash in a vacant lot. . . . This case involves the constitutionality of one such ordinance."

This move to inject a hypothetical fire-starting offender into the analysis is reminiscent of Holmes's introduction of the person who falsely shouts fire in a crowded theater; both characterize the reckless behavior more as conduct than expression. In this instance, Stevens would have described cross burning as an intentional act that justifies special rules of conduct and voted to uphold such a law if it were better worded to avoid capturing too many instances of protected expression.

For Justice Stevens, the bottom line was that "[a]lthough it is regrettable that race . . . is so incendiary an issue, until the Nation matures beyond that condition, laws such as St. Paul's ordinance will remain reasonable and justifiable." Notice that Stevens tried in vain to resuscitate the tactics of an earlier linguistic regime that had afforded greater latitude to the regulatory state. He did so initially by equating cross burning with "lighting a fire near a gasoline storage tank" and then by reusing the speech-as-fire metaphor. But Justice Stevens's attempt to characterize flag burning in "incendiary" terms met resistance by a majority of the Court, underscoring the durability of the prevailing linguistic regime.

The speech-as-fire metaphor failed to find favor in one more notable controversy. *Texas v. Johnson* held that the First Amendment protected flag burning as a type of symbolic expression. In a heartfelt dissent, William Rehnquist urged his colleagues to perceive the individual's performance as "so inherently inflammatory that it may cause a breach of public order." The statement amounted to an earnest but failed effort to revive the habits of an older age — at least until another grammatical reordering takes place.

The Marketplace of Ideas

Perhaps the single most influential encapsulation of contemporary free speech ideals is "the marketplace of ideas." Not only does the metaphor succinctly capture the libertarian tradition of the First Amendment; it has also proved to be enormously popular. The term of art did not experience the same discontinuities in its development as the rhetoric of fire, though the phrase, too, owed its genesis to the burgeoning antitotalitarian ethos that infused rights discourse across the constitutional spectrum.

In the heady days of early twentieth century jurisprudence, Justice Holmes advocated "free trade in ideas." But his proved to be a dissenting position, and, although it began to find favor in certain sectors of society, the phrase had little influence in juridic discourse until 1945, when the Justices overturned a contempt order against a labor leader for failing to register with a state agency before soliciting union members.[15] Rejecting the state's argument that the procedure did not restrict the flow of information, the High Court insisted, in *Thomas v. Collins*, that " 'free trade in ideas' means free trade in the opportunity to persuade to action, not merely to describe facts." Because the regulation complicated the union's ability to get the word out, it necessarily hampered efforts to mobilize the citizenry for political reform. With a clever turn of phrase, the psycholinguistic structures of the free market, self-government, and juridic trusteeship had been joined at last.

Besides endorsing the theme of free expression as an exchange of commodities, the Court harkened back to *DeJonge* so as to integrate the commitments of speech and assembly into an "inseparable . . . conjunction of liberties." In the face of an integrated First Amendment, the statute amounted to a "trespass upon the domain set apart for free speech and free assembly." Clues in *Thomas* suggest that individuals operating within the postwar ethos found market-based notions of liberty appealing precisely because such modalities aligned with the antitotalitarian mood of the interregnum. First, Justice Wiley Rutledge's analysis began with a strong statement identifying freedom of expression as a singular goal of the nation-state. Where before the First Amendment was simply one among many provisions mentioned in the Constitution, the Justices now accorded the First Amendment a "preferred place," to be seen as securing "indispensable democratic freedoms." Second, consistent with the militarization of constitutional discourse, the opinion repeatedly described rights in terms of "a sanctity . . . not permitting dubious intrusions," regulatory action as a species of "repression," and judicial review as a means of "immun[izing]" rights against such restraints. In fact, the opinion confronted the charge — leveled by the dissenters — that the registration requirement at issue presented a minor inconvenience. "If the restraint were smaller than it is," Justice Rutledge's opinion rejoined, "it is from petty tyrannies that large ones take root and grow."

This last statement is enlightening on a number of fronts. The European experience was distilled into a derived belief to ground the adjudicative act: institutional vigilance was essential to liberty because even minor encroachments may breed grave repressive measures. Immediately after quoting Holmes's statement on the importance of ensuring "free trade in ideas," the Justices alluded to the tragic mistakes of the past attributable to acquiescence: "Indeed, the whole history of the problem shows it is to the end of preventing action that repression is primarily directed and to preserving the right to urge it that the protections are given."

Moreover, the statement validated the idea of judicial participation in the cultivation of constitutional norms. Inattentiveness to "petty tyrannies" can so alter the environment that "[s]eedlings planted in that soil grow great and, growing, break down the foundations of liberty." Unjustified impingements on liberty had to be identified, named, and repudiated. The consequences of inaction, the gardening metaphor strongly suggested, could be worse than mistaken action.

In his concurring opinion, Justice Jackson underscored the reconstructive mind-set with his own set of metaphors. He warned darkly of a "public authority . . . assuming a guardianship of the public mind" and cautioned that "every person must be his own watchman for truth." To the extent that the arrangement put the interests of the individual in tension with those of the state, the notion of "free trade of ideas" fit comfortably within this spectrum of the language of rights.

The legal saying gained more currency in the 1965 case *Lamont v. Postmaster General*, albeit in a concurring statement. Controversy centered on a federal law that called upon the post office to destroy "communist political propaganda" mailed from foreign countries unless the recipient timely executed and returned a reply card. The High Court nullified the preclearance provision because it unduly inhibited the flow of information.

Nurturing the still-inchoate theme from *Thomas* that expressive liberty depends upon reasonably effective speech, Justice Brennan wrote separately to stake out a fundamental right to receive publications. As he explained, "The dissemination of ideas can accomplish nothing if otherwise willing addressees are not free to receive and consider them. It would be a barren marketplace of ideas that had only sellers and no buyers."[16] Justice Brennan concluded with a call to arms to resist authoritarianism wherever it is found: "That the governments which originate this propaganda themselves have no equivalent guarantees only highlights the cherished values of our constitutional framework; it can never justify emulating the practice of restrictive regimes in the name of expediency."

Early on, "free market" rights rhetoric arose from a collective desire to distinguish the nation from its Communist enemies, whose planned economies and regimented way of life evoked feelings of outrage among Americans. Eventually, however, it became just another part of our conversational toolkit, as accepted as any formal doctrinal argument arising from original text, historical practice, or constitutional design.

An illustration of how constitutional language is fabricated by borrowing material from other domains, this metaphor has emerged as the single most recognized encapsulation of the ideal of free speech. Infused with laissez-faire ideology, First Amendment vernacular elicits support for expressive norms by harnessing ordinary Americans' belief in the virtues of open markets, minimal governmental intervention, and competitive pricing. The speech-as-commodity metaphor entails a series of values, propositions, and expectations:

1. The forum is a bounded place dedicated to a particular purpose.
2. Communicating ideas within the forum involves alienating idea-objects and securing them.
3. The utterance or set of ideas behind the utterance can be created, packaged, moved, stored, used, and depleted.
4. An exchange of ideas not only gives buyers and sellers what they desire but also puts an objective valuation on the ideas.
5. This valuation can be enhanced or diminished through state action.
6. The exchange of ideas is primarily initiated by individuals.
7. Regulation, if can be justified at all, must be defended according to its predicted impact upon this private ordering of ideas.

As the metaphor gained strength in twentieth century public debate, methods for deploying or resisting this type of rights discourse multiplied. One practice was to argue analogically, as the Justices did in a formidable line of cases, that the "college classroom with its surrounding environs is peculiarly the marketplace of ideas."[17] According to this form of the argument, the market represents an idealized conception of the public forum; joining this abstraction with a contested site implicitly benefits the latter through cognitive association. A seemingly natural implication — once the association is made — is that the rules governing traditional expressive settings ought to be migrated over to run on these new sites or technologies.

A dramatic instance can be found in *Tinker v. Des Moines Independent School District*.[18] There, the Justices enjoined enforcement of a school policy that prohibited students from wearing black armbands while on school grounds. The expressive interests of the students could hardly be doubted: they wore strips of black cloth to convey their opposition to the Vietnam conflict, and they conducted themselves in a manner that otherwise respected the decorum of the site. Once the Justices analyzed the policy and found it wanting, they chanted the market formula for a specific purpose: to extend the notion of the relevant expressive site beyond the classroom. After paying homage to the metaphorical market, the Court followed with a disquisition on the importance of expressive liberty to the implementation of sound educational philosophy: "the principle of these cases is not confined to the supervised and ordained discussion which takes place in the classroom. The principal use to which the schools are dedicated is to accommodate students during prescribed hours for the purpose of certain types of activities. Among those activities is personal intercommunication among the students. This is not only an inevitable part of the process of attending school; it is also an important part of the educational process." Accordingly, the image-schema of the market transformed the entire school into an outsized forum, in which the interactions of students are subject only to the proviso that they take no action that "materially disrupts classwork or involves substantial disorder."

In 1997, the Justices labeled the Internet a "new marketplace of ideas," applying free speech principles to strike down a federal law against indecent online material. Conceptualizing this rapidly changing, trans-border technology in such terms had two principal consequences. First, the metaphor suggested that the Internet resembled a traditional public site. The opinion therefore gestured in the direction of a right to access the Internet, without committing to all of the interpretive consequences such a position would necessitate. Second, the arrangement reinforced the more specific instruction that one is to "presume that governmental regulation of the content of speech is more likely to interfere with the free exchange of ideas than to encourage it." That is to say, the popular aspects of the ruling ratified strict scrutiny analysis when a law on its face appears to inhibit expression.

By a significant margin, the most common formulation associated nongovernmental action with "neutrality in the marketplace of ideas." Ritually invoking the "uninhibited marketplace of ideas" initiates a script in which the populace instinctively appreciates that "truth will ultimately prevail" because of the same "invisible hand" that is believed to produce optimal decisions in the economic sphere. The speaker-as-seller possesses a valuable commodity to exchange with a willing listener-as-procurer, and the state's charge is simple enough: to stay out of the way. Once the regulation under review is re-described as an impediment to an efficient transaction, judicial action is understood as restoring the natural forces that drive such exchanges. What began as a casual comment in the work of a single jurist became embraced as an article of faith in post-war America: "the best test of truth is the power of the thought to get itself accepted in the competition of the market."[19]

Pro-regulatory versions of the metaphor were certainly possible but rarely succeeded in juridic debate. By far the most prevalent approach was to argue that "distortions" of the market, or the problem of market failure, justify regulatory action.[20] According to this countermetaphor, the existence of monopoly power over speech may be shown by the acquisition of sufficient resources and the will to manipulate information processes. For example, in *Miami Herald Publishing Company v. Tornillo*, the High Court considered the constitutionality of a statute requiring newspapers to afford a candidate for office the right to reply to an editorial that "assails the personal character" of that candidate. Defenders of the law argued that First Amendment principles were imperiled because " 'the marketplace of ideas' is today a monopoly controlled by the owners of the market" — that is, large-scale media — and this "monopoly of the means of communication allows for little or no critical analysis of the media except in professional journals of very limited readership." The implication of this reasoning: "Surely a command that the government itself shall not impede the free flow of ideas does not afford non-governmental combinations a refuge if they impose restraints upon that constitutionally guaranteed freedom."

The majority opinion authored by Chief Justice Burger invalidated the enactment pursuant to the Free Press Clause and, in doing so, rejected this attempt to rewrite the governing script. His partial answer to the monopoly claim was that a "true" market, defined by "relatively easy access to the channels of communication," appears to have existed only in the historical past. Working with the same set of underlying political beliefs if not the exact metaphor, he argued that newspapers might choose to avoid controversy entirely rather than submit to the right-to-reply rule. This resulting dampening of press vigor would inhibit "free discussion of governmental affairs." Justice Burger's opinion also expressed grave concerns about the governmental "coercion" and "compulsion" necessary to enforce a right-of-access. Introducing a boundary metaphor to set apart and preserve editorial discretion, he concluded that "the Florida statute fails to clear the barriers of the First Amendment because of its intrusion into the function of editors."

A line of campaign finance cases similarly underscores the force of laissez-faire conceptions of free speech. *First National Bank of Boston v. Bellotti*, resolved in 1978, involved a challenge to a Massachusetts law that restricted corporations' political expenditures to those affecting the property, business, or assets of the corporation. The High Court struck the provision for impeding public debate. In a dissenting opinion, Justice Brennan signaled his preference to afford the state leeway to determine that unregulated campaign expenditures by corporations "seriously threaten[] the role of the First Amendment as a guarantor of a free marketplace of ideas." The animating goal of the law was "preventing institutions which have been permitted to amass wealth as a result of special advantages extended by the State for certain economic purposes from using that wealth to acquire an unfair advantage in the political process."[21] Again, however, this countermetaphor won few supporters among the community of jurists. The ideal of a "free exchange of ideas" aided efforts to keep campaign finance laws in something of a holding pattern in which contribution limits are subjected to more lenient review than expenditure limits.

An interesting variation on the theme of monopoly power arises when the government itself chooses to speak. Sandra Day O'Connor sensed precisely this problem when the government sponsors overtly religious or sectarian symbols: "When the government associates one set of religious beliefs with the state and identifies nonadherents as outsiders, it encroaches upon the individual's decision about whether and how to worship. In the marketplace of ideas, the government has vast resources and special status. Government religious expression therefore risks crowding out private observance and distorting the natural interplay between competing beliefs."[22]

Taking it as a given that the public square shares a kinship with an outdoor bazaar, Justice O'Connor found the exchange of ideas primarily to be governed by a "natural interplay" between private parties. The general presumption of a market-oriented basis for expressive liberty confirms the modern tendency to treat religious expression as a presumptively valuable and non-regulable commodity. When the government speaks, however, it is able to draw on resources that elude the typical orator. At least in the context of religious statements, O'Connor's logic suggests that the government's "special status" as a market participant may require judicial defense of minority rights, rather than adherence to a strict policy of nonintervention.

In theory, it is always possible to argue that discrete sets of ideas "contribute little to the marketplace of ideas" or to suggest that a particular regulation "affects the quantity — rather than the quality or the content" and would therefore not "raise the specter of Government control over the marketplace of ideas."[23] Each of these strategies seeks to avoid the chain of inferences associated with the frame invoked by the speech-as-commodity metaphor. Nevertheless, this method of characterizing the "marketplace of ideas" increasingly became a losing tactic outside well-established areas of unprotected expression. More often than not, the pro-regulatory version of the metaphor was viewed as incompatible with the general expectation that a culture of wide-open debate perfects the polity.[24]

As the formulation has metamorphosed from a casual reference to an organizing concept, it has promoted a sustained and active interaction among the domains of law, mass culture, and politics. Demonstrating its tenacity and pliability, market iconography initially helped to free individuals from statutes that restricted labor organizing, school policies that punished war protest, laws that criminalized flag desecration, and university regulations that permitted sanctions for subversive expression.[25] In each of these disputes, respecting the symbolic trading post meant enhancing one's ability to think for oneself, express oneself politically, or refuse to say anything at all.

Return, momentarily, to the pair of flag-burning cases resolved in 1989 and 1990. The dissenters who sought to protect the flag's cultural status felt compelled to operate within the liberty-as-exchange paradigm. In *Texas v. Johnson*, which involved a state antidesecration law, Justice Stevens attempted a market corruption argument: "sanctioning the public desecration of the flag will tarnish its value — both for those who cherish the ideas for which it waves and for those who desire to don the robes of martyrdom by burning it. That tarnish is not justified by the trivial burden on free expression occasioned by requiring that an available, alternative mode of expression — including uttering words critical of the flag . . . be employed."[26]

In the federal law analogue, *United States v. Eichman*, Stevens again claimed that judicial vindication of controversial speech would stimulate Americans to engage in further erosion of the flag's unifying symbolism of patriotism and sacrifice: "In today's marketplace of ideas, the public burning of a Vietnam draft card is probably less provocative than lighting a cigarette. Tomorrow flag burning may produce a similar reaction."[27]

In both cases, the dominant webs of signification exerted their influence on the explanations by parties on opposite sides. Citing *Brandenburg* as an emblem signifying the order of things, the Justices in the prevailing coalition argued: "The First Amendment does not guarantee that other concepts virtually sacred to our Nation as a whole — such as the principle that discrimination on the basis of race is odious and destructive — will go unquestioned in the marketplace of ideas."

The building of free speech culture would not stop there. As social context tumbled into context and political priorities were reordered, this combination of legal ideology and economic philosophy would help to ease regulatory barriers to commercial advertising, shield many hostile speech-acts, and alter the trajectory of Establishment Clause jurisprudence.[28] For instance, Chief Justice Rehnquist once criticized a decision that "elevates commercial intercourse between a seller hawking his wares and a buyer seeking to strike a bargain to the same plane as has been previously reserved for the free marketplace of ideas," but the trend has been to do just that.[29] Indeed, as his colleagues explained, the prevailing view is that "the relationship of speech to the marketplace of products or of services does not make it valueless in the marketplace of ideas."

Consider *McDaniel v. Paty*,[30] resolved by the High Court in 1978. The Tennessee constitution contained a provision that disqualified ministers from serving as legislators. The state's separationist strategy was motivated by not only a barely disguised anticlerical sentiment but also a sense that "ministers of the gospel are, by their profession, dedicated to God and the care of Souls, and ought not to be diverted from the great duties of their functions." The High Court invalidated the provision under the Free Exercise Clause. In a fascinating concurring opinion by Justice Brennan, he argued that the provision violated both the commitment to nonestablishment and free exercise of religion. In response to the state's argument that such a barrier to participation was necessary to "avoid fomenting religious strife or the fusing of church with state affairs," he replied: "The antidote which the Constitution provides against zealots who would inject sectarianism into the political process is to subject their ideas to refutation in the marketplace of ideas and their platforms to rejection at the polls." The original separationist sentiment may have been a desire to avoid "religious divisiveness," but wide-open "public debate of religious ideas, like any other, may arouse emotion, may incite, may foment religious divisiveness and strife." On this occasion, barrier-style language met its match in the more free-flowing connotations of assembly-based discourse.

The general tactic engaged in *Paty* would be repeated with increasing frequency in the Justices' readings of the Religion Clauses. Among these many occurrences, one noteworthy controversy stands out: *Rosenberger v. Rector and Visitors of the University of Virginia*. A policy invited student organizations to apply for general funds to support extracurricular activities that advanced the "educational purpose of the University." The policy categorically excluded religious activities from consideration for financial support and defined the relevant term as any activity that "primarily promotes or manifests a particular belie[f] in or about a deity or an ultimate reality." When school officials denied a Christian student group's application for the subsidy, the students claimed that the action infringed their First Amendment rights.

In a strongly worded ruling, Anthony Kennedy found the denial of funds to be an exercise in viewpoint-based discrimination. In support of this rationale, he invoked the familiar image of the state interfering with the natural give and take between student speakers: "Our understanding of the complex and multi-faceted nature of public discourse has not embraced such a contrived description of the marketplace of ideas. . . . It is as objectionable to exclude both a theistic and an atheistic perspective on the debate as it is to exclude one, the other, or yet another political, economic, or social viewpoint."[31]

Instead of treating the policy as a legitimate prohibition of direct public expenditures on behalf of religion (and thus presumptively a violation of the Establishment Clause), the word-picture presented the challenged action as a denial of access to a nonphysical expressive site (and therefore a presumptive free speech violation). Market-oriented discourse was deployed to deflect the separationist argument that "public funds for the direct subsidization of preaching the word is categorically forbidden under the Establishment Clause."

Framing the issue in this way not only created the context for judicial analysis but also facilitated its resolution. The nature and extent of university control over the speech subsidy, Justice Kennedy suggested, "skewed" the normal terms of give and take. Once we envision this—or any other dispute—in these evocative terms, our cultural understandings do much of the work of normalizing the constitutional injury detected, as well as the remedy that is ultimately implemented.

The Limitations of Moment-Based and Incrementalist Accounts

The return of the free market to discursive practice defies easy explanation. Dominant models of legal change have particular difficulty accounting for this phenomenon and, indeed, often ignore the transformations in the First Amendment. Bruce Ackerman understands the New Deal era as a decisive defeat for laissez-faire constitutionalism, but the persistence of market-talk proves to be confounding for such Big-Bang accounts. For the marketplace of ideas not only entails a particular way of talking about our commitments but also affirms, at least implicitly, a particular set of economic attitudes and political values.

According to Ackerman's intricate "dualist" theory, American politics can be divided into two cycles: ordinary politics, during which official acts are measured against past achievements, and higher lawmaking, in which entirely new commitments are fashioned by a virtuous, mobilized citizenry by invoking Article V of the Constitution or through more unconventional methods.

Dualism posits that there have been three and only three moments in which the people "transformed their higher law to express deep changes in their political identities": the Founding, Reconstruction, and the New Deal.[32] As to this last revolutionary event, an activated citizenry received and responded to the signals of a charismatic leader in Franklin Delano Roosevelt. With the "switch in time" by the High Court in the late 1930s, the decisions of the Supreme Court codified a reversal of a property-oriented conception of the Constitution.

If one grants the monumental nature of the New Deal (and there is every reason to accept Ackerman's characterization of this seismic shift as revolutionary), then the people repudiated market ideology as a set of governing ideas. Because one searches in vain for compliance with the text or the spirit of Article V, however, dualism must understand the economic colonization of First Amendment thought as either a failed revolution or a successful but illegitimate one.[33] The difficulty with the first response is that it denies tangible changes to the text's meanings; the flaw in the second is that it places compliance with Article V above the deeply held beliefs of generations of Americans.

In fact, the return of free market discourse to constitutional debate is most credibly attributed to Americans' rising postwar defense of open markets and their pursuit of an antitotalitarian mission, rather than to a single episode of republican deliberation.[34] That is to say, the grammatical patterns arose because the techniques became useful to political elites in the reconstruction of the public mind; useful rhetorical forms then became increasingly generalized to become part of Americans' automatic behavior. Richard Primus has thoughtfully explored the manner in which "the cumulative American reaction against European totalitarianism became so powerful a force in the world of legal and political ideas that it sometimes surpassed, though without ever completely eclipsing, the influences of the ideas and experiences of older eras."[35] The emergence of these popular constructions of the First Amendment fits neatly within Primus's broader narrative of the transformation of rights discourse.

Rather than concede defeat, the dualist might be tempted to attribute the market's stranglehold on First Amendment thought to jurists' misplaced appreciation of their role in an "activist government," one of the principles that dualism derives from the New Deal experience. To attempt this tack, however, is to show that receptivity to the proactive state is not a foundational principle erected with clarity or finality but rather a dominant frame of mind. Instead of a substantive rule to live by, it is a mood whose intensity waxes and wanes with changes to the state of electoral politics and the terminology employed to debate constitutional ideas.

At all events, the experience teaches that even if a doctrine formally circumscribes or screens out certain considerations (*e.g.*, the *Carolene Products* decision's famous downgrading of economic claims traveling under the Fourteenth Amendment), ideological vestiges of earlier eras may persist in legal terminology, lying dormant until conditions become conducive to a revival. Far from securing overwhelming victory for any particular political belief, the matrix of reflective action and legal thought produced by a mobilized moment is a particular type of social consensus.

Taking seriously the proposition that politics transforms vocabulary also means that no linguistic regime is untouchable. The constitutional process may simply displace a defeated belief or rhetorical habit from one legal domain (Equal Protection) to another (First Amendment). In this case, the New Deal era may have been a triumph of complexity over simplicity with regard to the role that government may play in the lives of ordinary Americans, and even of one economic philosophy over another, but the impressive nature of the achievements is not reason enough to calcify the moment against subsequent efforts to alter the terms of debate.

Where the dualist praises human wonders of the grandest scale, the gradualist discovers progress in even the subtlest changes to legal topography. The law, Benjamin Cardozo famously claimed in *The Nature of the Judicial Process*, is "fluid and changeable," in "an endless state of *becoming*." For Cardozo, the past and present are transient stages toward ever better end-states. Stability to the incrementalist is not a social fact but a mirage, dangerously obscuring a system in "perpetual flux."[36]

Evolutionary models of law, usually captured in defenses of the "living Constitution," are enticing because they give the impression of flexibility and growth. In the main, however, they are hobbled by imprecision, for there is no process of natural selection that ensures that superior stewardship traits are reproduced and disadvantageous aspects of the law disappear. It is not reason or social approval that evolution rewards but adaptability alone. The gradualist senses this gap in protocol and therefore locates the jurist at the center of the life of the law. In the midst of doctrinal incoherence and political chicanery, the judge serves as the law's most faithful "guardian," entrusted with the authority to make law to fill its interstices or to levy war against obsolescence.[37]

Ironically, then, despite resort to naturalistic imagery, mastery of the law by specialists is a staple of gradualism. Law is conceived of as "a body of rules and principles and standards" to be "sorted, selected, moulded, and adapted in subordination to . . . bring[ing] certainty and order out of the wilderness of precedent."[38] While the ability to manipulate doctrine is certainly an important aspect of judging, there is more to the law than the internal considerations of the craft. Forces exogenous to the law not only offer raw material for legal innovation but can also dramatically remake the very linguistic field in which constitutional grammar is reproduced.

The gradualist has little objection to "the marketplace of ideas" so long as the rest of the analysis hews to criteria internal to matters of craftsmanship. Similarly, court-centered gradualism might explain the epic swings in the rhetoric of fire in implausibly instrumentalist terms: governing language changed for the sole reason that judges found it useful to make a change in word choice.

Cass Sunstein's provocative proposal for a "New Deal . . . for speech, one that would parallel the New Deal provided to property rights during the 1930s," is based on the gradualist model of legal change.[39] Troubled by a turn toward laissez-faire conceptions of free speech in recent years, Sunstein recommends that jurists "apply much of the reasoning of the New Deal attack on the common law to current questions of First Amendment law." The merits of the proposal aside, Sunstein's error is to treat laissez-faire constitutionalism as an endogenous rule, rather than as a practice buoyed by significant cultural support. Focusing less upon language than outcome, he mistakenly believes that "the marketplace of ideas" has had an influence on the development of the First Amendment only in the past quarter century. To see the two as entwined shows that the discursive practice has deep roots not only in founding attitudes about property but also in mobilized postwar beliefs about the appropriate mission of the state.

If, indeed, the impact of this economic philosophy on the First Amendment is merely a recent error in juridic reasoning, it should be a simple matter to correct once decision makers see the light of day. But if the gradualist is wrong about this — and if the entrenchment of the "marketplace" metaphor in constitutional practice for nearly two generations is any indication — then the reformation for which Sunstein hopes may generate far more opposition and demand more resources to accomplish than he anticipates.

In short, it is necessary to achieve a consolidated account of foundational change capable of explaining everyday miracles as well as spectacular monuments, one that can situate readings of text within broader cultural processes while accounting for the internal customs of the craft. The next task is to demonstrate why the idea of the linguistic regime fills the need for predictability on the one hand and the reality of cultural change on the other.

The Linguistic Regime as the Basis of Constitutional Stability

Once constitutionalism is understood as a species of political acculturation, the patterns of linguistic transformation suggest a more significant degree of fluidity to foundational discourse than one might expect, as well as a different set of structural constraints. Dualism again provides a useful counter-point. In this sense, one might say that dualism posits an extension of original-ism's formal methodology: each theory emphasizes explosive moments of po-litical creation that generate unmistakable principles to be dutifully preserved and implemented by jurists. Dualism finds in the New Deal at least one other moment of creativity that originalism rejects, but what unifies these otherwise disparate theories of legal change are dependence on a moment-based account of constitutionalism and a demand that citizens obey formal criteria legitimat-ing structural change.

What is excluded by strict adherence to such a rule of recognition, or at least requires a supplemental account, is the impact of social movements and cul-tural upheavals that have nevertheless shaped the public consciousness. These events are just as likely to generate fresh political beliefs and re-descriptions of textual commitments. Institutional responses to unplanned events can require a level of engagement that matches or exceeds that produced during debates over formal changes to constitutional text.

Taking the linguistic regime as the relevant unit of analysis promises greater insight. Any account of legal change must grapple with comprehensiveness and historicity if it is to be persuasive. Downscaling the theoretical point of reference enhances the search for continuities in discursive practices across time while illuminating subtle connections with other languages of power, as well as points of opposition. In this way, it becomes possible to speak not of single themes organizing the entire legal imagination but of discrete bodies of knowledge. It becomes possible to see the First Amendment as a set of ideas that depends upon and informs certain values while being relatively un-touched by other values. Principled integration of the various aspects of the law into a coherent whole may or may not occur at these points of contact, but a theory of linguistic convergence does not presume that such overarching consistencies exist.

Rather than seeking to explain constitutional development in light of a handful of events, the linguistic regime better accounts for the social and political dynamics that are constantly acting upon readings of text. Unlike the moment-based model, the model of linguistic transformation is concerned less with adherence to single substantive principles than with social-political con-sensus as to what actors believe to be acceptable terms of debate and the range of outcomes that constitutional actors find palatable. The approach hews to the observation that something other than meta-procedure dictates the de-velopment of the political imagination.

In training attention upon the linkages among language, rule, and external ethos, the linguistic regime is also superior to the incrementalist model. Contrary to the gradualist's vision of perpetual motion, it reveals that stability exists and locates that stability in the interaction of these overlapping domains. The approach also issues a kind of warning to the gradualist: if control over the meaning of text lies beyond any particular juridic statement, then court-directed programs of reformation might not only fall short but in some instances yield counterproductive consequences.

Does minimizing the shadow cast by Article V over the processes of constitutional construction cause us to lose something crucial with respect to fidelity to basic organizing principles? Absolutely not. The linguistic regime better captures popular sovereignty by recognizing the stability that social norms provide and identifies the range of rhetorical freedom that citizens enjoy. By situating the authoritative meaning of text in social practice rather than in an external rule of recognition, it actually makes the substance of the law more accountable to the people. This is so because controlling the meaning of text remains, at any given moment, a matter for institutional consensus.

While the model confronts the capaciousness of text, it also recognizes that there will always be a socially implausible set of understandings. This is where Article V retains its vitality. When attempts to secure institutional consensus around a preferred construction repeatedly fail, formal amendment is the only viable option. Article V serves as a functional backstop, rather than as an organizing set of commands intended to constrain the everyday construction of text.

Why is burning a flag constitutionally protected "speech" rather than a scurrilous act that threatens to precipitate disorder? Not because the text is self-defining or because extrapolating original intentions from any particular deliberative moment yields a single set of answers. Rather, flag burning is speech because for the time being a discernible but uneasy cultural consensus exists among the Judiciary, the political branches, and a nontrivial number of ordinary Americans behind this juridic definition. Any number of things, however, can destabilize the regime short of an amendment to text: a breakdown in cultural consensus over a particular practice, a decisive shift in judicial appointments, a concerted effort by the political branches to challenge a prevailing construction, the achievements of a highly mobilized political movement.

For those who find this a disquieting proposition, it is worth keeping in mind that it is not easy to manipulate any of the levers of political authority that might lead to a decisive shift in constitutional meaning. Altering context by organizing and sustaining a social movement, electing ideologically dedicated leaders, or securing the appointment of a critical mass of sympathetic jurists requires an enormous commitment of time and resources. Many contingencies have to break in favor of the challenger along the way. Lawsuits extend invitations to jurists to chip away at governing understandings of text and to present new constructions, but it may take several attempts before the Justices will take notice. It is not a simple task to alter prevailing conceptions of the Constitution through ordinary politics or litigation, but, then again, it is not impossible.

Fire Versus Market

The production of market-based constructions shares a number of similarities with that of fire-based vernacular. First, there is not, and has never been, a necessary connection between original text and the common rhetorical methods ultimately chosen to articulate the meaning of that text. To put it another way, at its inception each metaphor involved drawing upon a store of informal knowledge, rather than one-for-one borrowing from any authoritative writing. It is true that John Stuart Mill employed the speech-as-combat metaphor in defending the importance of liberty of expression in his writings, but this entailed a somewhat different set of resonances. It can also hardly be disputed that references to "property" appear prominently in the Constitution. Yet, not even the most strained theory of intratextual interpretation yields a comprehensive economic scheme for evaluating our First Amendment commitments.

Second, the lack of any sound textual basis for the market or fire has not, so far as anyone can tell, reduced its systematicity or durability in political thought. In fact, the evidence points in exactly the opposite direction: despite the aesthetically pleasing quality of the market metaphor, it was not until a mobilized society and a reinvigorated economy made open markets a priority that the trope ascended into the pantheon of First Amendment modalities. This suggests not only that text matters less than the structures of grammar over time but also that the complicated social dynamics that sustain the meaning of ordinary language do not necessarily obey the customs of doctrinal analysis. Everyday constructions are deployed purposively on behalf of preferred rules, but the mechanisms of cognition and dissemination ensure that these constructions have a life term of their own.

Third, there is a cumulative quality to the production of these pro-speech formulations. Actors are not shy about mixing metaphors or deploying a preferred metaphor to combat the ideological effects of another. For example, the flag-burning cases saw proponents of expressive liberty resisting the incendiary approach while taking full advantage of the dominant marketplace metaphor. Detractors simultaneously cast flag burning in inflammatory terms while resisting, as best they could, the implications of the uninhibited market.

Similar patterns of metaphoric extension and resistance can be found in other controversies.

Herein lies the basic difference between the grammarian and the facilitator. The former would recoil from such ungainly tactics, finding them to be abuses of language, while the latter would look for social utility in the practice if it appeared to be sufficiently pervasive. Before moving on from the historical patterns analyzed in this chapter, it might be worth pausing to evaluate the relative utility of these terms. If metaphors are treated as they are, namely fragments for mass consumption rather than nuanced formulas, too much should not be asked of them. After all, they are meant not as substitutions for rules to live by but as means of actuating and disseminating constitutional knowledge among a wider audience. Within these parameters, it is fair to ask to what extent they encourage productive attitudes and to what extent they might promote undesirable perceptions of political community.

One method of answering this question is to determine just how a given metaphoric framework conceptualizes the subject of law. On this score, the language of fire surely has its shortcomings. The earliest arrangement severely underdrew the human faculty. In permitting aggressive regulation at the first hint of counterproductive consequences ("a single revolutionary spark"), legal language treated citizens as generally helpless in the face of foreign ideologies, unable to exercise reason to help themselves. The possibility that recipients of socialist ideas might ignore, contradict, or reject them out of hand did not enter the realm of possibility; the strategy was to exclude first and ask questions later.

Take Justice Jackson's position in *Kunz v. New York* on why regulation of racially "incendiary" speech should be permitted while the brooding threat of totalitarianism remained.[40] In *Kunz*, the High Court protected the racially hostile rantings of a street preacher against police officers who arrested him under the auspices of a permit law. Justice Jackson dissented, voicing his concern — consistent with his feelings in *Dennis* — that "[e]ssential freedoms are today threatened from without and within." "In such a setting," he explained, "to blanket hateful and hate-stirring attacks on races and faiths under the protections for freedom of speech may be a noble innovation" to which he could not assent. Chanting the theater fire mantra, he argued that the speaker's "words, in the environment of the streets, have and will result in [street fighting or riots], unless a police escort attends to awe the hearers into submission." Justice Jackson loosed a pyrotechnic, pro-regulatory version of the house-on-fire metaphor: silencing a speaker by authorities as a measure of mob control is like dynamiting a house to stop the spread of a conflagration. It may be justified by the overwhelming community interest that flames not be fed as compared with the little interest to be served by continuing to feed them." Whereas the emerging pro-speech version of the language treated the house as a representation of the entire legal order, Jackson's variation reduced the house to a stand-in for the interests of a single citizen, just one expendable resource that may be "dynamited" to save untold lives in the path of the ideological "conflagration." A paternalistic theme thus unites the discourse of different eras.

This is hardly an image of the human subject, or an ideal of citizenship, that inspires love for the political community or one's fellows. The experiential gestalt reduces public reason to a series of commands and responses, rather than reflective action by autonomous subjects. It displays a potentially corrosive lack of trust in the people's political agency and a terrifying notion of the state empowered to quash unflattering images of itself. At a minimum, the vision of law is in tension with the terms of community articulated in *Barnette* in which the survival of democracy calls for faith in a mature citizenry.

A recalibrated variation of the discursive strategy seems to do better, but perhaps only because its usage promotes speech-protective outcomes. When its structure is analyzed more closely, it is apparent that the popular construct does little to enrich the notion of citizenship. The frame of understanding invoked by the regulation-as-fire metaphor succeeds primarily by reversing the polarity of the privileged alliance in the public mind from the *state:: court* to the *court:: speaker*. The political order is still presented with a psychic threat, but the overwhelming impression conveyed by the composition is that public officials are misguided or shortsighted. The net effect is that the citizen-as-orator is added to an already lengthy list of parties in need of rescue. The individual is presumed to be unable to engage in self-help, a prisoner of bureaucratic forces or a victim of malevolent designs.

Indeed, it would not be going too far to say that the rhetoric of fire has, on balance, promoted court-centered resolutions and an undifferentiated fear of authorities who might "torch" the proverbial house. One does well not to overstate the point, yet the rapidity of the device's saturation of popular culture threatens to overwhelm more nuanced portrayals of the constitutional order.

If the fire metaphor grossly undersketches the legal subject, the marketplace metaphor overdraws the individual in some peculiar ways. At its best, the "uninhibited marketplace" treats the legal subject as a producer or consumer of ideas entitled to respect. To the extent that metaphoric entailments align with broader understandings of the importance of autonomy and individual self-worth, the frame of understanding affirms the moral agency of the speaker and the listener. The concerns arise primarily from the danger of ideological spillover — that is, the possibility that the political beliefs associated with one rhetorical arrangement will extend beyond their initial context and influence another domain. In elevating the exchange as the central goal of text, the rhetorical device dictates that communal practices of engagement and valuation are subsidiary to this transaction. The state is treated, accordingly, as an interloper or, at best, empowered to correct market failure; it is never a creator whose actions (or inactions) are legitimately expressive and directive.

This is an untenable orientation in the long run, even if, against all experience, political beliefs can be cabined to a particular area of social life. Rousseau explains that in a republic each citizen "is bound by a double relation": "[A]s a member of the sovereign he is bound to [other] individuals, and as a member of the state to the sovereign."[41] Vernacular that posits expressive freedom as a state of existence untethered from (and perhaps preexisting) the state therefore threatens dual harm to group life insofar as it perpetuates the impression that the conditions of deliberative democracy may be satisfied through the accumulation of private preferences in a relatively unbounded end-state. Instead, public reason requires ascertaining the general will rather than the will of all, "which is no more than a sum of particular wills." The general will is purposive and reflective, dependent upon the citizen to demonstrate a measure of self-restraint and regard for others, whereas the individual will cares for little more than satisfying its own needs and wants: "Public good or evil would not be merely the sum of individual goods and evils, as in a simple aggregation, but it would reside in the liaison that unites them; it would be greater than this sum."[42]

It is not necessary to go as far as Rousseau, who believed that "private interest and the common good are mutually exclusive in the natural order of things," to sense risk along with reward. What, ultimately, is to be done? If every construction of law is partial, and institutional control of democratic culture incomplete, it is as foolish to pursue an extermination policy as it is to promote a single substantive conception of law. The solution is not to try to eradicate popular iterations of our commitments but to contain their counterproductive qualities, cultivate alternative formulations, and guard against the sedimentation of any single idea in the public mind.

4

Political Pathways

As soon as one accepts that the structure and valence of juridic language are inevitably altered by dynamics beyond the four walls of the courthouse, questions of process move to the foreground. What are the actual mechanisms through which dedicated advocates and activists encourage or pressure official decision makers to adopt new constructions of text? Where are the crucial points of entry into the system of language formation?

To alter the social foundations of legal language and stimulate linguistic development, motivated actors must exploit available political pathways. Broadly understood, a political pathway is any means by which constitutional knowledge is accumulated, stored, presented, reproduced, or manipulated. A nonexhaustive list includes governmental institutions, media, civic organizations, litigation, and electoral processes. The objectives of control include (1) to intensify and redirect the dialectical interactions between the people and their political institutions; (2) to present new knowledge to decision makers and language innovators; (3) to secure the legitimization of preferred short-term policies and long-term values; (4) to alter the valence of governing terminology; and (5) to acquire new modes of discourse in the service of long-term goals.

Controlling political pathways requires pursuit of some combination of the following strategies: (a) seizing the national stage by dominating media coverage; (b) altering social context through legislative enactment, citizen initiative, or the election of ideologically motivated officials; (c) securing the appointment of sympathetic jurists and administrators; or (d) employing the courts in nonconventional ways in order to mold public opinion.

Two social movements enjoyed historical success in exploiting these pathways to reshape dominant understandings of the First Amendment. Each movement had a distinctive reformist agenda. During the 1960s, persons committed to the cause of racial equality sought to end the multigenerational practice of social separation between blacks and whites. In comparison, the conservative revival that began in the 1980s and gained momentum in the 1990s had a more diffuse agenda, one that spanned the moral revitalization of community, a reconfiguration of the relationships between the national and the local, and a redefinition of the judicial role in such areas as crime and punishment, religious experience, and human sexuality. The First Amendment played an indirect role in civil rights workers' policy agenda; legal innovation occurred as a result of confrontations over movement tactics. In contrast, a direct assault on First Amendment meanings motivated and organized social conservatives.

In spite of these differences, the two instances of linguistic transformation share significant similarities. Each sequence of events involved collective political action to generate and propagate alternative textual understandings, rather than passive reliance upon cultural processes. Each movement engaged in extensive vocabulary building to organize itself and define its objectives; movement leaders pressed their speech-acts or constructions of text in various quarters simultaneously. Opponents vigorously resisted these constructions, and governing practices eventually absorbed these external critiques through transformation of legal language.

Another reason to focus on these events is that a second-order metaphor played a crucial role in each episode. For civil rights activists, elaboration of the speech-within-a-meeting metaphor became a necessary condition to the public demonstration of their commitment to racial equality. For those dedicated to a "spiritual revival," success depended partly upon discrediting the governing boundary metaphor that had served as the starting point of deliberations over religious liberty and pressing for institutional methodologies and grammar that better suited their values.

The Phases of Linguistic Coherence

Before undertaking an examination of these two social movements, it is useful to build upon our existing descriptive terminology. At the outset, we might understand the life cycle of a governing regime to consist of four stages: composition, reaction, adaptation, and dissolution. There is no consistent length of time associated with any of these phases, as the durability of linguistic consensus turns on personnel, ethos, ingenuity, and dedication, as well as a host of events beyond human control. Some stages may begin to dissipate after a decade or less; others may last for a generation or more. Each stage is associated with a distinctive institutional orientation, a set of official strategies for managing conflict, and a state of conceptual coherence regarding legal ideas.

When a motivated social group or coalition attempts to dislodge a dominant regime, it is in actuality seeking to advance the cultural infrastructure of a governing matrix through its life cycle more rapidly. That constitutional transformation, like constitution writing, involves a social process means that it is never as simple as winning a lawsuit or securing the election of a single candidate. Isolated acts may produce glacial change within a stage but are unlikely to significantly alter existing law-making dynamics. Intentionality, coordination, and social approval are crucial to regime change.

The initiation of any particular regime requires the purposeful, authoritative composition of text — whether it originates in the domain of the courts or with policymakers. A reading of the Constitution must be authoritative in order to distinguish it from the preferred reading of a particular citizen and any number of understandings that might be percolating in popular culture. Compulsion could arise from executive policy, legislative act or practice, or juridic approval; the sense of authority may flow from fear of enforcement or force of habit. Whatever its source, the general idea is that the reading must be imbued with sufficient sanction that others are likely to accord it respect, if not obedience.

If the appearance of authority to construe text is where one must begin to search for stability, a corollary principle is that consensus depends upon institutional participation, though the degree of involvement may vary from subject to subject. It is possible, though it may not be ideal, for congruence to exist without equivalent participation on the part of bureaucratic actors.

Such consensus can be built upon a political construction of constitutional text combined with judicial assent, just as a governing regime can consist of social cooperation to maintain a particular juridic construction. For now, Congress's Article I authority to declare war is dominated by the model of executive leadership over foreign affairs, regardless of what the text suggests; by comparison, for much of the twentieth century, our understanding of the First Amendment was based on the model of judicial initiative.

During the initial phase of creation, the institutions with the greatest stake in construing text engage in justification. This involves a commitment of the bulk of existing resources to the presentation of a vision of law according to the customs of that institution. The presenter makes a strong claim to know the best interests of the people, and his credibility turns on a host of factors, including the plausibility of a reading in light of existing forms.

It is at this first stage that a construction often enjoys the greatest coherence. This occurs not only because there is an expenditure of significant energy in the initial act of creativity but also because the interpretive presentation is — at least according to the reasonable expectations of the presenter — likely to stimulate the most interest among affected communities. A well-crafted presentation of law therefore anticipates the possibility of backlash and considers the social plausibility of the various textual readings available. Having selected a reading of text, an actor immediately sets about suppressing alternatives, leading analysts to say that an act of legal creation, or "jurisgenesis," is always accompanied by the act of destroying competing visions of law — manifesting what Robert Cover termed the "jurispathic" instinct.[1]

When the compositional process is complete, the reading re-enters the stream of public debate. Some constructions generate little interest or objection; others prompt a swift outcry. Once a serious challenge to the textual reading begins to coalesce, a regime enters the phase of reaction. It is now possible to understand the primary import of the social movement — its targeted deployments of social energy and political capital hope to accelerate the reaction stage of a regime's life cycle, to speed the formation of alternative conceptions of group life, and to prepare the environment for legal change.

Institutional outlook correspondingly shifts from articulation to conservation; an institutional actor's energies are redirected from questions of plausibility to defense and entrenchment of the textual construction. Having already made an investment of prestige and resources to defend a particular vision of law, the principal motivation now becomes to maintain the appearance of consistency, coherence, and accountability. This initial stage of external resistance often produces a burst of linguistic diversity, first as an institutional actor seeks to popularize and disseminate his creation and then as he seeks to cultivate social support for that vision of law.

If a presentation of text survives cultural resistance, it is because the vision of law has secured a modicum of social support. At this point, one enters a period of adaptation, because once an institution has had the chance to gauge the intensity and breadth of resistance, constitutional actors generally then settle into a pattern of developing and implementing techniques for absorbing some auxiliary criticisms that arise and deflecting others. It is not unusual for a regime to face a second and a third period of reaction — concerted efforts to dislodge the reigning worldview — each with its own peculiar characteristics.

During this second stage of linguistic maturation, the judicial outlook changes from conservation to management. The task is no longer to defend the original textual construction against charges of illegitimacy but rather to coordinate the dialogic interactions between the institution and other actors over the presentation of law. Although there is a certain degree of trial and error that characterizes this phase, such fluctuations are not believed to undermine the prevailing paradigm.

Every linguistic regime eventually breaks down. The predominant causes of dissensus can be traced to internal or external sources, though they almost always produce synergistic effects. Internally, dissolution occurs because adaptation no longer seems to be a viable management strategy to a critical mass of stakeholders. Patience has worn thin among those who had previously cast their lot with the prevailing order, the political beliefs that once animated a textual reading no longer command a majority, and factions among elites generally or within a particular institution have developed and multiplied. The suppressive instinct momentarily dampens, as the decapitation of one jurisprudential possibility seems only to bring five hungry ideas. As pressures to submerge disagreements lessen and suppression becomes toleration, thematic coherence becomes threatened.

Externally, dissolution may be accelerated because an institution's constituencies have begun to align against a particular reading, putting that institution's reputation at risk. A significant event — such as war, national tragedy, or social movement — also has the power to scramble existing ethical configurations or electoral alignments. The citizenry's confrontation of such an event may lead to a rejection of older modes of interaction and the production of more responsive governing grammar.

As one enters the last days of a linguistic regime, factions within institutions begin actively signaling their receptivity to new constructions of text. Showcasing the multiplicity of constitutional possibilities only hastens the end of the regime, for it emboldens committed actors to increase the intensity and frequency of their opposition. Consequently, one can say that the institutional orientation has moved from adaptation to reformation. Because every ending is also a beginning, an institutional actor takes a calculated risk and trades away the appearance of internal cohesiveness for a possible stake in a new regime, one presenting a better match between a reading of text and some emerging set of norms. As the collective search for order proceeds in earnest, the constitutional system experiences another proliferation of rules, vernacular, and models of political community.

Assembly: From Equality to Liberty and Back Again

Consider the civil rights movement's transformation of First Amendment law during the 1960s. An intergenerational coalition of committed activists and intellectuals sought to redefine prevailing sociolegal conceptions of equality, particularly as they affected the rights, status, and material opportunities of African Americans. Much of the groundwork had been done in the previous two decades, as equality became a feature of foreign policy and, more broadly, of Americans' collective self-understanding as the defender of liberty and opportunity. But the next phase of the project, which would call for an assault on prevailing perceptions of equality in private spheres such as the workplace and the home, would not be completed until citizens took to the streets.

Although modern civil rights statutes are the main legacy of the Freedom Rides and marches, the tactics of civil disobedience also left an indelible mark on First Amendment law. As protestors employed unconventional tactics to engage the public on the question of racial equality, they encountered aggressive and creative forms of adversity. These repressive measures ranged from ordinary law-and-order techniques to disperse and deter public gatherings, to the state's pursuit of civil litigation to stop civil rights events, to the enactment of professional requirements that inhibited the ability of advocates and activists to interact for constitutional change. When courts finally were called upon to review these official measures, they creatively absorbed the discourse of the streets in First Amendment vocabulary.

This reading of the leading decisions of this era resists Kalven's recommendation that they be read "not as [reflecting] political pressure on the Court which then as a political institution responded, but rather as a strategy to trap democracy in its own decencies."[2] Kalven's perspective obscures more than it illuminates. It is not that citizens' "rights in an important sense were always there" and that, as agents, the Justices were merely "bringing them to light." To the contrary: the series of rulings reflects the joint institutional recognition of entirely new political beliefs to animate the First Amendment's textual promise.

If Kalven would deny exogenous influences on the judicial mind-set, Robert Dahl stands for maximum permeability in the law. Dahl envisions the Supreme Court as a policymaking institution because it must make choices between plausible interpretive alternatives and, in making such choices, must either please or disappoint other members of a national political alliance. Surveying the Supreme Court's rulings striking down federal laws as unconstitutional, he finds that "the policy views dominant on the Court are never for long out of line with the policy views dominant among the lawmaking majorities of the United States."[3]

There are two possible readings of Dahl's thesis.[4] The first—which looks to broad swaths of public sentiment—hypothesizes that, despite an enduring myth of rights, courts behave in accordance with "the preferences of a national majority." A second and more sophisticated version — which treats the Justices as members of the political elite — searches instead for congruence between judicial outcomes and the initiatives of the "dominant lawmaking majority in Congress."[5] But the first rendition approaches the notion of popular assent crudely and invites retrospective analysis; the second unduly minimizes the contributions of direct action in building the political imagination.

Whichever reading one prefers, Dahl's conception of constitutionalism fails to confront the liminality of constitutional language and the centrality of political belief — the dynamic, forgiving phenomena that make the articulation of public policy possible. For Dahl, "democracy is a set of basic procedures for arriving at decisions." Juridic discourse is, accordingly, treated as little more than a means of expressing the aggregated preferences of an organized subset of the population (a majority, a minority, or an "aggregation of minorities"). Dahl assumes that at different moments, different coalitions may govern, yet what remains constant is his prediction of general congruence between judicial utterance and external policy. The symbolic, popular, and everyday features of group life elude Dahl's model.

With Dahl, and against Kalven, the precepts of eloquence attribute the generative force of the law to events outside the courts. Concerned solely with matching judicial outcome and aggregated policy preferences like so many swatches, however, Dahl is hard pressed to detect the undercurrents of foundational change or to explain the cultural processes that produce and sustain the idea of the people. The high-minded is unjustifiably blurred with the parochial; enduring rhetorical forms are confused with the short-term policies that a political actor might pursue. Against Dahl, then, this reading of the cases insists that the vehicles of constitutional interaction are important and that they reflect not simply a reordering of policy priorities but more profound changes to the content and structure of the nation's political beliefs.

In a series of rulings involving civil rights activists and their advocates during the 1960s, the High Court gradually came to favor expressive liberty as a commitment that occupies a unique position: simultaneously an antecedent to equality and an efficacious means for realizing it. That is to say, an institutional consensus materialized favoring the entrenchment of the First Amendment as a method of preserving gains on racial justice. In the process, this coalition secured the First Amendment's position as "the matrix, the indispensable condition, of nearly every other form of freedom."[6]

As the rhetoric of defiance grew more pitched in local communities, the Justices added their sympathetic voices to the cause of equality, cautiously at first, then with escalating confidence. Eventually, the Justices would feel sufficiently buoyed by popular sentiment to lament — ostensibly within the context of free speech—the "ugly stamp of racism" that continued to taint the states' dealings with their citizens.[7] The elaboration of First Amendment text, which portrayed disobedients' actions in virtuous and respectful terms, undercut segregationist arguments that African Americans were not ready for the responsibilities of citizenship.

From Composition to Reaction

Even as the people's fragile belief in racial equality deepened from this interaction, the strategy reconfigured the patterns of free speech discourse. Early First Amendment jurisprudence arose in reference to a paradigmatic situation consisting of a solitary speaker and a respectful audience. The street preacher and the lone pamphleteer benefited from this straightforward approach. "Hotheaded speech on a street corner" might draw legitimate sanction, as would the individual who hurled epithets "likely to provoke the average person to retaliation"; the soapbox orator who did not interfere with traffic and "created no disturbance" had a fighting chance at securing First Amendment protection.[8]

Yet it proved to be equally obvious that this embryonic jurisprudence was resistant, even hostile, toward group action. In part reproducing a republican skepticism of faction, in part responding to a latent fear of revolutionary violence, the law was quick to label collective action as "coercive," "unruly," or "disorderly," as it often did to quash boycotts organized to alter consumer practices. Moreover, the solo speaker model proved incredibly fragile, overly dependent upon the reactions of a crowd as opposed to the intentions and actual words of the speaker. *Feiner v. New York*, decided in 1951, illustrates the contours of this linguistic regime. Feiner gave a street corner speech on a large wood box to publicize an event for the Young Progressives of America scheduled for later that day. During the presentation, he called President Truman and the mayor of Syracuse "bums" and urged African Americans to "rise up in arms and fight for their rights." When he refused to end his talk upon a demand by a police officer, he was arrested for disorderly conduct. Authorities cited these reasons for intervening: the speech was delivered in a "loud, high-pitched voice" before a "mixed audience," there was some pushing and shoving in the crowd, and, after twenty minutes or so, a bystander called for the speaker to cease.

The Justices rejected Feiner's First Amendment defense, comforted by the notion that, strictly speaking, the speaker was being punished not for the unpopularity of his speech but for "the reaction which it actually engendered." Indeed, they ratified the conclusion of the New York Court of Appeals, which had, operating within the speech-as-fire field, concluded that Feiner's oration "so inflamed and agitated a mixed audience of sympathizers and opponents that, in the judgment of the police officers present, a clear danger of disorder and violence was threatened." Because of the prevailing paradigm's emphasis on the solo speaker's reception, the approach subordinated an individual's right to myriad possible negative reactions to controversial expression.

Adaptation: The Expression-Within-a-Meeting Metaphor

An alternative metaphorical model would be necessary if Americans wished to escape the constraints of the speech-as-fire framework. The meeting metaphor would fill that need nicely. On January 6, 1941, President Franklin Delano Roosevelt had given a historic speech to Congress outlining what he believed to be the four basic freedoms in postwar America: freedom of expression, freedom to worship, freedom from want, and freedom from fear. Norman Rockwell subsequently commemorated the "Four Freedoms" in the pages of *The Saturday Evening Post*. Rockwell depicted the ideal of expressive liberty in action: a lone man in work clothes standing to address a New England town meeting while his neighbors, clad in businesswear, remain seated, listening intently. This artistic representation of the First Amendment as public discourse consisting of courageous expression of one's mind and respectful turn-taking would become an essential element in popular iconography. Not only would the visual image become a "deliberative icon,"[9] but also its rendition of freedom of expression as a republican ideal would be repeatedly inscribed upon the law.

In response to the large-scale social movements of the twentieth century, First Amendment discourse gained a valuable prototype that shaped whether "concerted action" merited institutional sanction: the virtuous citizen-assembly, an idealized cognitive model that was contrasted with that of the angry mob. Whereas the former reflected genuine public-spiritedness, an effort to decipher the general will, the latter was viewed as the epitome of self-regarding behavior: irrational and destructive, more a guttural sound than a meaningful contribution to civic deliberation.

This emerging discourse had two sources of legitimacy beyond the contemporary events taking place in the streets, the first textual, the second historical: (1) the First Amendment's guarantee of "the right of the people peaceably to assemble"; and (2) the American tradition of patriotic citizens meeting out of doors in impromptu fashion to debate the pressing issues of the day.

Unleashed in early controversies like *DeJonge* and *Thomas*, this dyad infused judicial readings of the First Amendment. Its fulcrum was the actual behavior of the speakers, rather than the anticipated reaction of the listeners.

The more that a gathering could be re-imagined as a public-spirited meeting gathered to do the people's business, the more likely its participants would receive institutional sanction. By contrast, the more a group bore some resemblance to an unruly crowd with less virtuous motives, the less likely its performance would find shelter in free speech rhetoric. Recall that in *DeJonge*,[10] the Justices overturned the conviction of a member of the Communist Party pursuant to the speech and assembly clauses. Dirk DeJonge had spoken at a gathering of a few hundred, deploring the conditions at the local jail, decrying the tactics of local authorities during a maritime strike, and urging listeners to attend a Communist Party meeting in Portland the next day. The meeting was unceremoniously interrupted, the gathering site raided, and the organizers and speakers arrested under Oregon's criminal syndicalism law.

At trial and on appeal from his conviction, DeJonge's "defense was that the meeting was public and orderly and was held for a lawful purpose." Wiping the defendant's record clean, the Court concluded that one's "mere participation in a peaceable assembly and a lawful public discussion" cannot, consistent with the First Amendment, form the basis of a valid prosecution.

Eight years later, in 1945, the *Thomas* Court similarly deemed "orderly discussion and persuasion" between a union leader and potential union members fully protected by the First Amendment, despite Texas officials' characterization of such recruitment efforts as unlawful solicitation. Notice, too, that the Justices deployed assembly-inspired rhetoric to combat the still prevalent fire-inspired discourse. Because the meeting "had no other than a wholly lawful purpose," the Justices reasoned, "We have here nothing comparable to the case where use of the word 'fire' in a crowded theater creates a clear and present danger."

Like its graphic analogue, the rhetorical move painted a scene in which the speaker comprised an integral part of a deliberative body or process. Demonstrating just how the prototype was beginning to shape decision making, the speech-as-meeting metaphor would continue to defeat the earlier vocabulary that had gripped the political imagination. A telling postwar example can be found in *Kunz v. New York*.[11] Carl Jacob Kunz, an ordained Baptist minister, believed himself called to spread God's word on America's highways and byways. One day, police arrested him for speaking in Columbus Circle without a valid permit. A city administrator had earlier revoked his permit on the ground that he had, on prior occasions, denounced and ridiculed competing religious beliefs. Kunz had apparently twice applied for a permit, only to be rejected without explanation.

Overturning Kunz's conviction, Fred Vinson held that the permit regime allowing an administrator to deny permission to speak on religious matters lacked standards. In the process of articulating Kunz's free speech interest, the Court presented Kunz's racist, anti-Semitic one-man ramblings before a group as legitimate "religious meetings" at which "public questions" were discussed, rather than as hostile words hurled by a provocateur in order to anger a crowd and stir them to violence.

Justice Jackson's dissent appealed to the speech-restrictive thread of the interregnum. He would have treated people on the street as a "captive audience." Preferring to give the state complete dominion over "street speech," he felt that Kunz's speech was akin to "falsely shouting fire in a theatre." Jackson feared that because aggressive counterprotests could not be stopped or contained, the state must be empowered to arrest such developments at their source. Tolerance of "intrinsically incendiary and divisive" topics like race and religion, he thought, was misguided, for "[t]he end of the Court's method is chaos." As Jackson put it:

> [I]f Kunz may speak without a permit, so may anyone else. If he may speak whenever and wherever he may elect, I know of no way in which the City can silence the heckler, the interrupter, the dissenter, the rivals with missionary fervor, who have an equal right at the same time and place to lift their voices. And, of course, if the City may not stop Kunz from uttering insulting and 'fighting' words, neither can it stop his adversaries, and the discussion degenerates to a name-calling contest without social value and, human nature being what it is, to a fight or perhaps a riot. . . . These are the explosives which the Court says Kunz may play with in the public streets, and the community must not only tolerate but aid him.

This represented the repressive logic that political elites, with the aid of postwar vernacular, would increasingly reject. The other thread of antitotalitarianism, which sounded in greater autonomy for individuals and social groups, would in time permeate the basic grammar of expressive liberty.

Memorializing the People Out of Doors

The civil rights movement put this conflicting set of normative aspirations to the test. Movement leaders self-consciously organized themselves in the form of an alternative deliberative body, one in which racial egalitarianism, mutual sacrifice, and civic virtue reigned. They staged revivals, rallies, and large-scale, open-air meetings. These assemblies followed a predictable, and thus reassuring, pattern for participants and observers alike: songs, prayer, the sharing of news, the making of plans, an inspirational talk, and the taking up of collections. Activists conducted these alternative assemblies or "mass meetings" in churches, pool halls, taverns, public spaces—anywhere injustice existed and committed citizens could be located.

At the apex of the Montgomery bus boycott in the spring of 1956, opponents of segregation appeared at a mass meeting nearly four thousand strong to help convert a local matter into a national moral question. In both word and deed, in terminology drawn from the secular as well as the sacred, civil rights advocates portrayed democracy as an "endless meeting." Supporters organized themselves as a counterassembly in order to dramatize the unequal and illiberal visions of political community enforced with cruelty and ferocity.[12]

When defenders of segregation moved in to crush the movement, the crisis forced political elites to rethink traditional ways of conceptualizing rights. But the cognitive ideal of the citizen assembly, elaborated as it had been by jurists, still proved constrictive given the realities of the politics of agitation. In short order, the High Court found a way to liberalize its approach to protect more aggressive speech tactics intended to highlight structural inequities without undermining faith in the rule of law. In the 1961 dispute *Garner v. Louisiana*, several civil rights protestors sat down at whites-only lunch counters in department stores, drug stores, and bus terminals. After they were told they would be served only in areas designated for blacks, the patrons stayed put; they were then arrested for disturbing the peace. The Justices fell short of a majority to vindicate the protestors' First Amendment rights directly but ruled for them under the rubric of the Due Process Clause. This was an act of supreme creativity because the analysis resembled an insufficiency-of-the-evidence claim (ordinarily understood as a statutory argument) but bootstrapped the Due Process Clause in order to ensure that federal jurisdiction existed. The theory of the case was that the prosecutions were "so totally devoid of evidentiary support as to render them unconstitutional."[13]

After laying out this theory, Chief Justice Earl Warren construed the Louisiana law to prohibit only actions that "foreseeably disturb or alarm the public." He then turned to the crux of the matter: on the facts presented, the protestors' "mere presence" at the counters in defiance of local custom could not reasonably support conviction under the statute. Because participants in the sit-in did not engage in "outwardly boisterous conduct or . . . passive conduct likely to cause a public disturbance," their convictions violated the Fourteenth Amendment. Perhaps because the Justices were afraid to countenance aggressive speech tactics on private property, the opinion went out of its way to bleed the political and expressive significance of the protestors' actions out of the analysis — it was almost as if these individuals were like any other persons who happened to be dining out that day. Although the meeting metaphor was not used to bring matters to a close on this occasion, the general approach of focusing on the speakers' actions had once again proven invaluable.

Although they had resolved the cases immediately at hand, the *Garner* gambit could be only a stop-gap, for its legitimacy rested on a tenuous reading of state law that could be impacted by the highest state judicial body at any time. The Justices' entry into the civil rights debate, while dramatic, remained highly vulnerable. In a more confident exposition of expressive liberty two years later, *Edwards v. South Carolina* finally pushed the speech-as-assembly metaphor to center stage.[14] A number of black students who marched around the statehouse were arrested and later convicted of breach of the peace.

The Supreme Court reversed. Writing figuratively, Justice Stewart found that the student gathering had indicia of "persuasion" and "argument," because the students pursued a program of highlighting racial injustices, did not exhort bystanders to unrest or violence, walked in single file or groups of two along the sidewalk, and were careful not to obstruct traffic. By contrast, Justice Stewart suggested, a mob would have distinguished itself by contributing nothing to political discourse, would likely have consisted of participants "pushing, shoving, and milling around," and would likely have been led by a "speaker [who] passes the bounds of argument or persuasion and undertakes incitement to riot."

The meeting metaphor drew upon the political tradition of the convention, which Gordon Wood describes as "an act of coming together, used to refer to all sorts of assemblies, especially formal assemblies, convened for deliberation on important matters, whether ecclesiastical, political, or social."[15] Americans remembered such conventions as "legally deficient bodies existing outside of the regularly constituted authority" yet reflecting "in a special manner the epitome of the People" if they were temporary in duration, led by publicly spirited citizens toward specific ends, and employed as a means of last resort.

Implying that the civil rights protests were equivalent to "meetings of the people" thus recalled the restoration of Charles II to the throne by an informal or "defective" assembly; the tennis court assembly of members of the Fourth Estate who vowed to remain united until Louis XVI agreed to a written constitution; the Constitutional Convention's writing of a new instrument in spite of its participants' narrow charge; and other impromptu gatherings to resist tyranny and restore justice to governmental priorities. Civil rights activists' labors in the 1960s gained a great deal through their rhetorical association with these older vehicles of popular sovereignty.

The motif underwent refinement in *Cox v. Louisiana*, which reversed breach-of-the-peace convictions of several college students who had staged an antisegregation rally at the state capitol. Justice Arthur Goldberg's opinion seized on the fact that the boisterous "outdoor meeting" retained its protected quality given its setting, the speakers' virtuous intentions, and the actual conduct of the participants. Even though the participants cheered, sang, shouted, clapped, prayed, and gave speeches, there was no indication that the "mood of the students was ever hostile, aggressive, or unfriendly." Although the police moved in to disperse the crowd with tear gas, until that intervention "the entire meeting . . . was orderly and not riotous."[16]

In yet another landmark intervention, the Court refused to draw bright lines that would have extinguished First Amendment rights merely because individual acts of protest occurred on a site not explicitly dedicated to vigorous expression. *Brown v. Louisiana*, decided in 1966, overturned breach-of-the-peace convictions of several individuals who conducted a wordless sit-in at a public library. Library employees were reputed to have treated black patrons differently from whites. Despite the fact that the demonstration took place indoors rather than in the streets, Justice Abe Fortas ruled that the protestors' "orderly and quiet" statement against the segregated institution fell within the ambit of the First Amendment.[17]

Hugo Black, who in an earlier case had been swayed by "the decorum" of street protestors in the face of "jeers, insults, and assaults with rocks and eggs," dissented in this one. Joined by three of his brethren, Justice Black insisted that the protestors' silent "monuments of protest" should not have to be tolerated within the library. Invoking memories of mob rule during the French Revolution (and indirectly tapping Americans' fears of a spontaneous assembly gone wrong), he warned of "powerful private groups . . . taking the law into [their] own hands": "the crowd moved by noble ideals today can become the mob ruled by hate and passion and greed and violence tomorrow. . . . The peaceful songs of love can become as stirring and provocative as the Marseillaise did in the days when a noble revolution gave way to rule by successive mobs until chaos set in."[18] In spite of the close vote, the outcome proved to be consistent with the re-emerging sense that activism and constitutionalism were entwined in important respects.

Besides challenging the relative importance of forum analysis, the widening circles of protest raised another challenge: these demonstrations had a peculiar habit of provoking equally unruly counterprotests or violence. In the name of preserving order, could the coercive power of the state be harnessed to quell protest in the first instance? Resisting this temptation, the Court armed citizen-speakers on both sides of the racial divide with the Heckler's Veto in the name of society's emerging belief in the virtues of robust political debate.[19] The proponent and the opponent of racial equality would have to interact in the public square; neither one would be permitted to engage the apparatus of the state to silence the other.

Taken together, the confluence of street tactics and litigation generated novel re-readings of constitutional text. It mattered not whether lawsuits and demonstrations were coordinated (a few were, many more were not); the very fact of direct action—with its sympathetic goals, humanizing strategies, and captivating personalities—altered the political consciousness within which judges rationally reformulated and implemented legal rules. The lawsuits filed during this period became the medium through which constitutional vernacular was refined and new political beliefs coordinated and expressed.

It represented a triumphal moment of citizen activism memorialized in an act of judicial creativity, a gesture toward the need for periodic renewal of the law. Legal innovations continued as the American language of power absorbed the events unfolding in the public square. First, the experience validated the belief that the First Amendment existed to facilitate vigorous, sometimes contentious, public debate. In the past, the High Court sporadically accorded decisive weight to the intrinsic quality of one's expression; after this sequence of events, speech on matters of public concern would again be poised on the "highest rung of the hierarchy of First Amendment values."

Second, the ascendance of assembly-oriented idioms served to further marginalize the rhetoric of incitement, which had for so long dominated deliberation over free speech questions. Their emergence would help to change the social context sufficiently that a later controversy such as *Brandenburg*—involving a historically violent and virulently racist organization like the Klan—could be perceived as an easy case in the speaker's favor and a cross burning as a deliberative event. In the interests of protecting collective action, the past actions of a social group would not be imputed to its entire membership without contemporary evidence of misbehavior.

Third, courts routinely treated extrajudicial challenges to the constitutional order as efforts to "petition the Government for redress," even though no formal legal process had been initiated by a speaker and no particular reform was pending before a political body. Textual commitments to speech, assembly, and petition were interlaced to account for the desperate strategies of the oppressed.

Fourth, sweeping aside clever, sometimes hastily fashioned official obstacles to political-legal engagement, the Justices even recognized the right to engage in constitutional litigation as a form of political advocacy.[20] As the Court explained, lawsuits, like the tactics of the streets, may be "undertaken to express political beliefs." Under the "conditions of modern government," such nontraditional means may be "the sole practicable avenue open to a minority to petition for redress of grievances."

Fifth, as a lasting gift to future social movements, "the practice of persons sharing common views banding together to achieve a common end" would henceforth be sufficient to trigger First Amendment protection. Though we know better the contingent nature of our constitutional beliefs during a moment of sober rediscovery, jurists and ordinary Americans would in later years claim with a straight face that respect for the social utility of collective action "is deeply embedded in the American political process."[21]

The Wall of Separation as a Site of Contestation

It should be increasingly apparent that, despite the most ardent hope for finality expressed by a litigant or jurist, no rhetorical construction of the Constitution is safe from politics. This lesson can be drawn from the patterns of actual usage of the metaphorical wall of separation between church and state. Cited for the first time in a nineteenth-century case testing the state's authority to forbid polygamy, the phrase gained sociolegal power after Justice Hugo Black's dramatic use of it to foster support for the outcome in *Everson v. Board of Education.*

Decided in 1947, the case involved an Establishment Clause challenge to a New Jersey school district's practice of subsidizing the transportation of children to parochial schools. The metaphor's demarcation of the social world was clean, if somewhat chilling: "a high and impregnable wall of separation between church and state" was "indispensable" to Americans' hope for a world without protracted cycles of sectarian strife. Despite this unforgiving image of church-state division, Justice Black nevertheless concluded that "New Jersey has not breached it here" because school authorities had implemented the program on an even-handed basis. While the particular flourish he gave the imagery was all his own, Black himself drew upon Thomas Jefferson, who in turn may well have been inspired by Roger Williams's sermon *The Garden in the Wilderness.*

The word-picture created by the metaphor evokes the tradition of separationism that influenced the writing of a number of state constitutions, as well as the resolution of memorable church-state controversies. It stimulates our senses on many levels and fashions the following conceptual dualities:

separation: entanglement::
peace: strife::
protection: isolation::
liberty: oppression::
respect: hostility::
strong: weak::
empowerment: alienation

Circulation of this boundary metaphor spreads the philosophy that separation of the sacred and the secular promotes religious peace, safeguards individual liberty, ensures mutual respect among a diverse population, and empowers the people. Concomitantly, the move presents opponents as inattentive students of political history and stirrers of sectarian strife.

Interestingly enough, Justice Jackson's dissent in *Everson*, too, took up the boundary metaphor and, in his very manipulation of it, suggested that the majority had not been faithful to the premises animating its creation. Of the Establishment Clause, he wrote: "This freedom was first in the Bill of Rights because it was first in the forefathers' minds; it was set forth in absolute terms, and its strength is its rigidity. It was intended not only to keep the states' hands out of religion, but to keep religion's hands off the state, and above all, to keep bitter religious controversy out of public life by denying to every denomination any advantage from getting control of public policy or the public purse."

Joined by Frankfurter, Jackson in his opinion took a further step. Not only is this boundary meant to safeguard the public fisc, he suggested; it is also intended to protect the citizen's moral development in a liberal democracy: "It is organized on the premise that secular education can be isolated from all religious teaching so that the school can inculcate all needed temporal knowledge and also maintain a strict and lofty neutrality as to religion. The assumption is that after the individual has been instructed in worldly wisdom he will be better fitted to choose his religion."

Likewise, the dissent by Justice Rutledge lamented, "Neither so high nor so impregnable today as yesterday is the wall raised between church and state by Virginia's great statute of religious freedom and the First Amendment." He worried that the outcome would encourage additional attacks on the separationist frame of understanding: "New Jersey's statute sustained is the first, if indeed it is not the second breach to be made by this Court's action. That a third, and a fourth, and still others will be attempted, we may be sure. For just as [an earlier decision] has opened the way by oblique ruling for this decision, so will the two make wider the breach for a third."

In the early years of the compositional phase, the High Court consistently paid homage to the wall of separation by using it as the undisputed starting point for legal inquiry. Almost everyone on the Court assumed that the words of the First Amendment, "properly interpreted," had "erected" the wall.[22]

A year after *Everson*, in *People of the State of Illinois ex rel. McCollum v. Board of Education of Champaign County*, Justice Black had occasion to reactivate the frame of understanding. This time, he invoked the metaphor to declare unconstitutional a policy that paid local clergy to give religious instruction during school hours: "For the First Amendment rests upon the premise that both religion and government can best work to achieve their lofty aims if each is left free from the other within its respective sphere. Or, as we said in the *Everson* case, the First Amendment had erected a wall between Church and State which must be kept high and impregnable."

For the separationist, the apparatus of government and the workings of religion must be maintained in dual spheres. Given the strength of the discourse, even those who agreed with the outcome had something to say about the wall. Justice Frankfurter stressed the importance of "confinement of the public schools to secular education" and warned of the dangers of "commingling . . . sectarian and secular instruction," which would stimulate a "feeling of separatism" on the part of believers whose faiths are not included.

On this view of political community, division preserves the unique social role of each institution and promotes feelings of mutual respect: "In no activity of the State is it more vital to keep out divisive forces than in its schools, to avoid confusing, not to say fusing, what the Constitution sought to keep strictly apart. . . . If nowhere else, in the relation between Church and State, 'good fences make good neighbors.' " Only one jurist — Stanley Reed — broke ranks to say that "a rule of law should not be drawn from a figure of speech."

In the abstract, there is nothing wrong with civic myth-spinning of this sort. On dozens of occasions, the Court has described the intellect or human spirit as "the inviolable citadel of the individual heart and mind . . . that it is not within the power of the government to invade."[23] In our constitutional tradition, sometimes the psychological wall of liberty is erected to nurture the secluded consumption of ideas or formulation of beliefs, as Justice Marshall did in *Stanley v. Georgia*; occasionally, the boundary is built, as it is in *McCollum*, to isolate and deter an undesirable social phenomenon or to suggest that the state lacks the ability to mediate disagreements of this nature.

In the usual case, the psychological barrier is erected against overzealous officials. The driving concern is intrusion into a particularly intimate human function or zone of decision making that ought to be kept largely free from official control. This rendition of the boundary metaphor, though, was potentially more pernicious from the standpoint of republican theory: the operations of the state were to be shielded from the people themselves for fear that excessive interaction might corrupt either the state or religion. What was to be segregated was either a substantial segment of the population (the God-fearing majority) or the fact of political contest over religious values. Yet, no good reason could be found to assume that the devout are less virtuous than those without divine inspiration or that they are less able to put aside social differences. If that were the implication, the phrasing would be as insulting as it would be wrongheaded.

If, instead, the goal was to preserve the law in a pristine condition untouched by thoughts of the divine, it may have been a fool's errand. For one thing, the nation's political culture is filled with references to hallowed beginnings and spiritual inspirations. For another, popular acceptance of the rule of law is nourished by many of the same cognitive and social structures of authority, iconography, and fraternity that make sectarian belief possible. To threaten the latter with banishment from the public sphere is to cut off a people's civic mythology from its indigenous sources.

Perhaps the greatest stumbling block for many was, and remains, the exclusionary power of the vision conjured by the original metaphor — its proponents insisted that "not even the slightest breach" could be countenanced. In fact, the wall's formidable quality proved to be its undoing. Taking the Supreme Court at its word, opponents quickly exploited this opening, showing how ludicrous it would be for decision makers to take the image literally — in other words, as a comprehensive rule rather than as shorthand. Would the Constitution be read to call for the scrubbing of our public culture to erase signs of the divine? Bar the religious motivations inspiring public policies that might uplift as easily as oppress? These objections, raised by civic leaders and ordinary Americans alike, would begin to coalesce into organized resistance to *Everson*'s presentation of the rule of law.

Contest and Proliferation

Given these critiques, few should be surprised that this juridic construction of law emerged as the site of political contest. Taking their cue from *Everson*, separationists and their allies defended the original composition under siege. They did so in direct mailing campaigns, press releases and media commentary, litigation, and communications with public officials by propagating the wall's positive connotations.

At the same time, in the years following *Everson* civic leaders regularly denounced the metaphorical wall to galvanize ordinary people and change the polarity of the device's connotations from positive to negative. The coalition that led the reaction to the wall proved to be diverse and highly motivated. many associated it with overreaching on the part of liberal judges; others found the metaphor emblematic of a Godless society; yet a third strand of opposition came from those, like President Reagan, who wished to "restore" "neutrality" to judging after decades of judicial leadership on social issues. Accordingly, the wall became a target of conservative politics aiming to roll back everything from perceived Warren Court excesses to general concerns about the activist state.

Opponents of the existing regime engaged in a strategy of rhetorical proliferation, according to which a coalition of actors seeks to entrench a set of political beliefs by multiplying (a) the modalities for conveying these values (b) in as many venues as possible. The key to informational saturation is that these constructions must enter the system of constitutional language at different points, flooding the zone of action. To control the political pathways is to take advantage of the permeability and inspirational quality of constitutional language.

Early reactions during the 1950s and 1960s, on the whole, appeared tentative. Some critics suggested that the boundary metaphor failed to "accommodate" the religious beliefs of citizens, which played upon the seeming inflexibility of the construct. Another favorite tactic was to insist that the phrase was not "self-defining" or that it did not "preclude a clash of views as to what the wall separates." Both of these strategies of argumentation sought to limit the ideological effects of the metaphor and to open up the possibility of closely parsing context so as to avoid separationist outcomes.[24] During this period, some disputes were resolved in favor of the individual and some in favor the state, but jurists generally accepted that the *Everson* framework continued to dictate the terms of debate. By and large, judges defending the prevailing gestalt did so openly and confidently.

Friends of the Court staking out an Establishment Clause position, too, eagerly identified themselves as defenders of the linguistic regime "who do not want to see the wall of separation between church and state either dismantled or replaced."[25] They warned of the "reciprocal embroilments" and "intercreedal rivalries" that would occur in the absence of the wall and vociferously argued that "union of government and religion tends to destroy government and degrade religion."

McGowan v. Maryland, which reviewed a set of Sunday closing laws, is a case decided within the dominant frame of understanding. Chief Justice Warren began his analysis by quoting the "wall of separation" formula. Because closing laws were "undeniably religious in origin," this seemed a serious problem, even though it was obvious that most thought the matter presented a minor concern. The solution Warren seized upon allowed him to adhere to the governing paradigm by dissolving any conflict between church and state; he proceeded to argue that the laws had been so drained of their religiosity that their existence on the books no longer presented a threat to our ruling belief in separationism. The secular purpose that now animated the closing laws was the laudable desire "to set one day apart from all others as a day of rest, repose, recreation and tranquility." And, from the perspective of contemporary social meaning, "the air of the day is one of relaxation rather than one of religion."

Although the metaphorical field remained intact, one could detect an emerging counterdiscourse that suggested that excessive separation might, under some circumstances, express animus against a religious believer: "To say that the States cannot prescribe Sunday as a day of rest for these purposes solely because centuries ago such laws had their genesis in religion would give a constitutional interpretation of hostility to the public welfare rather than one of mere separation of church and State."

Despite rumblings of discontent, jurists continued to quote the wall formula with approval and even "strongly reaffirm[ed]" its legitimacy.[26] In 1961, the Justices went out of their way to "renew our conviction that 'we have staked the very existence of our country on the faith that complete separation between the state and religion is best for the state and best for religion.'" The following term, the Supreme Court handed down *Engel v. Vitale*, which came to represent the high water mark for the barrier metaphor. There, the Justices overturned a teacher-led morning prayer, finding that the practice "breaches" the separation mandated between the sacred and the profane. In elaborating their rationale, the Court wrote of the First Amendment: "Its first and most immediate purpose rested on the belief that a union of government and religion tends to destroy government and to degrade religion. . . . The Establishment Clause thus stands as an expression of principle on the part of the Founders of our Constitution that religion is too personal, too sacred, too holy, to permit its 'unhallowed perversion' by a civil magistrate."

Importantly, the Court rejected the notion that striking down school-sponsored prayer was itself a manifestation of governmental hostility to religion: "It is neither sacrilegious nor antireligious to say that each separate government in this country should stay out of the business of writing or sanctioning official prayers and leave that purely religious function to the people themselves and to those the people choose to look to for religious guidance." Only Justice Stewart reproached his colleagues' "uncritical invocation of metaphors like the 'wall of separation,' a phrase nowhere to be found in the Constitution." Most everyone else operated according to the precepts of eloquence governing the era.

Adaptation

An interesting, and somewhat counterintuitive, pattern arose during the adaptive period that typified legal discourse on religious freedom in the 1970s. In the face of direct challenges, proponents of separationism and judicial engagement tried to save the wall by softening its appearance.

Lemon v. Kurtzman, resolved in 1971, represents the paradigmatic instance of adaptation as an institution grapples with external reaction. First, Chief Justice Burger's opinion for the Court—from which no one dissented—reaffirmed the rule of *Everson*. But it did so by presenting a fresh doctrinal synthesis in the form of a three-prong test, one that, by its terms, rejected an across-the-board no-aid or no-involvement rule. The Court ruled that, henceforth, state action must have a secular purpose, its primary effect could not advance nor inhibit religion, and it could not foster "excessive government entanglement with religion."

Second, a shift in vernacular mirrored the change in the legal rule; the opinion emphasized the malleability of legal language, in terms of both constitutional text and judicially authored texts. In elaborating upon the three-prong test, the Court claimed that the language of the Religion Clauses itself was "at best opaque," lacking "precisely stated constitutional prohibitions." Similarly, the Justices now backed away from Hugo Black's earlier statement that the wall was designed to be high and formidable, instead describing it as "a blurred, indistinct, and variable barrier depending on all the circumstances of a particular relationship."[27] "[T]otal separation," they wrote, "is not possible in an absolute sense."

Third, the Supreme Court signaled that despite the obvious shift in approach, on some matters it would revert to taking a stronger separationist position. Striking down the policy under review, the Court explained: "Under our system the choice has been made that government is to be entirely excluded from the area of religious instruction and churches excluded from the affairs of government."

Characteristic of the adaptive period, separationist rhetoric remained a plausible tool. The majority opinion reminded readers that "[t]he history of many countries attests to the hazards of religion's intruding into the political arena or of political power intruding into the legitimate and free exercise of religious belief." This synthesis acknowledged that "religious values pervade the fabric of our national life" but remained concerned that inordinate state focus on religious matters might "divert attention from the myriad issues and problems that confront every level of government" as well as stimulate "[p]olitical fragmentation and divisiveness on religious lines." Adding new vernacular that stressed the mixing of functions as the primary wrong, the Justices urged the citizenry to remain watchful for "intimate and continuing relationship[s] between church and state."

Likewise, in *Committee for Public Education v. Nyquist*, decided in 1973, the Justices insisted that the metaphorical wall coined by Jefferson was not "as winding as the famous serpentine wall he designed for the University of Virginia" and certainly did not mandate a "regime of total separation." Far from giving up on the wall, decision makers attempted to soften its appearance in order to rescue it. As the Justices clarified in the face of seemingly unending criticism: "Separation in this context cannot mean absence of all contact; the complexities of modern life inevitably produce some contact" between the sacred and the profane.[28]

By contrast, opponents of separationism gained momentum by continuing to lay siege to *Everson*'s image of the "impregnable" wall. In actuality, the most effective strategies during this period consisted of attacking the wall to ensure that popular discourse pressured doctrinal analysis and inviting institutional actors to treat the situation as a unique set of contingencies.

Reaction Redux

The linguistic regime held through the next decade. Although cracks had begun to show, jurists referred to the wall as "a useful signpost" well into the 1980s. Collective resistance to the symbolic wall entered a second, more intensive phase a few years into the decade. Several factors contributed to the resurgence against the barrier metaphor. First, Ronald Reagan had been elected president on promises to reverse the work of "activist" judges, to appoint jurists who respected "traditional family values and the sanctity of innocent human life," and "to embark upon a national crusade to make America great again," a "shining city on the hill." Accepting the Republican nomination before a national audience, he closed by asking, "Can we begin our crusade joined together in a moment of silent prayer?" Throughout his presidency, Reagan consistently decried "modern-day secularism," called for a "spiritual revival in the land," and singled out "the right to worship" as "the most important human right being violated" in totalitarian orders such as the Soviet Union. "As President," observers pointed out, "Reagan showed an extraordinary inclination to use the bully pulpit *as* a pulpit."[29]

Having taken executive leadership in a time of fiscal and moral anxiety, Reagan was led by a landslide victory in 1984 to declare his hope that "[t]hese will be years when Americans have restored their confidence and tradition of progress; when our values of faith, family, work, and neighborhood were restated for a modern age." Between 1980 and 1992, a single party dictated much of the nation's political agenda. This meant not only that ideologically compatible jurists were appointed to the federal bench but also that an electorally driven ethos — with a reassessment of religion's role in public life as its centerpiece — began to pervade formal decision making across institutions.

Second, institutional personnel matured and became comfortable in their roles within the constitutional order. As both carriers and shapers of legal culture, seasoned actors began to sense the range of their rhetorical freedom. Experience brought added skill with relevant forms and self-assurance in their usage; from time to time, it also led actors to seek a degree of consistency in their discursive strategies. For instance, elaborating upon the rhetorical techniques initiated by the president, briefs filed by the Solicitor General on behalf of the United States lamented the "artificial and undesirable sterility in public life" imposed by the regime and attacked any lower-court judgment that smacked of "total separation."[30]

Third, within this environment, ideologically compatible activists became increasingly hopeful of securing readings of text that matched their policy preferences and belief systems, while dissenters, for a time, became correspondingly demoralized. The dialectics of empowerment and discouragement brought about by the operation of the ordinary election cycle involved both a sudden change and the prospect of lasting gains. These dynamics fueled more chances to reconsider past practices and outlooks and, consequently, frequent creative deployments of existing rhetorical forms to make the most of opportunities that arose.

Control of political pathways facilitated a profound shift in the valence of the wall. Civic leaders claimed that the metaphoric boundary was intended to protect religion but had been erroneously transformed into "a wall of oppression." In their view, the wall was never meant to "quarantine" believers, "isolate" God from politics, or "cleanse" political culture of the sacred.[31] Perhaps the most critical intervention came from President Reagan in May 1982, when he introduced a constitutional amendment to permit voluntary school prayer. At the time, many observers were puzzled, believing such an amendment unnecessary because the High Court had never banned voluntary acts of faith; others found it little more than cynical pandering to the grass-roots members of the Republican Party. In fact, Reagan's public commitment to the reformation of religion's role in public life helped to mobilize others in the cause and put pressure on other branches of government to do the same. On March 8, 1983, President Reagan gave remarks at the Annual Convention of the National Association of Evangelicals. Campaigning for the school prayer amendment, he uttered a formulation of the wall that would in short order become appropriated by the Supreme Court: "When our Founding Fathers passed the first amendment, they sought to protect churches from government interference. They never intended to construct a wall of hostility between government and the concept of religious belief itself."[32]

Throughout the 1980s, Reagan consistently expressed his view that constitutional text had not been "properly interpreted," that "the first amendment has been twisted to the point that freedom of religion is in danger of becoming freedom from religion."[33] Although he seized upon a single issue — school prayer — on which he made little concrete headway, his symbolic actions galvanized the country to consider far-reaching changes in the ways that questions of faith and community were framed and addressed.

Emboldened actors inside and outside the courts increasingly argued that state practices that treated religious matters differently from nonreligious matters amounted to "disparagement" of faith. They contended that differential rules were "blatantly discriminatory," denied believers' "self worth," and forced them to practice their faith by "sneaking around the administration's back." A friend of the Court described a school policy that denied students the ability to meet for Bible study as an effort to "banish the Respondents from the public community" and likened the policy to racial segregation: "In denominating the Respondents' group as unacceptable to meet on school property, the school authorities treated the Respondents in a manner analogous to the school children in *Brown v. Board of Education*. . . . Discriminating against religious students with 'the sanction of law' by not allowing to meet on equal terms with other students surely sends the message that they are inferior outsiders."[34]

Rhetorical appropriation extended from equal protection discourse to First Amendment terminology. With a new sense of momentum, advocates drew upon free speech ideas to reduce the Establishment Clause's sphere of influence: "to segregate [religious] expression from the intercourse of ideas . . . is intellectual death of the highest form." Reformers summed up their approach in this way: the Religion Clauses safeguarded "freedom of religion rather than freedom from religion." This general strategy turned the relevant questions into ones of equal dignity, full participation in civic life, and informational freedom.

These alternative constructions of the First Amendment appeared in speeches, policy statements, and legal briefs, saturating all relevant fields of action. Given the sheer quantity of these counterformulations and the ferocity with which they were pressed, it would be only a matter of time before the governing linguistic regime was overthrown.

Absorption

Criticisms of the wall not only became more open and notorious; they also became more organized within the Judiciary. The pressure of competing constructions came from below (in the form of lower-court judgments) and from without (in the form of statements by elected leaders, commentators, and activists). Eventually, the mobilized criticisms of the rhetorical device would be absorbed by juridic discourse with a sense of urgency and confidence. Take then-Chief Justice Burger's statement in *Lynch v. Donnelly*, a 1984 fight over the constitutionality of a city-sponsored crèche, that "[n]o significant segment of our society and no institution within it can exist in a vacuum or in total or absolute isolation from all the other parts." This statement amounted to a naked appeal to the widely shared belief in a unified, sovereign people. The wall's vision of freedom exacts too high a cost by denying Americans their political agency, he suggested, and cannot be practically sustained.

Just two terms before, Justice Burger had felt obliged to both invoke and laud the separationist frame of understanding he had inherited. Now, he felt liberated enough to suggest that separationist rhetoric might breed "callous indifference" to the needs of the citizenry by signaling that government was disconnected from the people or, worse, hostile to their customs. Whatever one might ultimately think about the merits of his position in the dispute at hand, he rightly assumed that the tone of governing discourse matters: it sets a mood, indicates what is politically practicable, and identifies the things to be valued within the temporal community.

Opponents of secularism and judge-centered models of group life took up other cudgels by which to soften cultural support for the boundary strategy. Among the most active and elastic terms during these years was the word "hostile"; its rapid entry into the Establishment Clause lexicon indicated that governing rhetoric was responsive to impassioned voices from the political domain. Originally an inquiry into the motives of a policymaker, the term "hostile" metamorphosed into a general epithet.

Pushing the expressive function of law to its logical limit, the favored move described a ruling that went against an adherent (or even an entire jurisprudence) as "bristl[ing] with hostility toward religion." This discursive tactic drew from long-standing practices from two sources: equal protection and free expression. Since at least the turn of the twentieth century, official "animus" toward an individual based on characteristics beyond the individual's own control has been understood as the paradigmatic instance of inequality. Viewpoint-based discrimination, too, has been forbidden under First Amendment law, the attitude seen as a type of "hostility" toward a particular perspective. The union of the two traditions yielded a newly powerful modality.

Justice Kennedy, for instance, repeatedly derided the endorsement approach for achieving "neutrality in name but hostility in fact." Weaving free speech vocabulary together with free exercise ideas, the Court reoriented itself to be watchful for the perceptions of state action and to be ready to aid believers who might "suffer" from "viewpoint discrimination" perpetrated by the state.[35]

Reintroducing privacy-style grammar in a school vouchers controversy, Justice Clarence Thomas even suggested that a policy that took into account the "pervasively religious" nature of a private organization seeking government funds would be tantamount to "reserv[ing] special hostility for those who take their religion seriously" and "trolling through a person's or institution's religious beliefs." And when Chief Justice Rehnquist upheld the State of Washington's scholarship program in *Locke v. Davey*, he went to great lengths to point out that the state constitution's exclusion of religion from eligible courses of study did not evince "hostility toward religion."[36] All of this talk of animus recentered legal questions upon the social status of the religious faithful and culminated a collaborative program to reform dominant perceptions of religion's role in a democratic society.

Where the pro-separationist metaphor had associated a firm division of social domains with state neutrality, the barrier metaphor now equated sturdiness with antireligious sentiment. "[E]nforced recognition of only the secular," Justice Kennedy insisted in the 1989 case *County of Allegheny v. American Civil Liberties Union*, "would signal not neutrality but a pervasive intent to insulate government from all things religious." Set among several fractured decisions disapproving the City of Pawtucket's display of a crèche, he described aggressive separationism as a varietal of religious discrimination. Overall, the reformation of constitutional grammar suggested that protective measures were not simply constrictive but also foolhardy.

By the early 1990s, through the constant dialogic interactions between the people and their leadership, the connotations of the barrier metaphor had been entirely reversed from positive to negative. With the transformation of the nomos complete, a parochial vision of law became an authoritative one. The network of word associations dominating the trope became: unrest — isolation — discrimination — oppression — alienation.

Casting the decisive vote to ban sectarian prayers at public school graduations, Justice Kennedy said in so many words that there are walls and there are walls. His analysis in *Lee v. Weisman* utilized the barrier metaphor closely associated with the right to be free of coerced expression, rather than Jefferson's variation. Reviving this version, he accused the school of "disavow[ing] its own duty to guard and respect that sphere of inviolable conscience and belief."

He later implicitly rejected the pro-separationist formulation of the wall: "A relentless and all-pervasive attempt to exclude religion from every aspect of public life could itself become inconsistent with the Constitution. We recognize that, at graduation time and throughout the course of the educational process, there will be instances when religious values, religious practices, and religious persons will have some interaction with the public schools and their students."

Coupled with Justice Kennedy's earlier emphasis on "the right of conscience," his particular use of the boundary metaphor fortified the Court's growing sense that the barrier was not an appropriate method of encapsulating the relationship between the people and the state. While it may have been useful in cases like *Lee v. Weisman* because of an element of coerced conformity, the prevailing sentiment now held that the wall was too crude an instrument to be of much use. Interestingly enough, Kennedy's opinion decided the legal question for the religious objector, but his choice of words continued the long-term project of dismantling the wall.

Lee v. Weisman illustrates the truism that while outcome and word choice are interlaced in a given event, they are entirely separable in future contests. The event itself can be redescribed in new terminology, just as the language of the past can be recycled to characterize fresh situations. It is now possible to discuss the different methods of combining or untangling disparate discourses, that is, manipulating a governing form at the molecular level to achieve a new synthesis of the popular and the specialized. There are three major tactics for engaging the public imagination at this level: cooptation, containment, and substitution.

To coopt an opponent's vernacular, one accepts the shell and thereby impliedly acknowledges the present strength of a construct, but not its particulars. By highlighting and shading different aspects of the constitutional order, one hopes to harness and redirect the people's familiarity with an already visible tool. This describes the general tactic undertaken by opponents of separationism to reinvent the wall as a manifestation of "judicial tyranny." These motivated actors took existing concepts — boundary, equality, citizenship — and, through a well-coordinated program, altered the people's primary ideological and emotional associations with these terms.

To contain the undesired effects of a construct or to slow rhetorical borrowing, one emphasizes context — this is Justice Kennedy's tactic in *Lee v. Weisman* to circumscribe usage of the boundary metaphor. The key is to suggest enough differences in terrain that reproduction or transplantation of an idea seems rash, even counterproductive. To a surprising extent, this appeared to be the Court's primary management strategy during the adaptive phase, as its members strove to dissipate, segment, or otherwise address the social energies spent challenging their presentation of the First Amendment.

The risk-reward calculus is most uncertain when an actor seeks to substitute one popular formulation with another. Because one is presenting a comprehensive regime of vocabulary and belief, one can achieve the greatest control of perceptions if the tactic is successful, but there is no guarantee that even clever alternatives will capture the imagination of one's audience. When a linguistic regime is destabilized, however, debate over replacement becomes unavoidable as the collective search for alternative ways of encapsulating the stakes takes center stage.

Fragmentation and Reformation

The wall's waning influence on juridic discourse had several consequences for the rule of law. It simultaneously reflected and contributed to the
discrediting of separationist philosophies of self-government, a dramatic reduction in the wall's power to move key decision makers, and a profusion of
methods by which to order religious existence within a pluralistic democracy.

Uncertain odds of success did not prevent jurists from offering alternatives
to the scenes of political community conjured by the wall. It was no accident
that the "endorsement test" materialized as the *Lemon* test's chief competitor.
According to this approach, the state cannot pursue a course of action that
"sends a message to nonadherents that they are outsiders, not full members of
the political community, and an accompanying message to adherents that they
are insiders, favored members of the political community."[37]

Justice O'Connor, the test's originator, credited no particular source for her
innovation, which gained its share of supporters and detractors. Plucked from
everyday usage, it was a political creation made legal. In common parlance, to
"endorse" is to express favoritism, extend patronage, affirm another's social
status, or benefit one party at the expense of another. While the devil remained
in the details, the legal rule afforded significant latitude for political action.
Under the endorsement test, official practices that benefit religious communities but do not rise to the level of approval or sanction should survive judicial
scrutiny.

Dismissive of searches for impermissible "entanglements" on the ground
that they are too intrusive and suspicious of the endorsement test as overly
malleable, Justice Kennedy favored the term "neutrality." A word that invokes
an entrenched notion of judges as impartial and neutral, it promised a great
deal without giving away too many particulars in advance.[38] The general turn
toward more flexible terms such as "neutrality" or "endorsement" represented
a calculation of sorts: pragmatic answers grounded in specifics will better
ensure support for the Constitution and the institutions charged with giving
meaning to text.

The end of the brief hegemony enjoyed by the separationist tradition presented opportunity and danger. The Justices' struggles to find workable principles reflect the downside of having to react to external pressures — whether to
exogenous developments or to already internalized political values. Destabil-
ization of a linguistic regime always introduces a degree of uncertainty in both
terminology and doctrine. While the prevalence of vernacular in the political
ecosystem enhances popular control of the law, it also raises special concerns.
Intense hydraulic pressures exerted by these constructions upon governing

institutions can reduce a substantive commitment to a series of wavering rationales and difficult-to-administer legal strategies. Even when external influences are accommodated with care, appearances alone can present difficulties for the rule of law. If, as Paul Kahn argues, judging involves the oversight of the public's perceptions of the law, then a crisis of legitimacy may arise from the impression that the law is in a state of perpetual conflict.[39] This suggests that the judicial actor must be responsive to external developments while not appearing to capitulate to such occurrences for fear of breeding cynicism about the law.

The dawn of the twenty-first century brought a change in the reigning images of religious freedom. The wall was to be ridiculed, shunned, the speaker-believer glorified. Treating a public policy position differently "based on its religious nature" prompted charges of "viewpoint discrimination."[40] Radiant images of rights-bearing people gathered for socially productive ends overtook early postwar patterns of insulation-based rhetoric, particularly when it came to the Religion Clauses. To be sure, a good number of people continued to cling to the word-picture's romantic promise of a world free of religious difference. But separation as an organizing principle was significantly discredited for its antiseptic characterization of our actual political life and for its capitulation to Americans' paranoid style, its supporters reduced to an increasingly frustrated minority.[41]

There are more specific lessons to be drawn from this episode. First, in rejecting separationism as a general principle, the people themselves proved to be remarkably receptive to rule-making complexity, contradicting the general assumption that the simple rule is the most promising because it is easiest for the average person to grasp. A bright-line approach can lose social support precisely because it fails to account for the subtleties of political existence and therefore feels inauthentic or contrived.

Second, the linguistic regime is a participatory matrix, one that permits nonlegal actors to shape the course of constitutional language, even if they are not formally guaranteed a role in constitutional change. Cooperation is necessary to create, entrench, or end a linguistic regime. No single actor inside or outside the courts can determine the pace of its development. Yet, a regime is a temporary social fact, subject to the actions of individuals who must live within its parameters.

Third, experience bears out the hypothesis that the features of any linguistic regime are interconnected. Dissatisfaction with a popular term can stimulate institutions to reform associated rules. Just as attractive prose can enhance the life-term of a doctrinal rule, an ungainly or controversial formulation can destabilize the most thoughtful arrangements of legal doctrine and political precept. These episodes demonstrate that an institution's function is not simply to undertake an internal search for wisdom but also to engage an inside-outside coordination of the beliefs of a diverse populace. The life cycle of a linguistic regime may be extended through sensitive calibration of these attitudes and utterances; it can also be cut short if elites do no more than try to reflect majority preferences.

Fourth, conceptual innovation may be a fact of life, but so are techniques of resistance. For every move to germinate, transplant, or cross-breed legal material, there is a countermove available by which to prune, contain, or eradicate. Success in the legal domain is never complete; defeat is rarely final. Separationism became disfavored as a set of reigning ideas, but it would be a mistake to believe that the tradition had been vanquished for all time. Likewise, the prevailing antidiscrimination rhetoric and the powerful nexus of freedom of speech and the right to religious exercise — like any discursive approach — can be taken too far. When it does, one should expect to experience a reaction.

A Note on Popular Constitutionalism

When the entrenchment of the meeting metaphor is laid alongside the juridic marginalization of the metaphorical wall, the juxtaposition confirms the intuition that neither text nor genealogy is decisive in determining the salience of a rhetorical construction. The meeting metaphor has a strong textual basis in both the First Amendment and Article V, and it is a fixture of the Anglo-American tradition. But a series of transformative social movements was required to secure its place in the lexicon. The wall of separation between church and state, too, has an enviable pedigree: it can be traced to the writings of members of the Revolutionary generation, as well as to some of the High Court's early readings of the Establishment Clause, and yet these historical facts have been insufficient to sustain it against the mobilized sentiments of the people.

These experiences do not refute the relevance of text, only its claim to exclusive control of constitutional meaning. Successful instances of concerted action such as those embarked upon by the civil rights protestors of the 1960s and the social conservatives of the 1980s demonstrate in poignant terms the possibility of popular control of everyday constitutional meaning outside the processes enumerated in Article V.

Larry Kramer's important work on the American tradition of petitioning and pamphleteering seeks to legitimate these unruly forms of protest. In his study *The People Themselves,* Kramer points to a wealth of illuminating — and occasionally shocking — moments during the Founding era in which exuberant or angry gatherings of citizens made their views known to their leaders. To Kramer, these incidents of street action coupled with the consistent rhetoric of popular sovereignty during the Framing experience demonstrate that, notwithstanding our collective agreement to live by a written constitution, "final interpretive authority rest[s] with the people themselves."[42]

Kramer's theory of "popular constitutionalism" pursues aims with which the model of linguistic transformation is sympathetic, not the least of which are a desire to reclaim a place for ordinary citizens in democratic constitutionalism and a goal of reversing a pervasive misapprehension of the courts as the final arbiters of text. There are, however, two major points of disagreement between Kramer's theory of popular constitutionalism and the account provided here. First, insofar as Kramer appears to defend popular reaction regardless of method, the precepts of eloquence must reject certain types of unruliness as insufficiently tethered to the goals of democratic engagement. Second, Kramer's description of the people as the "ultimate" or "final" judge of the Constitution's meaning is descriptively inapt insofar as it discounts the importance of institutional interactivity and social consensus.

A critical point of departure is that Kramer's conception of social activism refuses to make judgments about appropriate participatory behavior. In his account, proponents of popular meaning are not measured by the good faith of the actors or their fidelity to established rhetorical forms. This is most obvious in Kramer's defense of "mobbing" as first a primitive form of crime control and then as "an accepted, if not exactly admired, form of political action." From the standpoint of popular constitutionalism, it appears to be just as permissible for an angry crowd to shout down Alexander Hamilton over the Jay Treaty and to throw rocks in his direction as it is for concerned citizens to agitate peaceably for human rights, apparently as legitimate for those bent upon derailing desegregation to block access to the school house as it is for individuals to conduct sit-ins to advance the principle of racial equality. The theory's unwillingness to distinguish between virtuous social movements and illegitimate mob action (except on grounds that such gatherings are populated or led by local gentry) weakens its claim to a seat at the table of *constitutional* meaning-making.

If the ultimate goal of constitutionalism is the formation of durable political beliefs to underwrite our textual commitments to one another, then matters of intelligibility and form assume central importance. The differences between the civil rights protestors and the religious activists on one hand and mobs bent upon the destruction of democratic ideals on the other are twofold. First, activists publicly committed themselves to the goals of renewal rather than either violent revolution or ordinary criminality. This was borne out by their message and actions as they repeatedly engaged the public on the appropriate meaning of the First and Fourteenth Amendments. Thus, activists implicitly swore fealty to the Constitution even as they rejected the particular construction put upon that document by those who ruled in their name.

Second, though inconsistent with prevailing state and local practices, the unconventional tactics of these activists were nevertheless deemed compatible with the broader principles of eloquence and reason that animate democratic constitutionalism. Even as the Justices and other political elites rightly took account of events unfolding in the streets and other quarters, they also correctly struggled to distinguish the tactics of these citizen-speakers from other forms of illegal and undemocratic reaction.

In the protest cases, the Justices wisely searched for, and settled upon, principled ways to say that social activism prohibited by state law could nevertheless be compatible with broader notions of constitutional process. Indeed, a good deal of the debate focused on whether and how civil rights disobedients (and other agitators) behaved differently from fascists and violent reactionaries who took to the streets. Similarly, in the church-state controversies, the Justices sought to reconcile good-faith criticisms of embedded norms. The statements of civic leaders and advocates were afforded a certain amount of respect precisely because they bore indicia of reasoned reflection on the part of actors committed to the constitutional process. All of this constitutes evidence not of courts crudely trying to match First Amendment law to what a majority of Americans desire but rather of judges engaged in an interactive process to synchronize political traditions to arrive at socially plausible readings of text.

There is another, deeper point of divergence. Kramer locates "final" authority to interpret the Constitution in "the people themselves." A pluralism of meanings may be a valuable thing, but interpretive conflict is inevitable in such a world, and popular constitutionalism provides little by way of tools to sort this out once complexity is multiplied. If by "final" Kramer means that the people reserve the authority to overturn or resist governing constructions of text, the point is undeniable.

But Kramer's approach may in fact be more daring. If, instead, he means to cull a stronger duty to favor a majoritarian reading of text over an elite construction whenever the two conflict or an obligation on the part of the Court to cede ground entirely as to certain subject matter, the implications are potentially far-reaching. Such a claim necessitates discussion of many questions, including when, if ever, the authentic sentiment of the people can be accurately discerned.[43] At all events, the theory inverts the very interpretive hierarchy that it critiques, and the notion of popular supremacy stands in sharp relief to the model of calibrated equilibrium sketched here.

Instead of claiming the existence of a single popular constitution, linguistic transformation accepts that reigning practices necessarily consist of an uneasy amalgamation of elite and popular values. Generally, these ideals are difficult to separate cleanly, are usually hotly contested, and are almost always managed by institutions. If, indeed, consensus is both a sociological fact and a structural ideal that can be normatively justified, there can be no such thing as an undiluted popular constitution. Indeed, the point is not to try to figure out the authentic feelings of the populace as to issue X or Y but to arrive at readings of text that can be defended in principled terms while securing the support of a critical mass of constitutional actors.

Separating governing constructions from parochial understandings acknowledges the necessity of a dominant understanding of text while respecting the inviolate right of dissenters to remake their commitments. In so doing, it may be possible to hold fast to the ideal of popular sovereignty and the practice of institutional governance without allowing one to swallow the other.

5

War and Syntax

A misconception has circulated for some time that war is purely an irrational event, a social paroxysm, even the breakdown of the rule of law. The Framers were certainly concerned about the destructive nature of war. "When the sword is once drawn," Hamilton wrote, "the passions of men observe no bounds of moderation." Whether out of fear of ascribing normative significance to actions taken under exigent circumstances or fidelity to a text-bound theory of self-governance, scholars, too, have hesitated to confirm that judgments made during a time of war can or should generate foundational change.[1]

Indulging this instinct to downplay the impact of war on the constitutional process is a mistake. The history of the First Amendment has been inextricably bound up with Americans' perceptions of the global conflicts for which they made sacrifices. The first encounter of the twentieth century rendered text relevant on a subnational scale by spurring interpretation of the Fourteenth Amendment; the second turned the First Amendment into a national and international priority. Citizens and their leaders worked out the legacy of war through use of existing democratic idioms, without the intervention of formal amendments to the Constitution. Therefore, the pertinent question is not whether armed conflict has influenced debates over governance but how individuals have molded a people's war experiences to generate constitutional meaning.

Presidential leadership played a crucial, though underexamined, role in entrenching the rights to free expression and religion during the interwar period. Although judicial references to the centrality of free speech and religious exercise to the democratic order appeared in the 1920s and 1930s, statements claiming a "preferred position" for the First Amendment did not command a majority of the Supreme Court until after a series of presidential orations extolling the virtues of the rights to speech and religion.[2] The twentieth century crises that gave rise to charismatic leaders of social movements also presented opportunities for industrious presidents to invoke the name of the people to transform settled understandings.

The American presidency enjoys a number of advantages in controlling the political pathways of constitutional language. First, a single individual is elected to the office, which allows the occupant to personify the nation's priorities, achievements, and traditions. Because Americans have grown accustomed to looking to presidents to set the agenda for the country, the executive branch faces many opportunities to capitalize on expectations of moral leadership. Second, a president can claim to be most responsive to the people's interests because the holder of that office is the only national leader elected by the people of every state. Despite the indirect system of government signified by the Electoral College, presidential rhetoric tends toward universal themes that all people can understand regardless of their state of residency. Third, the Oval Office has available significant resources with which to advance preferred readings of the Constitution. A president can direct lawsuits or legal briefs to be filed, give public addresses, sign executive orders or signing statements, issue position papers or proclamations, author and distribute legal memoranda, and hold press conferences.[3] Fourth, as a result of popularly approved instances of executive initiative in the past, historical and legal precedents favor executive leadership on a host of matters. Even though certain presidential actions in the past may have exceeded the rule of law or the average person's sense of justice, presidential initiative remains an enduring and desirable feature of constitutional practice. For all of these reasons, when a president has determined to engage in constitutional politics, the odds are good that the public and other branches of government will take notice.

Discursive Opposition and Convergence: A Case of Presidential Initiative

An instructive instance of reconstitution initiated by the president occurred in the early 1940s. In a span of three years, the Supreme Court initially approved a local policy requiring schoolchildren to salute the American flag and then reversed course to hold that such a requirement violated the First Amendment. In *Minersville School District v. Gobitis*, the Justices decided that "the promotion of national cohesion" favored the school board policy, even when religious objections are lodged. *West Virginia School Board v. Barnette* overruled *Gobitis* in ringing terms, finding that coercing a flag salute under such circumstances "invades the sphere of intellect and spirit which it is the purpose of the First Amendment to our Constitution to reserve from all official control."[4]

This sequence of events should be understood in light of rhetorical interventions by President Roosevelt to destabilize the Justices' reading of the Constitution in *Gobitis*. This interpretation of the events rejects a strict internal account of the switch, according to which the change is attributed to little more than personnel changes, the switch of votes by key Justices, or intervening changes to legal doctrine. It also rejects a purely extrinsic account, which explains the switch as taking place "in a wartime atmosphere in which the justices of the Supreme Court were clearly conscious of the need to articulate the fundamental differences between democratic and totalitarian values."[5] The rapidity and decisiveness of the turnabout by an institution that prizes respect for precedent, the diametrically opposed visions of group life enunciated in each opinion, and the rhetorical intervention of the president all cut against the internal account. At the same time, the fact that Justices Black, Douglas, and Frank Murphy began to rethink their position after they had had an opportunity to gauge reaction to their reading of text suggests that the transformative deliberation happened in stages.

A convergence of language practices rendered a change in juridic orientation appear not only reasonable in light of the circumstances but also progressively more difficult to resist. The public incongruity between an electorally charged political vision and an increasingly isolated judicial construction of text precipitated institutional receptivity to reexamination. Political rhetoric then presented jurists with the material to reshape official First Amendment understandings. Beyond a claim of causality — that a shift in context destabilizes a construction's support and renders another composition more attractive — the consensus-based approach demonstrates that the source and structure of juridic language often lie beyond existing legal referents. G. Edward White argues that the special status of the First Amendment can be attributed to the rise of a "modernist consciousness" that prized, among other ascendant values, "the capacity of humans to master their experience and in effect to create their own destiny."[6] While these intellectual developments surely influenced the ultimate picture of liberty painted in many important decisions, they could not have gained currency as foundational ideas until a critical mass of political elites and ordinary persons signaled their support of them as essential to democratic self-government. That happened as a result of a vigorous dialogic interaction among the branches of government in the early 1940s. Once FDR presented these ideas in a form acceptable under the precepts of eloquence, they appeared to all concerned as popularly authorized modes of deliberation.

Despite never initiating the formal requirements of Article V beyond fidelity to rhetorical form and respect for institutional consensus, political elites led the country through a remarkable and lasting shift in governing understandings of political and religious dissent. Transformative change occurred when politicians innovated from the store of foundational ideas to suit the exigencies that arose, judges borrowed from democratic idioms to explain their rulings, and ordinary Americans gained a degree of facility with a vocabulary of rights that emerged from this discursive interaction.

When the High Court encountered *Gobitis,* in 1940, the nation had not yet entered a conflict that was rapidly engulfing Europe. Tensions, however, were palpable. Although Paris would not fall until days after the Justices' decision was released to the public, Germany had already invaded Denmark, Norway, Holland, Belgium, and France in rapid succession. William Leuchtenburg reports: "the country felt naked and vulnerable."[7]

Lillian and William Gobitas, devout Jehovah's Witnesses, affirmed in testimony that saluting the flag amounted to paying homage to a false idol and threatened their spiritual standing.[8] Expelled by the school for their "act of insubordination," they challenged the policy on First Amendment grounds. The Justices sided with the school district, with only Harlan Fiske Stone dissenting on the ground that the First Amendment should protect "freedom of mind and spirit" and with a suggestion that the *Carolene Products* formula could have been utilized in the religious dissidents' favor. In his opinion for the Court, Justice Frankfurter framed the citizen's plea as involving "conflicting claims" of "liberty of conscience" and the "authority to safeguard the nation's fellowship." Despite the seemingly equivalent balance of interests at stake, it soon became apparent which interest would be determinative. Frankfurter described the "promotion of national cohesion" as a "great common end," "an interest inferior to none in the hierarchy of legal values"; he waxed eloquent that "national unity is the basis of national security."

Justice Frankfurter went so far as to appeal to the people's memories of the Civil War: "Situations like the present are phases of the profoundest problem confronting a democracy—the problem which Lincoln cast in memorable dilemma: 'Must a government of necessity be too strong for the liberties of its people, or too weak to maintain its own existence?' No mere textual reading or logical talisman can solve the dilemma." Frankfurter lifted this quotation directly from President Lincoln's Address to a Special Session of Congress on July 4, 1861, convened for the purposes of making the case for military action against the seceding states. In that famous oration, Lincoln accused the states of attempting to "destroy the Federal Union" and characterized the conflict as "a people's contest." After presenting a conflict between security and liberty, he answered his own question: "no choice was left but to call out the war power of the Government."

The Supreme Court's reference to this earlier crisis was meant to recreate a sense of anxiety, engender love of country, and remind the populace that liberty might have to give way to security in a time of crisis. Endorsing the local school board's assertion of national unity, the Justices mimicked Lincoln's plea to support the state's decision "to resist force, employed for its destruction, by force for its preservation." On that "extraordinary occasion," Lincoln had observed: "the response of the country was most gratifying; surpassing, in unanimity and spirit, the most sanguine expectation."

As strident as the tone may sound to contemporary ears, the High Court was hardly alone in its sentiments. The Minersville School District, which claimed to speak for "countless other school districts throughout this country," had explicitly appealed to the extraordinary times as a reason for extending the state's police power to protect the "morale" of students, employees, and average Americans:

> In these days of social, economic and political unrest, the preservation of the state is dependent upon the maintenance of a proper morale as much as the maintenance of the health, peace, safety, and morals of the people. The state is much more susceptible to insidious attacks in these days of strain and stress than would appear from casual observation, and the maintaining of a proper esprit de corps or morale of this country may conceivably have a more devastating effect upon the nation than a catastrophe resulting from disease, breach of peace, or even an invasion of the realm.

To arrest "the breakdown of government," the school district claimed the authority to quell "disrespect" to "the government, its institutions and ideals," and to address feelings of "demoraliz[ation]."[9]

Even more important than the feelings of school officials, presidential rhetoric in the late 1930s had similarly called for national cohesiveness. Indeed, this is likely a significant reason why the students' repeated cries that a compulsory pledge was a hallmark of "totalitarian governments, such as the Hitler regime," initially found no purchase.[10] In his 1939 state of the union address, FDR had urged Americans to display a "united patriotism" and "united democracy," to demonstrate the "united strength of a democratic nation." On the eve of oral argument in *Gobitis,* in 1940, as the overseas fighting continued to dominate the news, Roosevelt stressed again the value of "national unity . . . in a very real and a very deep sense, the fundamental safeguard of all democracy."[11] "American integrity and American security" can only be preserved, he proclaimed, if we do not "face the future as a disunited people."

The Supreme Court made their interpretive choice as to the scope of the First Amendment against this background. Noting the right of conscience in the abstract, Justice Frankfurter's opinion nevertheless endorsed the school board's action as aimed at "the ultimate foundation of a free society," which is the "binding tie of cohesive sentiment." *Gobitis* located school officials' authority to coerce students to perform the flag salute ritual in a people's collective right to "self-protection." Uncertainty about the fate of Europe and the president's endorsement of the theme of national unity made Frankfurter's resort to the language of preservation appear perfectly reasonable.

Three short years later, the entire interpretive field became altered by swiftly moving political trends, rendering the juridic vision of communal life incongruous from the one consistently depicted by other elites. On January 6, 1941, Roosevelt turned in a masterful address on the state of the union that later became known as "The Four Freedoms Speech." Interpreting the election as a mandate to battle authoritarianism around the world in spite of America's official policy of "neutrality," the chief executive took advantage of the bully pulpit to present a fresh harmonization of New Deal principles, an emerging rights-based national agenda, and the global conflict under way.[12] In the address, he committed the nation to building a "world founded upon four essential human freedoms":

> The first is freedom of speech and expression — everywhere in the world.
>
> The second is freedom of every person to worship God in his own way — everywhere in the world.
>
> The third is freedom of want — which, translated into world terms, means economic understandings which will secure to every nation a healthy peacetime life for its inhabitants — everywhere in the world.
>
> The fourth is freedom of fear — which, translated into world terms, means a world-wide reduction of armaments to such a point and in such a thorough fashion that no nation will be in a position to commit an act of physical aggression against any neighbor — anywhere in the world.

What FDR described as an "unprecedented" speech proved to be the culmination of various rhetorical moves perfected between the mid-1930s and 1941. The first theme entailed the principled integration of economic rights and certain noneconomic rights in a way that elevated the latter as matters of contemporary salience and national priority. A second major theme was the gradual sharpening of the First Amendment as the favored instrument for building consensus in favor of the war. A third crucial move consisted of the retelling of the history of American constitutionalism as a struggle against evolving incarnations of "autocracy," from the colonists' resistance to repressive English measures to the engagement with the forces presently arrayed against self-rule. Weaving these themes together skillfully, Roosevelt repeatedly appealed to the people themselves, urged the kinds of sacrifices on behalf of country offered during other foundational moments, and rekindled "the faith of America" in its "democratic aspiration."

As early as 1936, FDR had begun to direct the people's attention beyond their immediate borders. In his state of the union address, Roosevelt recalled taking the oath of office in March 1933, when "the world picture was an image of substantial peace." Now, grave dangers threatened the "economic constitutional order" fashioned by the New Deal, which had broken the "domination of government by financial and industrial groups" without returning to a form of government predicated upon the "ruthless and the strong." To defend these hard-won gains, the U.S. would seek "every legitimate means . . . against autocracy and in favor of freedom of expression, equality before the law, religious tolerance and popular rule."[13]

It would not be long before efforts to mobilize the nation against an omnipresent threat were in full swing. "[T]he dangers within are less to be feared than dangers from without," FDR proclaimed on January 4, 1939. "This generation will 'nobly save or meanly lose the last best hope of earth.'" FDR began to shift his rationale from preserving the gains of the New Deal toward saving the constitutional system from external threats, an objective that demanded fresh strategies: "The tools of government which we had in 1933 are outmoded. We have had to forge new tools for a new role of government operating in a democracy — a role of new responsibility for new needs and increased responsibility for old needs, long neglected. Some of these tools had to be roughly shaped and still need some machining down. The American people, as a whole, have accepted them."

He urged fellow Americans to think of the "nation's program of social and economic reform [as] . . . a part of defense, as basic as armaments themselves." Having militarized the New Deal, FDR turned to characterizing the enemy's aims as the antithesis of the American way of life:

> Dictatorship, however, involves costs which the American people will never pay: The cost of our spiritual values. The cost of the blessed right of being able to say what we please. The cost of freedom of religion. The cost of seeing our

capital confiscated. The cost of being cast into a concentration camp. The cost of being afraid to walk down the street with the wrong neighbor. The cost of having our children brought up, not as free and dignified human beings, but as pawns molded and enslaved by a machine.

FDR had become adept at building support for the war in terms of global constitutional ideals. In his 1940 state of the union address, he again appealed to cherished First Amendment values: "We must look ahead and see the kind of lives our children would have to lead if a large part of the rest of the world were compelled to worship a god imposed by a military ruler, or were forbidden to worship God at all; if the rest of the world were forbidden to read and hear the facts — the daily news of their own and other nations — if they were deprived of the truth that makes men free." Linking the freedom of America's youth to the plight of oppressed children worldwide, Roosevelt suggested that a judgment of hypocrisy would fall upon all Americans if they stood on the sidelines while the fate of democracy was decided on the battlefield. In this way, he portrayed the war effort as more than an international effort, but also as a multigenerational endeavor.

Roosevelt's "Four Freedoms" address on January 6, 1941, differed from these earlier orations in its clearly stated purpose, its organization, and its elegance. Whatever doubt might have been entertained that the First Amendment was a subject of passing interest to the administration should have been laid to rest by this state of the union address. With the campaign now behind him, FDR presented his constitutional vision with increased determination and urgency. He called "this Annual Message to the Congress . . . unique in our history" because "at no previous time has American security been as seriously threatened from without as it is today." Making the case that the present conflict raised constitutional questions of the first order, he summarized our experiment in self-rule: "Since the permanent formation of our Government under the Constitution, in 1789, most of the periods of crisis in our history have related to our domestic affairs. . . . It is true that prior to 1914 the United States often had been disturbed by events in other Continents. . . . But in no case had a serious threat been raised against our national safety or our continued independence." He continued: "Every realist knows that the democratic way of life is at this moment being directly assailed in every part of the world either by arms or by secret spreading of poisonous propaganda." Quoting Benjamin Franklin, he cautioned that "those who would give up essential liberty to purchase a little temporary safety, deserve neither liberty nor safety." In its reversal of the priority of liberty and safety, the president's oration appeared to repudiate the logic of *Gobitis.*

No longer content with reacting to hostile forces, FDR proposed taking the offensive if America were to become "the great arsenal of democracy"—a phrase he had earlier employed in a fireside chat to great fanfare.[14] Rather than mention the First Amendment as part of a hodgepodge list of rights, he now prioritized a national commitment to expressive freedom and religious worship above all other constitutional duties and universalized their significance. The subordination of the "new economic constitutional order" to First Amendment ideals underscored the legal significance of the transformation under way. As FDR himself confessed, he had embarked upon a bold gambit to "make [the nation's] people conscious of their individual stake in the preservation of democratic life in America," to "toughen[] the fibre of our people," "renew[] their faith and strengthen[] their devotion to the institutions we make ready to protect." Nothing less than "the happiness of future generations of Americans" depended upon the project's success.

The president would return to these themes in his inaugural address two weeks later, but at a higher level of abstraction. First, he situated the present conflict among other crucial moments of constitutional creation. Placing the global conflict on par with the American Revolution and the Civil War, and associating himself with two of the nation's greatest leaders under fire, he declared:

> In Washington's day the task of the people was to create and weld together a
> nation.
> In Lincoln's day the task of the people was to preserve that Nation from
> disruption from within.
> In this day the task of the people is to save that Nation and its institutions
> from disruption from without.[15]

Second, he sought to "muster the spirit of Americans, and the faith of America" in order to extend national interests beyond U.S. shores. Constitutional self-government had found its evangelist in FDR, and he was all too ready to take the lead, committing the nation to the advancement of First Amendment ideals "everywhere in the world."

In 1942, after the emperor of Japan's attack on Pearl Harbor, the president proclaimed: "Our own objectives are clear; the objective of smashing the militarism imposed by war lords upon their enslaved peoples the objective of liberating the subjugated Nations—the objective of establishing freedom of speech, freedom of religion, freedom from want, and freedom from fear everywhere in the world."

Without mentioning the case by name, the 1941 address came as close to a repudiation of *Gobitis* as one could expect from the president without incurring the wrath of significant numbers of patriotic Americans. Other executive branch officials made similar statements bolstering the president's emphasis on the rights of speech and conscience.[16] If the Justices believed that the president might wish to have the authority to inculcate patriotism through the power of local and state laws, FDR made no claim on such authority. Indeed, his celebration of dissent appeared to reject such power by implication.

Follow the Leader: Judicial Revision and the Legacies of War

On June 8, 1942, came a curious decision from the Supreme Court that revealed that the alliance that had produced *Gobitis* had started to fray. In an opinion penned by Justice Reed in *Jones v. City of Opelika*,[17] the Court rejected a First Amendment challenge by a Jehovah's Witness to a local ordinance that imposed a license tax on printed materials; the defendant had failed to pay the tax before distributing pamphlets on the city streets. Echoing the community-first ethos of *Gobitis*, Justice Reed stressed the "sovereign power explicitly reserved to the state . . . to ensure orderly living." In an attempt to sidestep charges of totalitarianism, he then drew a dichotomy between the individual spirit (ruled by "ethical principles") and action (ruled by law), "so the mind and spirit of the man remain forever free, while his actions rest subject to necessary accommodation to the competing needs of his fellows." Turning to the specific enactment, he greatly minimized the impact of the tax on the free flow of information: "it is difficult to see in such enactments a shadow of a prohibition of the exercise of religion or of abridgment of freedom of expression or the press. It is prohibition and unjustifiable abridgment that is interdicted, not taxation."

Harlan Fiske Stone, newly installed as Chief Justice, dissented on the ground that the Constitution had put the rights of speech and worship in a "preferred position" and that the ordinance was a "prohibited invasion of the freedoms thus guaranteed." Opposing the idea that the law had a trivial impact on the exercise of First Amendment rights, he insisted that these "commands are not restricted to cases where the protected privilege is sought out for attack. They extend at least to every form of taxation which, because it is a condition of the exercise of the privilege, is capable of being used to control or suppress it." Justice Stone's opinion can be understood as an attempt to reverse the language of military necessity in favor of liberty. It also appeared to be the first time that he or any other member of the Court had placed the First Amendment in a "preferred position," endorsing the contemporaneous moves of the president.

This time, Justice Stone was not alone in dissent. Justice Murphy also dissented, choosing to write a separate opinion. Resisting the majority's effort to separate constitutional text from individual spirit, he wrote: "Freedom to think is absolute of its own nature; the most tyrannical government is powerless to control the inward workings of the mind. But even an aggressive mind is of no missionary value unless there is freedom of action, freedom to communicate its message to others by speech and writing."

Justices Black, Douglas, and Murphy then dropped a bombshell: they had decided to renounce their support for *Gobitis* because they saw *Opelika* as a "logical extension of the principles upon which that decision rested," a decision they could no longer abide. "Since we joined in the opinion in the *Gobitis* case," they announced in a joint dissent, "we think this is an appropriate occasion to state that we now believe that it also was wrongly decided." The Justices subsequently set *Opelika* for reargument and, with the addition of Wiley Rutledge for the departed James Byrnes, changed their collective mind.

After this series of presidential orations and judicial responses, the Supreme Court revisited the question of the coerced flag salute.[18] By then, political oration and private art had joined to make the right of conscience a subject of national importance. Norman Rockwell's contribution to free speech iconography — which depicted individual voice as essential to communal deliberation — appeared in the pages of *The Saturday Evening Post* on February 20, 1943, mere weeks before *Barnette* was argued in Washington. This widely seen image confirmed the growing sense that dissent need not be subordinated to the war but might be treated as one of the prizes of a war well fought. As Robert Westbrook observes, and as Rockwell's reflections on the inspiration for his painting confirm: "It was not political community that Rockwell saw himself celebrating in the painting, but tolerance of individual dissent, the use of free speech to protect private conscience from the state." Bathed in light, the standing figure's eyes are trained in a heavenly gaze as he speaks at the town meeting. The faces of others at the gathering, too, are turned upward, not only drawing attention to the individual speaking his mind but also reinforcing a general atmosphere of reverence. If the speaker's work clothes and the pamphlet in the hands of another citizen did not tip off the casual observer that the painting depicts a town meeting, one might easily mistake the scene to take place at a house of worship. In art, as in politics, the right of dissent needed myth-makers. Judges would next have their chance to participate in creating a culture of rights.

Walter Barnett and his co-plaintiffs filed a brief inviting the Justices to follow the president's lead and repel the "intolerable invasion" of their rights, repeatedly invoking FDR's "Four Freedoms" address. The Jehovah's Witnesses argued that, as native-born citizens, they posed less "danger to the nation" than "the hundreds of thousands of enemy aliens, lo millions, who are in possession of liberty and freedom while the nation battles their fatherland for the preservation of the four freedoms."[19] Recounting the "storm of violence and persecution" of the sect in the aftermath of *Gobitis*, Barnett reported: "In three of the cities mobocracy 'took over' and the 'four freedoms' were blitzkrieged." The brief juxtaposed *Gobitis*-inspired violence with the president's more hopeful message for the purpose of discouraging continued adherence to the first set of ideas and encouraging validation of the second. Unable to deny the symbolic power of the flag, the schoolchildren instead proposed that the flag be converted from a tool of terror into a "practical daily lesson" on the First Amendment, "a liberty which is one of the four great freedoms for which inhabitants of this land now fight!"

On June 14, 1943, the Justices overruled *Gobitis* and composed a contrasting picture of group life — one that was tolerant, hopeful, and cosmopolitan. The opinion memorialized a constitutional transformation resulting from a discursive convergence between the political branches and the Judiciary. Four major themes figured prominently in both FDR's state of the union address and the public opinion codifying the Supreme Court's switch on the constitutionality of the coerced pledge: (1) a re-imagination of the First Amendment as the main armament in the struggle to rid the world of totalitarianism; (2) the establishment of the First Amendment in a "preferred" position vis-à-vis other constitutional rights; (3) the introduction of an equality principle; and (4) the production of popular rhetorical forms with which to disseminate these norms.

Justice Jackson, who joined the Court from the Roosevelt administration after *Gobitis*, penned the ruling in *Barnette*. The opinion proceeded to reconcile the tension between the president's own mobilized, forceful construction of the First Amendment and the Supreme Court's parsimonious reading in the earlier decision. Mirroring the rhetoric of the president, Justice Jackson's opinion projected a vision of America as guarantor of the "freedom to be intellectually and spiritually diverse," a society in which "exceptional minds" flourished alongside "occasional eccentricity and abnormal attitudes." This political vision joined the principle of antidiscrimination, a legacy of the Civil War, with the principle of expressive liberty, a principle at stake in the global struggle to save democracy. Throughout FDR's oration, he had repeatedly spoken of a unified America whose "national policy" included the steadfast defense of democracy and embattled peoples around the world "without regard to partisanship." Justice Jackson similarly wrote that Barnette's claim raised questions of equality: "Free education, if faithful to the idea of secular instruction and political neutrality, will not be partisan or enemy of any class, creed, party or faction." Just as the survival of democracy demanded a generous, undifferentiated display of force in its self-defense abroad, so, too, the continuation of a democratic people rested upon unstinting enforcement of the First Amendment at home.

This daring pluralistic vision distinguished American from "our present totalitarian enemies," who were hell-bent upon "coercive elimination of dissent." Its rhetorical innovations differed starkly from the Framers' fears of factionalism and dissensus. If democracy now defined itself in opposition to crushing uniformity, then diversity of opinion and background would have to be embraced openly as a virtue.

To carve out "the very heart of the *Gobitis* opinion," Justice Jackson went out of his way to contest its claim on the legacy of the Civil War. Quoting Frankfurter's words, he quickly drained them of institutional support: "It was said that the flag-salute controversy confronted the Court with 'the problem which Lincoln cast in memorable dilemma: "Must a government of necessity be too strong for the liberties of its people, or too weak to maintain its own existence?" ' and that the answer must be in favor of strength." For the *Barnette* Court, the claimed interest in unity paled in comparison with the necessity of national cohesion during that earlier conflict: "It may be doubted whether Mr. Lincoln would have thought that the strength of government to maintain itself would be impressively vindicated by our confirming power of the state to expel a handful of children from school."

Beyond establishing the right of conscience, a distinctive language emerged from this institutional evaluation of Americans' experience with war, past and present. This language of rights contained an explicitly oppositional and anti-majoritarian structure: one's fundamental rights "may not be submitted to a vote," for rights "depend on the outcome of no elections." Moreover, fear of overreaching government officials now led jurists to employ territorial metaphors to signal the importance of certain rights. To license judicial action, Justice Jackson pronounced: "The very purpose of the Bill of Rights was to withdraw certain subjects from the vicissitudes of political controversy, to place them beyond the reach of majorities and officials, and to establish them as legal principles to be applied by the courts." In a theme that would be replicated with greater precision in later years, rights were plotted along an imaginary stretch of land and "withdrawn" from the field of action as if troops were being redeployed to stand watch over a community's most precious possessions.

Legal language that had earlier facilitated the display of military prowess was now reconfigured to showcase the ideal of individual liberty. Reclaiming militaristic vernacular on behalf of the rule of law, Justice Jackson declaimed against the "invasion of rights." The First Amendment "reserved" a "sphere of intellect and spirit" in each citizen; the school board's policy under review "invades" that sacred realm.

In arguably the greatest repudiation of *Gobitis*, the Court concluded that, far from predictably instilling a feeling of patriotism in the citizen, the policy under review did little more than empower local officials to behave as "village tyrants." Democracy remained threatened when rights were threatened, but now grave danger came not from faithless citizens but from overzealous ones. The American story had its villains for the postwar age: these "petty tyrants" or "village tyrants" were ordinary people who were given enormous responsibilities by the democratic process but who were occasionally motivated by malice, acted carelessly, or lacked foresight.

It is important not to mistake the erasure of *Gobitis* for a total rejection of the state's educative interest in the ideals of citizenship. Nor should one fall into the trap of thinking that there is ideological content to be internalized by the people only when a state practice is affirmed but not when judges act to delegitimate such a practice. After *Barnette*, the honest question is not whether the state should enjoy the power to mold how it is perceived but, rather, to what extent and for what reasons the state makes such demands of the citizen. In coordinating parochial beliefs and public ideals, First Amendment language simultaneously affirmed the integrity of individuals' intensely held outlook and ethics and required that they subscribe to a particular set of democratic values. Thus, the price of a right of conscience proved to be toleration of others; in exchange for equal dignity, one gained a civic identity to be incorporated into one's portfolio of the self.

America's war experience merely increased the sense of urgency in defining the concept of citizenship in a nation-state. Eric Hobsbawm has suggested a social link between nationalism and democratic identity: "the mere decline of the older socio-political bonds would have made it imperative to formulate and inculcate new forms of civil loyalty." As old attachments declined, modern "states required a civic religion all the more because they increasingly required more than passivity from their citizens."[20] This myth-making imperative, and the corresponding psychological demands on the citizen, gained strength as political systems multiplied. In postwar America, citizens had to be capable of envisioning the state as a beneficent, all-knowing actor firmly committed to the economic and political health of each American. Thus, citizens needed to be able to not only respond viscerally to the personification of the state but also envision the state in unitary, ideal terms. Yet, individuals' psychological makeup had to be sufficiently supple that they could detach such legitimating sentiments from state actions when the uglier aspects of humanity intruded and a government representative behaved like a "village tyrant." Claims that an official had either "safeguarded" or "invaded" this symbolic space triggered a series of emotional and intellectual reactions. Rhetorical manipulation of the people's receptivity to and revulsion toward "the state" proved to be a central feature of late twentieth century discourse.

If citizens had a new way of making sense of their place in the reconstructed order, so the judge had additional obligations to fulfill. The judge would be a defender of human faculties such as "individual freedom of mind" and "the senses." In enforcing First Amendment values, the jurist labored under instructions to care for "the development and well-being of our free society . . . and its continued growth"; ensure the means of "political and social changes desired by the people"; and, at least indirectly, sponsor the arts and sciences.[21] The antiauthoritarian ethic permeated the smallest units of constitutional language, energizing and complicating the social role of the Judiciary.

Cordoning off particular sectors of social experience from politics—in *Barnette*, the exercise of free will over one's moral and intellectual development—became the preferred mode of describing the exercise of judicial review. The enforcement of rights was intended by judges to short-circuit an inevitable spiral of social strife:

> As first and moderate methods to attain unity have failed, those bent on its accomplishment must resort to an ever-increasing severity. As governmental pressure toward unity becomes greater, so strife becomes more bitter as to whose unity it shall be. Probably no deeper division of our people could proceed from any provocation than from finding it necessary to choose what doctrine and whose program public educational officials shall compel youth to unite in embracing. . . . Those who begin coercive elimination of dissent soon find themselves exterminating dissenters. Compulsory unification of opinion achieves only the unanimity of the graveyard.

In his speeches to the nation, FDR had made the case that the "inner and abiding strength of our economic and political systems" is dependent upon the protection of civil liberties.[22] Taking its cue from presidential rhetoric, the Supreme Court endorsed and elaborated the point. Rejecting the argument that vindication of the schoolchild's right somehow disabled government and betrayed New Deal principles, Justice Jackson pointed out: "To enforce those rights today is not to choose weak government over strong government. It is only to adhere as a means of strength to individual freedom of the mind." A "strong" government had at the Framing and during the New Deal been set in opposition to vigorous enforcement of rights (a "weak" government had prized state sovereignty and freedom of contract). The Justices' reconciliation of the New Deal with war experience altered these connotations such that enforcement of certain political rights was compatible with "strong" government. If the emphasis on the priority of individual dignity within democratic constitutionalism were seen as a studied revival of an earlier "philosophy that the individual was the center of society," that would be an error. Instead, Justice Jackson urged that *Barnette* be understood under "changed conditions": "the laissez-faire concept or principle of non-interference has withered at least as to economic affairs, and social advancements are increasingly sought through closer integration of society and through expanded and strengthened governmental controls."

Notably, the Justices harmonized the deliberative moments of the past without erasing the fact of cultural change over time. The original Bill of Rights articulated principles that "grew in soil" in which colonial Americans treated the term "liberty" as synonymous with the "absence of governmental restraints." As *Barnette* suggests, the Justices understood themselves and their contemporaries to be operating under a charge to "transplant these rights to a soil" in which Americans now had more complex conceptions of liberty. The Justices' use of gardening metaphors underscored, and made more transparent, the fact that their re-reading of constitutional text required choosing among plausible solutions, regular caretaking, and adaptation to social context.

If Justice Jackson's opinion for the Court signified a new rhetorical alignment, then Justice Frankfurter's dissent in *Barnette* represented the remnants of an earlier epoch.[23] In his failure to anticipate the emerging convergence or to acknowledge that the earlier one had been destabilized by armed conflict and presidential resistance, he desperately defended an unyielding reading of the New Deal moment: "Judicial self-restraint is equally necessary whenever an exercise of political or legislative power is challenged. . . . Our power does not vary according to the particular provision of the Bill of Rights which is invoked." What was next, Frankfurter wondered aloud, now that the compulsory flag salute offended the First Amendment—would compulsory Bible reading would be the next to go?

Frankfurter stubbornly refused to reconcile the New Deal with Americans' most recent generational experience. Though Frankfurter surely would not have admitted it, the structure of his dissent mirrored the eulogy of a regime that is passing away: refusal to acknowledge ongoing cultural-historical patterns, nostalgia for a glorious past, fear of the great unknown, a willingness to employ force to try to arrest the passage of time. Seizing for himself alone the mantle of neutrality, he accused his colleagues of "writing . . . private notions of policy into the Constitution." Frankfurter rejected out of hand the idea that the text offered any more flexibility "when dealing with one phase of 'liberty' than with another" and even went so far as to deny that the law can be concerned with "the inner life of man."

The fact that two committed New Dealers—Frankfurter and Jackson—

could arrive at such divergent interpretations of their generational experiences should not be underestimated. These were not just men of different dispositions; they also epitomized particular institutional attitudes toward social change. Jackson was prepared to treat the war experience as the formative lens through which prior constitutional obligations were to be reexamined. He therefore undertook a reformation of the existing linguistic regime. Frankfurter, on the other hand, held fast to an inalterable vision of the New Deal transformation. Having participated in one revolutionary moment, he was not prepared to recognize yet another reconfiguration of these barely settled understandings. For Frankfurter, the revolution was over.

The collaborative use of the First Amendment to reconstruct the public mind in the 1940s reflects the model of presidential initiative in action. As part of concerted efforts to mobilize the American people for war, a democratically elected leader seized the opportunity to define the national agenda. Working within the precepts of eloquence, the president claimed a mandate to reassess existing constitutional understandings and chose to describe his agenda by reinventing democratic idioms. In this case, the chief executive's constructions of the First Amendment's place altered the vector of public debate, destabilizing past understandings while laying the groundwork for a more expansive right of conscience. All of this happened even though the administration decided not to file a brief in either lawsuit.

When the opposed visions of the war's legacy collided, repeatedly, in the public domain, the Supreme Court found itself pressured to reconsider and adjust its rhetorical vision of community. The High Court, like any other political actor, must sense that there is sufficient support for its readings of the Constitution. The Justices proved more than willing to reconsider their position in the face of strong, repeated political constructions that resisted their interpretation. In the end, some members of the media sensed that the High Court's dramatic switch on the flag question realized FDR's constitutional vision. On June 20, 1943, less than a week after news of *Barnette* filtered throughout the country, the *New York Times* called the decision "impressive evidence of the high regard in which the Bill of Rights is held by this country which is fighting, along with the rest of the United Nations, to establish the 'Four Freedoms.' "[24]

Enforcing rights had become another way of doing battle with the nation's enemies. Totalitarianism, according to Hannah Arendt, consists of the mobilization of isolated individuals into faceless "masses" bent upon "the permanent domination of each single individual in each and every sphere of life." Because totalitarianism succeeded by "dominating and terrorizing human beings from within," a competing ideology would have to be inculcated, one that would exhibit respect for individual dignity and autonomy, an ethic of anti-instrumentalism, and a belief in the virtues of pluralism. Antitotalitarian thought — and the wholesale reorganization of rights inspired by American's unique experience with the threat of annihilation both real and perceived — owed its origins to the practical politics of the age as intellectuals struggled to define their society against the looming "other," first during actual hostilities and then during the Cold War. As Richard Primus explains, "the cumulative American reaction against European totalitarianism became so powerful a force in the world of legal and political ideas that it sometimes surpassed, without ever completely eclipsing, the influences of the ideas and experiences of older eras."[25]

The Constitutional Politics That Presidents Make

The techniques employed by FDR to capture the political imagination did not always succeed, but they succeeded on enough occasions to inspire those who would come after him. Presidents who followed Roosevelt emulated many of his rhetorical strategies, including the use of rights-based rhetoric, to pursue objectives of national importance. Harry Truman, who shared FDR's commitment to internationalism, continued to stress that "[r]eligious freedom, free speech, and freedom of thought are cherished realities in our land."[26] For Truman, and for citizens living in an America reconstructed by the war, the term "constitutional rights" had become interchangeable with "human rights." It was not readily apparent whether the indigenous language of rights had colonized the language of international law and practice or the other way around, but for a time these questions hardly mattered. The president could confidently assert that "[a]ny denial of human rights is a denial of the basic beliefs of democracy and of our regard for the worth of each individual" and expect many in the audience to approve of his claim that enforcement of certain universal values enhanced democratic constitutionalism.

As the Cold War deepened, Truman drew upon the people's support for the First Amendment in pursuit of other goals. More so than his predecessor, Truman proved willing to use the resources of the Oval Office to make progress on racial equality. In his 1951 state of the union address, the president sought to inspire listeners with these words: "And above all, we must remember that the fundamentals of our strength rest upon the freedoms of our people. We must continue our efforts to achieve the full realization of our democratic ideals. We must uphold the freedom of speech and the freedom of conscience in our land. We must assure equal rights and equal opportunities to all our citizens."[27]

Truman's primary objective was to mobilize society against "[t]he threat of world conquest by Soviet Russia." But a second priority involved building support for initiatives on racial equality. In that sense, the cultural demands of maintaining America's self-image created an opportunity for presidential action on rights. By placing these particular constitutional values side by side, Truman's call to arms accorded them equivalence in addition to prominence.

Ronald Reagan came closest to matching the constitutional ambition of Roosevelt, and he proved every bit FDR's match in exercising moral leadership within the precepts of eloquence and reason. Where Roosevelt was the patrician bred in the Northeast, Reagan was the plain-speaking actor hailing from the West; yet each had a knack for appearing unflappable in times of crisis. The tactics Reagan employed to reverse the work of the Warren Court rivaled Roosevelt's effort to dislodge the constitutional understandings of the Taft and Hughes Courts. Both made appointments to the Supreme Court with an eye toward reversing the valence of constitutional text in the years before their election. Roosevelt appointed nine members to the Supreme Court in the twelve years between 1933 and 1945; Reagan made four appointments in the eight years between 1981 and 1989.

The issues that motivated each president had important points of contact, but they cannot be considered mirror images of each other. Insofar as ideology mattered, Roosevelt appointed judges with compatible economic philosophies and, later, certain political rights in mind. The most prominent priorities on Reagan's agenda included abortion, religion, state's rights, and criminal punishment; judicial selections were made to enhance the chances that the law would adopt the administration's language and ideas on these matters. Reagan's political philosophy departed most from FDR's around the role of the national government vis-à-vis the states and the relationship between the market and the nation-state,[28] and on those public matters Reagan provoked vigorous reconsideration in the final decades of the twentieth century.

Whereas FDR's Department of Justice demonstrated itself to be highly selective in the cases in which it intervened or filed briefs, especially in matters where a federal law was not at stake, Reagan's Justice Department aggressively made its position known in a wide array of cases pending in the federal courts. A good deal of the difference can be explained by the department's limited litigation authority and resources in its early years, even as its lawyers tried to defend New Deal legislation against legal challenges. By contrast, the DOJ had grown into a formidable, well-staffed institution by the time of Reagan's tenure, with the capacity to monitor and respond to any legal development that might impact the president's constitutional vision. Reagan may not have been any more ideologically motivated than FDR, but the resources available to the presidency had grown significantly in the years between their tenures, and by the 1980s there existed a significant body of achievements against which to mount a sustained reaction.

Both charismatic leaders appreciated the artistry and the power of public oratory, and each seized the opportunities afforded him to reconstruct constitutional democracy in his own image. Many of FDR's efforts in the 1930s were directed at altering the notion of negative rights in favor of an affirmative conception of economic rights that could be secured by government. To the extent that FDR deployed First Amendment rhetoric in the 1940s, it was largely in service to external goals, and the work of internationalism had been completed by Reagan's time. Reagan, by contrast, deployed rights-based rhetoric aggressively in pursuit of a broader range of domestic issues. In general, he favored the notion of negative rights as a way of rhetorically reducing the role of the state in an individual's everyday existence. Still, each president's exercise of rhetorical autonomy inspired countless Americans.

One lesson Reagan surely drew from Roosevelt's rhetorical successes had to be the sheer power of the First Amendment as a set of popularly accepted beliefs. Like FDR, Reagan invoked the ideas of religious and expressive freedom in foreign policy to define the American nation-state as an exceptional moral community. He adhered to the premise established during the war years that a "united people" and expansive notions of "individual liberty" could co-exist.[29] Reagan paid tribute to "The Four Freedoms" and frequently stressed these values in public addresses. A number of his domestic initiatives came in these areas as well, though with a different emphasis: enhancing commercial speech, promoting religious exercise, and reducing the sphere of the Establishment Clause. If FDR bore significant responsibility for creating the speech-centered society, Reagan did an effective job of maintaining its appearance. As powerful as Reagan's rhetorical presidency proved to be, the techniques perfected during his tenure could be traced to the plebiscitarian leadership of the Roosevelt years.

Marching Our Sons and Daughters Off to War

After the Second World War, it became effective to castigate a particular position as exhibiting a "totalitarian cast," as bearing the "hallmark[s] of the totalitarian state," or as "a long step down the totalitarian path."[30] In legal decisions, the term "basic to a free society" rapidly became synonymous with the traditional formula for identifying fundamental rights — "implicit in a scheme of ordered liberty" — and eventually surpassed the formula in popularity. The former never rolled off the tongue smoothly and raised more definitional questions than it resolved; the latter captured the anti-authoritarian ethic for a generation that had lived through the Nazi and Fascist threat, with its fearful image of the "closed" and "regimented" society. As Justice Douglas wrote in the 1949 case, *Terminiello v. City of Chicago*, which overturned a breach of the peace statute as unduly vague: "The right to speak freely and to promote diversity of ideas and programs is therefore one of the chief distinctions that sets us apart from totalitarian regimes. . . . The ordinance as construed by the trial court seriously invaded this province."

The legacy of the Second World War remained as contested as any other deliberative moment, including the framing of the original Constitution. A speech-restrictive interpretation of the war experience would occasionally prove attractive, especially when the specter of "the masses" in the streets could be raised. Many remembered that the Nazis came to power with the help of the masses.[31] Nevertheless, the weight of judicial reconciliations favored the speech-protective tradition. The individual-centered language of rights resolved far-reaching controversies such as *Stanley v. Georgia*, a crucial link in the chain of precedents establishing the ideas of decisional and information privacy; *Brandenburg*, which enlarged expressive protections for controversial and intolerant groups; and *Tinker v. Des Moines Independent School District*, the ruling that established the right of public schoolchildren to engage in nondisruptive protest.

Recall *Stanley*, in which the Justices determined that the First Amendment prevented authorities from punishing a person for possessing obscene materials in the home. Justice Marshall presented the matter as an epic struggle over a person's mind: "If the State can protect the body of a citizen, may it not, argues Georgia, protect his mind?" His answer: "our whole constitutional heritage rebels at the thought of giving government the power to control men's minds." Justice Marshall stated that "this right to receive information and ideas, regardless of their social worth, is fundamental to our free society." This commitment obligated judges to act when doing so would help the individual "satisfy his intellectual and emotional needs" or otherwise "protect Americans in their beliefs, their thoughts, their emotions, and their sensations."[32]

Brandenburg continued the discursive trend. In his separate opinion concurring with the result, Justice Douglas resorted to the metaphor of the Constitution-as-barrier. "The government," he wrote, "has no power to invade that sanctuary of belief and conscience." According to this perspective, the state's effort to suppress the advocacy of controversial ideas is equivalent to the "investigator [who] roams at will through all of the beliefs of the witness, ransacking his conscience and his innermost thoughts."[33] To suppress an individual's expression, Douglas suggested, is to violate a "sanctuary" and, even if nothing is taken, still may leave the impression of control.

Tinker, decided the same year as *Brandenburg*, brought expressive liberty to the youth of America, who were formerly treated as temporary charges of the state, attending school to "learn, not teach." School officials suspended several student activists for doing no more than wearing black armbands to convey their opposition to American activities in Vietnam. Finding the punishment a transgression of free speech principles, Justice Fortas explained: "In our system, state-operated schools may not be enclaves of totalitarianism. School officials do not possess absolute authority over their students."[34] Expressive liberty entails some risk of disturbance, "[b]ut our Constitution says we must take this risk; and our history says that it is this sort of hazardous freedom—this kind of openness—that is the basis of our national strength of the independence and vigor of Americans who grow up and live in this relatively permissive, often disputatious, society." The state could not legally "confine" student views to "those sentiments that are officially approved" out of a desire to "foster a homogeneous people."

Even as late as 1969, memories of the last just war remained fresh: Justice Fortas pointed out the irony in the fact that the school policy under review permitted students to wear "the Iron Cross, traditionally a symbol of Nazism," but not these "passive" symbols of dissent. His statement had resonance not because the Nazi token is intrinsically evil but because it is presumed to elicit strong reactions given our unique political experiences.

The valorous dead are recalled to active duty during the most mundane of public controversies, though we have become so accustomed to this practice that one scarcely notices when it happens. Consider *Watchtower Bible and Tract Society of New York v. Village of Stratton*.[35] The appeal raised the question of whether a municipality could require a person to obtain a permit before engaging in door-to-door canvassing. Local officials believed that their law addressed the goals of protecting residential privacy, deterring fraud that might occur through solicitations, and preventing crime.

A majority of the Supreme Court easily found the law a violation of the First Amendment. Justice Stevens began his exposition by employing the wartime decisions to set a mood: "Although our past cases involving Jehovah's Witnesses, most of which decided shortly before and during World War II, do not directly control the question we confront today, they provide both a historical and analytical backdrop for [the] claim that the Village's ordinance offends the First Amendment." Not only did Justice Stevens argue from earlier precedent that door-to-door canvassing and pamphleteering are traditionally protected "vehicles for the dissemination of ideas"; he also stressed the medium as indispensable to "the little people"—the underfinanced, those lacking a lobby, the despised. The Court's unapologetic usage of the Jehovah Witnesses as iconic dissenters continued. The historical experience of the sect offered proof as to the "chilling effect" of permit regimes such as the one under review: "As our World War II-era cases dramatically demonstrate, there are a significant number of persons whose religious scruples will prevent them from applying for such a license."

Having established the pedigree for the deterrence claim, Justice Stevens then generalized its scope: "There are no doubt other patriotic citizens, who have such firm convictions about their constitutional right to engage in uninhibited debate in the context of door-to-door advocacy, that they would prefer silence to speech licensed by a petty official."

One might forgive Stevens's obsession with the "patriotic" dissenter given the romantic prototype of the silent contrarian depicted in earlier controversies such as *Barnette*. Still, if deterrence of speech is the concern, hyperpatriotic citizens might not be the segment of the community most at risk of self-censorship, for many such highly motivated persons will exercise their rights regardless of the legal consequences. It is, rather, the risk-averse members of society who are most likely to curb their expressive activities when faced with significant obstacles or the prospect of punishment.

At all events, the opinion concluded the same way it began, with a reference to the Judiciary's midcentury awakening to the responsibility of defending democratic freedoms: "The rhetoric used in the World War II-era opinions that repeatedly saved petitioner's co-religionists from petty prosecutions reflected the Court's evaluation of the First Amendment freedoms that are implicated in this case. The value judgment that then motivated a united democratic people fighting to defend those very freedoms from totalitarian attack is unchanged. It motivates our decision today."

In one sense, the statement is romantic and idealized. In another sense, Justice Stevens's portrayal of the adjudicative process comes across as refreshingly honest. It offers a rare synopsis of the harmonization of political beliefs that occurred during the interregnum period of the First Amendment's development. The people made a "value judgment" during the war years. That moral decision motivated a "united" people "to fight" and inspired American institutions to reevaluate the foundations of the political order. The value judgment was eventually "reflected" in judicial "rhetoric." It continues to "motivate" the judgment of decision makers in the present.

So ingrained is the rhetoric of war that it cannot be claimed as the exclusive province of any particular segment of society. In *City of Erie v. Pap's A. M.*, the High Court sustained a public indecency ordinance that had been read to forbid nude dancing in commercial establishments. Concluding that the law had only a "de minimis" impact on "overall expression," Justice O'Connor wrote: "few of us would 'march our sons and daughters off to war to preserve the citizen's right to see' specified anatomical areas exhibited at establishments like Kandyland."[36] This jarring linkage of a sober, high-minded political decision (war-making) with a hedonistic, commercial enterprise (erotic entertainment) diminished the social importance of the enterprise seeking the benefit of the free speech tradition. Indeed, the rhetorical move implied that enforcing the First Amendment in such circumstances would demean the sacrifices of soldiers past.

Justice O'Connor copied the phrase from Justice Stevens's earlier statement in a case called *Young v. American Mini Theaters*, demonstrating how war-inspired legal sayings can cross ideological divides. In *Young*, Stevens had authored an opinion that upheld various ordinances regulating "adult" establishments against a First Amendment challenge. Justice Stevens explained why regulating the availability of sexually explicit material was compatible with "the free market in ideas": "Whether political oratory or philosophical discussion moves us to applaud or despise what is said, every schoolchild can understand why our duty to defend the right to speak remains the same. But few of us would march our sons and daughters off to war to preserve the citizen's right to see 'Specified Sexual Activities' exhibited in the theaters of our choice."[37] In militarized language, he suggested that the rule against content-based laws could be relaxed when the state regulated low-value expression. While the First Amendment protects information from "total suppression," he concluded, at times it may be appropriate for the state to treat adult material "in a different classification from other motion pictures."

The collaborative reading of text over time resulted in additions to the political lexicon that sketched a more robust picture of the human subject. The individual was entitled to "respect," "dignity," "a free mind," and the right to chart his "destiny." And yet, its successes were not unqualified. There remained jarring divergences between word and deed. The system of thought sanctified organized violence against the perceived enemies of the state, both at home and abroad. Despite the rising American pride in egalitarianism, the wartime internment of Japanese-Americans appeared at the time to be compatible with the revitalized rights discourse, especially given the precedence accorded the First Amendment. Critics charged that internment policy proceeded upon a race-dependent "inference [that] has been used in support of the abhorrent and despicable treatment of minority groups by the dictatorial tyrannies that this nation is now pledged to destroy." Yet, Justice Black's opinion in *Korematsu v. United States* resisted the comparison with totalitarianism. "Our task would be simple, our duty clear, were this a case involving the imprisonment of a loyal citizen in a concentration camp because of racial prejudice . . . we deem it unjustifiable to call them concentration camps with all the ugly connotations that term implies."[38] For Black and others, Japan's attack justified the unequal treatment of Americans on racial grounds, and they saw no reason to interrogate further the premises upon which that decision was reached.

Eventually, the militarized language of liberty curried support for the development of rights across a broad spectrum of areas. Although casting one's priorities in the language of rights could not guarantee victory, doing so appeared to enhance one's chances. Certainly decision makers believed that the language of rights made outcomes more palatable to average citizens. Consider the right to privacy articulated in *Griswold v. Connecticut*. Without these war-inspired motifs, it is hard to imagine Justice Douglas's arresting, and in some quarters ridiculed, portrait of the right's genesis. An underappreciated fact is that Douglas opened and closed his discussion by casting the right to privacy — the "intimate relation of husband and wife" — in First Amendment terms.[39] "The association of people is not mentioned in the Constitution nor in the Bill of Rights," Justice Douglas began. "Yet the First Amendment has been construed to include certain of those rights." In fact, although much has been made of Douglas's reference to "penumbras" emanating from various textual provisions, he actually devoted the majority of his opinion to discussing First Amendment freedoms, including the right to resist foreign language instruction, freedom of association, and even the right to assemble peaceably. For Douglas, these popularly accepted rights provided a basis for judicial protection of "the intimate relation of husband and wife." This interpretive strategy implicitly recognized the power of First Amendment ideas in reconstructed America.

After stating that these textual commitments created "zones of privacy" — a move that recalled the postwar division of Germany as a strategy for a just peace — Justice Douglas repeatedly characterized the Constitution as providing "protection against all governmental invasions." Having situated the anti-contraception law as an intrusion into such a "zone," he offered perhaps the most coherent theory for a right of privacy: "Marriage is a coming together for better or for worse, hopefully enduring, and intimate to the degree of being sacred. It is an association that promotes a way of life, not causes; a harmony of living, not political faiths; a bilateral loyalty, not commercial or social projects. Yet it is an association for as noble a purpose as any involved in our prior decisions."

Reverence for the First Amendment shaped the articulation of other rights. Where appropriation from this rich store of ideas occurs, as in *Griswold*, one expects to encounter an increase in the novelty of arguments and doctrinal mixing. On the other hand, as *Korematsu* hinted, the long shadow cast by the reformulated hierarchy of liberties and the increased attention to "four essential human freedoms" arguably stunted the articulation of other rights. If the people adored the First Amendment, the courts made sure to return this affection by resolving a steady stream of such cases year after year; other areas of the Constitution received considerably less attention.

When borrowing from free speech ideas occurred, however, there was no assurance that a synthesis would be coherent, and, in fact, there is some reason to believe that the strength of social support for the First Amendment could lead an interlocutor to prefer generality over specificity. In a society reconstructed according to the ideals of expressive liberty, it became all too tempting to gesture in the general direction of the First Amendment, to invoke its powerful ideas and recite its most cherished sayings, without always doing the hard work of making lasting connections.

Take the landmark decision *Lawrence v. Texas*, which overruled a Texas law that banned same-sex sodomy. Justice Kennedy's ruling for the Supreme Court began by deploying the rhetorical legacy of the Second World War and raising the specter of the state unbound: "In our tradition, the State is not omnipresent in the home." Justice Kennedy then announced matter-of-factly: "Freedom extends beyond spatial bounds. Liberty presumes an autonomy of self that includes freedom of thought, belief, expression, and certain intimate conduct."[40]

Notice what is often overlooked: three of the four illustrations of liberty can be traced to the First Amendment. The opinion commenced with a description of rights that already enjoyed broad support—thought, belief, expression— before adding the more contested right of sexual autonomy to the end of this list, hoping that the right would gain something from its association with expressive rights.

The opinion went on to stress that an individual's liberty interest arises, as it did here, "[w]hen sexuality finds overt expression in intimate conduct with another person." Analyzing the practical effects of the law on the lives of sexual minorities, the Justices concluded: "The State cannot demean their existence or control their destiny."

Having assessed the structure of postwar rights discourse, we find it easier to appreciate why the High Court might have been tempted to rebuild the right to privacy through the First Amendment in the first place. Recall that *Bowers v. Hardwick* had left the privacy doctrine in tatters, with the right seemingly dependent not on particular conduct but rather on the sexuality of the individuals committing certain acts.[41] The rhetorical strategy of *Lawrence* reflected a shrewd calculation: above all else, the language of expressive liberty had the potential to foster broad social support.

It is now possible to mount a response to the most strident attacks against *Lawrence* as "illegitimate" and "anticonstitutional."[42] Simply put, the modalities employed in the judicial composition did not contravene the idea of popular sovereignty; rather, such terms had been authorized by the people themselves. Nor was the composition the fabrication of a few unelected judges but a sincere construction of text in which a consensus of jurists paid due respect to the achievements of previously constituted people. The fact that the outcome may have aligned with certain philosophies, such as libertarianism or humanism or natural law, did not deprive the ruling of its public character or reduce the words in the ruling to the jurists' "personal" preferences. All in all, the decision fit comfortably within the rhetorical tradition and the political belief system forged during a time of intense mobilization.

To say that the decision should be accorded respect, however, is not the same as saying that the opinion is as persuasive as it might have been. It is possible to recognize the ruling's importance as an inspiration to a great many Americans and for its removal of *Bowers* as an obstacle to judicial articulation of minority rights while noting that the popular elements of the ruling exist in tension with its doctrinal aims. Should the opinion's references to free speech be understood as little more than mood lighting or as an effort to sketch a durable rationale? When is sex "speech," and when is it merely "conduct"? If a casual sexual encounter behind closed doors is an "overt expression in intimate conduct" entitled to judicial protection, why not life-long declarations of affection and mutual support? Surely these relationships "express" something more meaningful to the outside world.

Whatever the ultimate answers to these questions, we might at least agree on this: to the extent that the seriousness of the First Amendment rationale remained in doubt, the ruling left behind material for almost everyone with which to engage these matters. The Justices made a choice to rely on popularly accepted forms while leaving the right to privacy noticeably undertheorized, perhaps in the hope that strategic ambiguity would promote discussion on the rights of sexual minorities and make a social convergence on such matters more obvious in the future. If the general right to privacy is to move beyond support for specific outcomes, however, there will have to be greater attention to eliciting the support of political elites as well as ordinary people. Beyond the strategic use of popular rhetoric, one must also make a commitment to a coherent set of rationales.

A final complaint about the rhetoric of "mind control," "regimentation," and "aggressive breaches" of rights can be lodged with the educative function of law in mind. The concern is that antitotalitarian rhetoric may inhibit a more sophisticated understanding of the nature of rights and the constitutional process more generally. Many of the preferred moves revolve around the enforcement model of constitutional debate. According to this model, there is a designated "victim," "vested" or "well-established" rights that must be vindicated, and a "violator" to be repelled by the courts. The basic structure of the discussion encourages the framing of social ills in rights-based terminology, a belief in rights as ontologically fixed rather than socially contested, and a preference for court action over other strategies to vindicate rights. It is difficult to measure the truth of any of these claims to a mathematical certainty, but there remain a surprising number of individuals who believe that constitutional questions must be addressed in an orderly manner, through the courts alone, and that the rulings of judges are, and should be, the last word on a subject.

Even those inclined to favor rights should detect a certain irony in the fact that Hamilton's prediction that the specification of rights may, paradoxically, circumscribe rights rather than ensure their survival has been realized during the golden age of rights. Mistaken though it may be, the common belief today is that if a right is not named, it is presumed not to exist. As Hamilton warned in *Federalist 84*: "[A Bill of Rights] would contain various exceptions to powers not granted; and, on this very account, would afford a colorable pretext to claim more than were granted. For why declare that things shall not be done which there is no power to do? Why, for instance, should it be said that the liberty of the press shall not be restrained, when no power is given by which restrictions may be imposed?" There is a sense in which the people have been imprisoned by the language of rights. Public debates careen between vigorously defending "spheres" of rights and expansive state prerogative, even if lived experience falls somewhere in between.

The durability of the enforcement model is one reason that First Amendment forms enjoy such staying power and that constitutional actors feel authorized to intersperse their elocutions with references to expressive values. It also helps to explain why instances of judicial enforcement of rights are widely celebrated while the actions of others on behalf of rights can be so easily forgotten. In this respect, antitotalitarian discourse entrenches, rather than overcomes, the idea of judicial leadership favored in certain circles.

Does a viable alternative to the enforcement model exist? Indeed: one that stresses the management of crises rather than valorizes their resolution and permits the coordination of ascendant political discourses instead of pretending that they do not influence the meaning of legal texts. It is a model that treats adjudication as an act of facilitation, and it is worth recovering from the American political tradition.

6

Adjudication as Facilitation

The establishment of a political order based upon First Amendment
ideals during the twentieth century was a collaborative effort of genuine creativity, one that entailed sacrifice and foresight. In helping to maintain or
erode linguistic regimes within the law, judges played a major part in the
reproduction of constitutional norms. Their participation in the creation of
the speech-centered society should prompt a general reevaluation of the judicial function. Some courts claimed to be doing no more than dutifully enforcing self-evident meanings of the Constitution. Others resisted the temptation
to obscure their rhetorical autonomy from the public and instead described
themselves as reading text and tradition in changed contexts to arrive at practical strategies for governance. How is one to decide between these representations of judging?

A great deal of contemporary constitutional discourse is premised on the
enforcement model, in which disputes over foundational values should be
shepherded into the courts, where judges can be expected to safeguard either
individual rights or the prerogatives of the state. It is said that the court-
centered model has several virtues, namely that it is orderly for interested
parties, efficient in its resolution of claims that might be presented, and predictable from the standpoint of rights-holders.

The model depends upon a conception of judicial review — often described as translation — according to which a decision maker is charged with the solemn task of capturing the intentions or expectations of past parties formally authorized to write legal text. Despite its superficial appeal, this adjudicative ideal suffers from ambiguity about what exactly is being translated, an overly narrow sense of the judiciary as a political and cultural institution, and a troubling lack of transparency about how interpretation actually occurs.

Stitching together earlier threads of argument based on what jurists did and not merely what they said they were doing, this chapter defends the cultural model of adjudication displayed in the formation of First Amendment law. This facilitative model, in which regularized judicial participation offers an alternative to the intermittent enforcement model, reorients a jurist's attention toward a different order of responsibilities: the mediation of cultural conflict, the development and management of political grammar, the cultivation of civic ideals, and the rhetorical empowerment of others. This model of constitutional interaction is compatible with the Framers' own writings on the task of judging. It also better integrates their ideas on adjudicative power with their expectations for a democratic ethos that ensures respect for fundamental rights.

Translation's Discontents

The dominant conception of judging under the enforcement model is translation, a task that presupposes the existence of a foreign statement or dead language incomprehensible to the nonnative reader. The obligation of the judge-as-translator "is always to determine how to change one text into another text, while preserving the original text's meaning."[1] In other words, a person judges best when he appears not to be judging at all — when individual voice is subjugated to the intentioned statements of others. As Lawrence Lessig explains, this adjudicative prototype of judging treats "the power to translate as a delegated power from an author to an agent." While there is some play in the joints of Lessig's particular version of translation, as there is for other versions of translation, it cannot escape a more general critique.

For the dead — even the heroic dead — have no voice. If a single authentic voice ever existed, a dubious proposition at best, it no longer exists to be "translated." The trope of the judge-as-seer therefore trades away descriptive accuracy for the appearance of fidelity.[2] The moment one grasps that readings of text involve complicated normative judgments about the multiple contexts in which differently constituted peoples wrote and read, the approach begins to lose its explanatory power. Having lost the power to explain what judges have actually done in the past, its potential as a normative model becomes severely compromised.

The jurist is not passively describing governing language but actively using it and, in the using of it, reshaping its meaning. This has been true at every step of the First Amendment's development, and it is surely true in other areas, as well. Thus, the relevant question is rarely whether a reader of a text has frolicked and detoured from text but how the reader — an actor with a moral agency of his own — goes about making synthetic readings and why.

Nor is it any more helpful to suggest that judges engage in interlanguage translation. A people's governing discourses arise from a dynamic language spanning several generations. Certain terms have cycled out of usage, just as previously unimagined rhetorical forms have become active in the lexicon, and there are even contradictory ideas and formulations. But these variances do not justify treatment of modern trends and local idiosyncrasies as comprising separate tongues. Perhaps, then, what is meant by translation is that judges should convert archaic legal traditions into ordinary terms. This is closer to the idea of facilitation, for there is an educative component to the adjudicative process that entails a responsibility to communicate in accessible terms. But if this is all that is meant by translation, then judges are doing no more than translating themselves.

One might try to rescue translation by replacing a written text with the voices of presently constituted peoples. For example, a proponent could claim that the judge's responsibility is to turn political events into legal language. Even if one is sympathetic to an account of courts as culturally responsive institutions, however, the pertinent functions revolve around the production and management of constitutional norms, as well as the modeling of political habits, and not simply the faithful channeling of original expectations. Because the underlying principal-agent ideal suppresses or denies these dynamic socio-institutional functions, translation ultimately fails to capture the full range of linguistic tasks. This last critique — a lack of transparency about what judges past and present actually do — should be reason enough to set translation aside as a plan of action.

Instead of disguising the authorship of the jurist, one might instead openly acknowledge the creative and coercive nature of the interpretive act by imagining this law-making power to be the major threat to democratic constitutionalism. The modified strategy locates elected officials, rather than jurists, at the center of constitutionalism. From this perspective, which reprises the Antifederalist critique of the draft Constitution, the unelected judge's power to nullify laws underwritten by popular majorities is uneasily reconciled with the people's political agency.

Yet, a mobilized citizenry considered and ratified the Constitution notwithstanding these objections, suggesting that whatever tensions exist between the judicial power and majority rule are not insurmountable. This historical fact aside, the argument as modified departs from classical translation by retaining a reduced juridic authority to compose but otherwise throwing the responsibility for producing constitutional norms in the lap of other actors within the system. Unless certain conditions of democratic breakdown could be said to predominate, the jurist operates under instructions to stay clear of the institutions better placed to cultivate constitutional norms. Accordingly, Robert Bork, who favors readings of text in light of the Framers' expected application of those words, argues that "we govern ourselves democratically, except on those occasions, few in number though crucially important, when the Constitution places a topic beyond the reach of majorities." John Hart Ely, who, unlike Bork, favors a process-oriented reading of text whenever "intervention" is practicable, nevertheless hews to the same underlying conception of majoritarian translation. Under our constitutional design, Ely argues, "the selection and accommodation of substantive values is left almost entirely to the political process."[3] Given this baseline, it is no surprise that forbearance is the majoritarian jurist's highest virtue. A court must "check itself," Bork insists, if it is to avoid "a political role."

All of this is to say: the majoritarian judge operates either at no power or at full throttle. For whenever a judge can identify especially crucial rights, because they are consonant with either a particular theory of self-rule or the writers' expectations, the judge is told to try to protect them from the corrupting influences of politics. As Ely argues, it is the responsibility of the jurist to "build protective barriers around free expression as secure as words can make them." Such a two-track effort to define and insulate may be a popular discursive form to identify important stakes, but as an actual enforcement strategy it is doomed from the start. Neither authority nor right can be sealed off from the political process, and no amount of praying for an impermeable judiciary can make it happen.

The frequently made claim that the people are "helpless before the authority wielded by judges" is vastly overreported.[4] There have been instances when jurists have intemperately tried sweeping resolutions that precipitated movements to rewrite foundational texts or enhanced the intensity of cultural conflict, but these have been few and far between. Most of the time, judicial resolutions present opportunities to seek new discursive convergences, without closing down all avenues for contestation. The cruelest readings of text have prompted organized reactions; even the most convincing visions of political life can be distinguished or repudiated.

There is, in the final analysis, an unbearable tension in the concept of majoritarian translation. The adjudicative ideal points in two directions at once:

maximal readings of law followed by judicial silence. The jurist finds himself caught between two tendencies, neither of which is positive for self-rule in the long run: the first, an impulse to clothe ever more social values in legal language so they might have a fighting chance in debate; the second, an equally ardent hope that nonintervention is healthy for the democratic order. Treating the Judiciary as an antimajoritarian institution turns translation into a model of intermittent judicial enforcement.

Can the idea be dismissed out of hand that the wild swings between vindication and nonaction produce feelings of rapture and despondency in observers? That the enforcement model contributes to passive-aggressive decision making — and a good deal of uncertainty over whether and under what conditions courts should participate in constitutional debate — underscores its limitations.

Judicial Review Within the Precepts of Eloquence

Once the presumptions that juridic constructions are antidemocratic and impossible to resist are relaxed, an opening emerges for a more interactive model of judicial review — one in which rhetorical engagement by the jurist is the norm, rather than the exception. Properly considered, the jurist's role within the constitutional order is significantly more complex than what translation envisions. Instead of mechanically enforcing established rights, the jurist articulates them openly and notoriously for a diverse audience. Rather than deny the open texture of the law, the judge should be more transparently concerned with rhetorically facilitating the interaction of relevant cultural domains affected by text. The parameters of the judicial function are defined not by the scientist's formulas but by the rhetorician's precepts of eloquence.

In rejecting translation as a normative ideal for interpretation, the facilitative model affirms that historical arguments are important to adjudication. It locates arguments arising from formative events and drafters' expectations among other valid techniques for honoring their achievements, such as reasoning from text, structure, precedent, or ethos. Moreover, the model would distinguish specific claims about the historical past intended to persuade lawyers, judges, and public officials from more generic references to the historical past as a method of cultivating popular support for text, with each modality having a part to play in the continuation of the state.

If the Constitution is to be more than an artifact housed for public admiration, then judges, as much as any other constitutional actor, must tend to the political imagination. The social functions expected of the judge as facilitator include:

1. Harmonizing popular discourses;
2. Building a people's political vocabulary;
3. Managing and nurturing a society's organizing beliefs; and
4. Enabling other constitutional actors to speak on behalf of the people's interests.

Unlike a translator, the judge is authorized to speak to the people's long-term interests in a distinctive voice rather than required to efface the public record of his own participation. As Robert Post puts it cogently: "If the Constitution is not to degenerate into merely repressive law, authoritative only because of the need for clear and predictable rules, courts interpreting the Constitution must be allowed to speak from the authority of a national ethos, in the form of either historical or responsive interpretation."[5] Still, an institution must be more than responsive to social conditions; it must also signal, at some level, that it is being responsive. Otherwise, citizens would not fully understand the constitutional system in action, or judges would be overly tempted to pass off private preferences in the guise of neutral language. Transparency of process therefore is not only a precondition to socially accountable adjudication; it is also necessary to satisfy the rhetorician's goal of instruction. Because of their training and experience, as well as an ingrained preference for clarity and order, there exists the ever-present danger that judges will rhetorically exclude others from the law. This temptation must be resisted and every effort made to portray constitutionalism as an interactive process. Greater clarity about the judge's coordinating functions creates incentives for the judge to identify and soberly evaluate socially plausible readings of text.

The courts' duty to say what the law is thus encompasses more than the power to articulate the meaning of text; it extends to the authority to initiate, suppress, and coordinate prevailing rhetorical trends. This management function of judging has many interesting implications. For now, it is enough to stress the organizing idea that courts serve not as disinterested actors when constitutional crises occur but as institutions dedicated to the development and maintenance of a democratic vocabulary.

Jurists appropriate language from the domains of popular and political culture in aid of their readings of text. They validate particular forms by modeling their usage or exhorting others to experiment with them. Once such forms are licensed or disapproved, they are more or less likely to become ingrained features of discursive practice. Juridic silence denies an overlay of legitimacy to a style that might be preferred by others, though such a style may still flourish separate and apart from the workings of the legal process.

Adjudication as facilitation shares some of the assumptions of the theory of judicial review posited by Robert Burt. In *The Constitution in Conflict*, Burt envisions a role for courts in mediating social conflict, premised on the observation that "judicial review . . . is a logical response to an internal contradiction in democratic theory between majority rule and equal self-determination."[6] For Burt, judicial projects to suppress cultural conflict are hopeless and should not be undertaken. These are starting points that the facilitative model also accepts. Yet, Burt's account assumes that judges have perfect, or at the very least reasonably accurate, information about how other constitutional actors might behave in response to the exercise of judicial review. It also labors under certain mistaken premises of the backlash thesis.

Burt's optimistic view of the quality of information available to judges is especially acute. Although an effort to anticipate the reaction of others is essential to achieving socially plausible results, it remains difficult to gauge likely reaction to any degree of certainty. Imperfect information is the primary reason a jurist can only identify a range of plausible outcomes *ex ante*: a judge can proceed only on the basis of available information, and such knowledge is severely limited by the rules of procedure that structure the litigation process. In many situations, the signals from key participants as to the strength of possible support of or opposition to a course of action are vague or contradictory. Even when such information is accurate at the moment of decision, individuals and groups may change their minds in the face of judicial action or new information.

None of this is to suggest that political actors are any better at gauging the source and strength of reaction to a construction of text. Indeed, there are reasons to expect that such actors will overplay the negative reactions of judicial action for electoral gain or bureaucratic advantage. Facilitative adjudication would begin with a presumption in favor of judicial participation in the elaboration of constitutional ideas. A claim of judicial forbearance would have to overcome this high threshold by demonstrating either that a political tradition favored nonaction in a particular context or that existing management strategies would not be efficacious. This presumption is justified not only because of the political tradition of judicial review but also because the sources and severity of popular reactions cannot be fully gauged in advance.

If there is a substantive principle that unifies Burt's approach to judicial review across subject matters, it is "to identify and reject the secessionist impulse throughout our social relations."[7] On this ground, Burt approves judicial action in *Brown v. Board of Education* but is less sympathetic to *Roe v. Wade*. He believes *Roe* to be a mistake because it "drastically narrowed the participants' perspectives and truncated their educative efforts." Yet, the sharpest criticisms of *Roe* are misplaced precisely because they overdetermine the impact of judicial review on the actions of others. In both *Brown* and *Roe*, popular reaction arose to a judicial construction of text. Vicious resistance to *Brown* appeared despite the Justices' flexible approach; it is not apparent that an alternative reading in *Roe* would have done anything to reduce the political polarization that ensued. If there is no such thing as constitutional settlement but only the temporary appearance of it, predicating judicial review on the capacity to dictate the behavior of others in advance is bound to cause jurists to overplay their hand or, if they cannot control others, to find ways of avoiding social conflict entirely. Burt modifies some of the normative implications of the backlash thesis, but he nevertheless labors within its assumptions.

Because Burt occasionally overstates the risks of judicial participation, he does not fully confront the possibility that some reactions and misperceptions can be ameliorated through strategies of eloquence. In the end, he favors occasional judicial nonparticipation, thin substantive readings of text, and certain procedural methods of avoiding reaching substantive rulings in the face of cultural conflict. Thus, Burt ultimately inclines toward judicial strategies favored by proponents of modified translation, even if he does not accept the countermajoritarian difficulty as an accurate characterization of the judicial function.

Adjudication as facilitation stakes out a more nuanced position with regard to a jurist's options. The facilitative model does not mandate a single mediating strategy, but it does expect judges to choose their words carefully. If judges do not act when duty demands, they should say why. When a litigant's claim of right is adjudicated, the rationales and interests can be described in ways that leave no impression of final victory. Presentation of the stakes in irreconcilable terms and judicial outcomes as categorical solutions should be avoided whenever possible. Embracing the rhetoric of a losing party or resisting the intemperate rhetoric of the prevailing party can help to avoid the impression that courts have simply taken sides or imposed personal preferences. These are merely a few of the strategies available to judges to mediate conflict while remaining rhetorically engaged.

At the end of the day, there is only so much that judges can do to end the constitutionalization of moral questions or the politicization of legal issues. The symbiotic relationship between higher law and politics is captured in a pair of sayings from one of the nation's religious traditions. The first is attributed to Isaiah and is by far the more familiar of the two. When Yahweh arrives "in the final days" to "judge between the nations and arbitrate between many peoples," it is said that the people "will hammer their swords into ploughshares and their spears into sickles."[8] This prophesy illustrates one of the basic dynamics of higher law, secular or sacred, in which the act of judging takes the cultural vehicles of contest and converts them into tools for cultivating the peace.

It is inevitable that the people eventually will take the words of resolution and turn them into weapons for political disputation. The *Book of Joel* captures this reversal of the prophetic dynamic as the rarefied becomes mundane once again. Just as legal rhetoric domesticates the people's most charged ideas, so politics shall again demand that the people "[h]ammer your ploughshares into swords, your bill-hooks into spears."[9]

Recognizing the inevitability of political reaction leads to another insight about judicial disposition. Sustaining the political imagination requires acclimation to a certain degree of messiness; more than any other constitutional actor because of a habituated instinct toward hierarchy and simplification, the jurist must learn to appreciate the beauty of cacophony. Thus, it might be said that the highest juridic virtue is not humility or empathy but an appreciation of the aesthetic. According to Joseph Campbell, "the people who can keep [myth] alive are artists of one kind or another. The function of the artist is the mythologization of the environment and the world."[10]

The aesthetic sensibility demands apprehension of not only the plurality of forms but also their incompleteness. Again, every creation of law is based upon imperfect information. Judges may be selecting textual constructions from among many possibilities, but that choice necessarily remains tentative, revisable. In determining which discourses to validate and which ones to reject, the judge must be receptive to the call and response between public officials and the ordinary people in whose name they act. The nation's governing belief system, as with all mythological structures, "come[s] out of an elite experience, the experience of people particularly gifted, whose ears are open to the song of the universe. These people speak to the folk, and there is an answer from the folk, which is then received as an interaction."

It is often said that translation has several beneficial features: order, efficiency, and predictability. Facilitation indeed trades hierarchy for pluralism, deliberation for efficiency, and specialty for commonality. The model embraces the systemic values of order, efficiency, and predictability, but not at the cost of dislocation or alienation on the part of average citizens. It therefore locates the realization of such virtues not in a juridic plan to dictate the law's development but in the words, beliefs, and expectations of others. Adjudication as facilitation considers an interactive discursive order to be most consonant with the participatory aims of democratic constitutionalism.

This juridic ideal—which calls upon the decision maker to treat constitutional disputes as part of broader cultural conflicts and to inform and redirect such conflicts rather than resolve them — shares some similarities with the dualist model of adjudication. First, both defend the instinct of judges to evaluate the state of political beliefs as they transpire in real time. Not only is it appropriate for jurists to consider political developments for their bearing upon existing commitments, but also courts are most accountable when such responsive calculations are made as transparently as possible. Second, both approaches affirm the possibility of articulating legal principles while retaining the centrality of political context. That is to say, institutional responsiveness must not decline into incoherent submission to external pressure.

That is where the similarities end. Dualism adheres to the strategy of insulation in that it envisions the jurist's role to "preserve" past achievements and only in rare moments to "codify" mobilized reactions. Describing "transformative precedents" such as the ones written by judges in the New Deal era, Ackerman argues that, because these rulings "memorialize the rare determinations of a massive and sustained conversation by the American people," they deserve status as special landmarks. "Since lawyers did not make them," he insists, "lawyers cannot unmake them."[11]

If one accepts the logic of popular sovereignty, then no judicial reading of text can be insulated from the politics of reimagination. It is only when jurists capitulate to what Hamilton called "a momentary inclination" that "lay[s] hold of a majority" or if they unvirtuously "connive" with others that a reading should be inherently suspect. Otherwise, operating in a responsive capacity, jurists must be free to construe text in good faith as the precepts of eloquence and logic permit. It is up to the other participants in the process to affirm, challenge, or erode the juridic presentation of text. The Judiciary's imposition of text on certain litigants may be final, but its construction of the Constitution is a first draft, due equal respect, if not equal allegiance — at least if we are to respect the rhetorical freedom of others. As Madison explained during the Virginia Ratifying Convention, on June 20, 1788, the Judicial Power was conferred "with confidence," premised upon the assumption that "this power cannot be abused, without raising the indignation of all the people of the states."

Historical Authorization for the Facilitative Tradition

We have up to this point been tiptoeing around the edges of a foundational question. It is time now to confront it head-on: what authorizes a magistrate to coin aphorisms, claim to know the people's long-term interests, and reassemble past controversies as templates for the future? Thus far, the answer has been twofold: first, judicial production of vernacular is, in the abstract, compatible with the structure and goals of democratic constitutionalism; second, all of these behaviors are embedded in historical practice. The answer to the authorization challenge, in part, is that this is what judges have done since the earliest days of judicial review. Generations of practice have confirmed, rather than dispelled, the rhetorical autonomy inherent in judging.

Far more can now be said about the judge's responsibility to the popular consciousness from within the revolutionary tradition. In its infancy, the Constitution "address[ed] itself immediately to the hopes and fears of individuals; and to attract to its support those passions which have the strongest influence upon the human heart." That is to say, the Constitution was seen not simply as a problem-solving instrument but also as a vehicle to foster a public ethos and mission. Writing under the nom de plume "Publius," Alexander Hamilton makes a special point of mentioning the courts in his description of the ultimate goals of constitutionalism, which he suggests were to be neither superior nor inferior to other agents in the articulation and defense of the Union's "common concerns and preserving the general tranquility."[12] This theme, in which judges derive their ultimate authority from and therefore may properly appeal directly to the sentiments of the people, is echoed in stronger terms in *Federalist 78*. Explicitly taking on the "perplexity" that "has arisen from an imagination that the doctrine of [judicial review] would imply a superiority of the judiciary to the legislative power," Publius emphasizes the partial and derived nature of judicial review: "It only supposes that the power of the people is superior to both." This passage is conventionally understood to mean nothing more than independence. In fact, however, it also imparts the source of the jurist's rhetorical authority (a virtuous claim to know the long-term interests of the people) and approves, implicitly, direct appeals to the populace.

There are two insights worth untangling from each other. The first is the indissoluble relationship between strategic considerations and systemic virtues as the Framers and their opponents engaged in a rich metaphorical discourse on the nature of the citizenry's political attachments. The debaters' manipulation of latent ideas was not merely a strategy of convenience but also a technique for building a lasting vocabulary that might describe and legitimate their experiment in self-governance. Second, the speakers' numerous and direct appeals to "the people" were not empty gestures but directed toward stimulating and empowering others to deliberate over the pressing issues of the day.

This interactive tradition has been obscured in part because of professionals' obsession with the Federalist papers as monuments of lawgiving rather than partisan texts in a multifaceted debate about the real-world applications of popular sovereignty. The Judicial Department was itself purposely under-drawn, even more so than either of the other branches — not because the Framers themselves actually agreed as to the appropriate scope of the Judicial Power (in fact, the available evidence suggests a good deal of disagreement about its particulars) but because they almost certainly wished the details of the judicial function to be part of continuing conversations about the political system as a whole. The text of Article III, which sets out the Judicial Power, concerns itself almost entirely with the subject matter bases of jurisdiction and their relation to one another. Beyond saying that "the Judicial Power shall extend to all cases, in law or equity, arising under this Constitution," the provision leaves the crucial questions of how the judicial function is best performed to the wisdom that comes with experience.

Publius's writings on the subject must be parsed in light of his overriding concern with defending an enlarged conception of judicial review against its critics; it is a motivation that almost certainly leads him to minimize its signifi-cance. Still, Publius's defense of judicial review is revealing in that his meta-phors for judging project a vague, rudimentary picture of the mechanics of judging, while the more literal aspects of his writings reveal a more significant institution in development. The magistrates are characterized by their "natu-ral feebleness," he says, because they have only "judgment," not "will," mak-ing clever use of the classical image of the body politic. Further, the Judicial Department should not be feared because it is "in continual jeopardy of being overpowered, awed or influenced by its co-ordinate branches."[13]

Having explained that an independent Judiciary will be called from among the educated, the experienced, and those steeped in tradition (thus implying the existence of what he will come to call "judicial discretion"), Publius abruptly shifts gears and makes what Jack Rakove calls a "bland assertion of the 'impar-tiality' of federal judges" as an account of what judges actually do.[14] The magistrate is to "secure a steady, upright, and impartial administration of the laws." When two statutes collide, Publius states, the jurist is to "liquidate and fix their meaning and operation." And, "whenever a particular statute con-travenes the Constitution, it will be the duty of the judicial tribunals to adhere to the latter and disregard the former." All of this is interesting as far as it goes, but just how far does it go to clarify original expectations of the office?

When Publius writes that the judge is to serve as "barrier to the encroach-ments and oppressions of the representative body," he is doing what debaters do best: coopting the tactics of his opponents. He is also shifting from the literal to the metaphorical in order to conjure a threat of political oppression that, despite his earlier passive description of judging, implicitly argues for a robust judicial role. At the time that Publius was writing, the legislature, because of its metonymic identification with human passion, was thought to pose the greatest risk of oppressing the people. Publius's appeal to a common belief in limited government and his use of an ambiguous account of judging to defend a coequal Judiciary is therefore best read not as an attempt to circumscribe juridic authority. If anything, his metaphorical tactic hints at, and even may be said to support, more robust judicial exercises of eloquence and reason.

Compare Publius's general sketch of the judicial function with Brutus's more practical observation that Article III, if approved, would "give a certain degree of latitude of explanation."[15] This is an accurate assessment of the text — the Constitution specifies no methodologies of construction. He then goes on to remark that the text appears to authorize courts to "give such meaning to the constitution as comports best with the common, and generally received accept[ance] of the words in which it is expressed, regarding their ordinary and popular use, rather than their grammatical propriety." This, too, is both a correct statement of Article III and not denied by Publius. Brutus's comments are meant to be damning, but they instead prove to be incredibly insightful observations as to the rhetorical discretion to be afforded the federal judge.

The Antifederalist attack elicits a pointed rebuttal by Publius in May 1788. Publius takes pains to repeat Brutus's words and to deny that the plan authorizes judges to "constru[e] the laws according to the *spirit* of the Constitution, [so as to] enable that court to mould them into whatever shape it may think proper."[16] Notice the form of the Federalist response: the hysterical charge leveled by the Antifederalists is "made up altogether of false reasoning upon misconceived fact."

Importantly, Publius does not deny that ordinary language ought to be a part of judicial constructions. Nor does he take Brutus's bait by insisting that judges are to serve as grammarians. Prodded repeatedly, Publius one way or another rejects a text-bound or static conception of judicial review. The tenor of his response is to dispute the charge that the jurist's authority to construe text is completely unbounded, rather than to deny that discretion exists.

Publius begins his defense of Article III by resorting to a textual argument: "there is not a syllable in the plan under consideration which *directly* empowers the national courts to construe the laws according to the spirit of the Constitution, or which gives them any greater latitude in this respect than may be claimed by the courts of every State." Notice that Publius does not deny that such authority exists; he merely concedes that this remains a contested interpretive matter. Indeed, Publius reverts to first-person perspective to illustrate the point. He "admit[s]" his own preferred reading that "wherever there is an evident opposition, the laws ought to give place to the Constitution" and honestly acknowledges that "this doctrine is not deducible from any circumstance peculiar to the plan of the convention, but from the general theory of a limited Constitution."

Publius goes on to appeal to existing practice in the states, saying that federal magistrates have a function analogous to that of the independent courts created by many enlightened state constitutions and that attacking the idea of a federal judiciary is therefore to "condemn every constitution that attempts to set bounds to legislative discretion." Publius's comparative point has more bite than the thought that questioning the scope of judicial review impugns the states, but the implication of the entire line of argument is unmistakable: judging has, and will continue to develop, an internal set of criteria by which to "give place to the Constitution" — what we have been describing as the precepts of eloquence. At this stage in the life of the nation, it is unwise to demand more than what has already been said about "the nature and reason of the thing."

Publius then makes several structural points to buttress his general defense of interpretive discretion. First, if the objection to Article III is that the judges are not part of the legislature, as they are in Great Britain, "the authors of the objection must renounce the meaning they have labored to annex to the celebrated maxim, requiring a separation of the departments of power." That is to say, the notion of divided government supports an independent judiciary. Second, opponents of judicial review have it wrong if they think that state legislatures can formally revise a state court sentence in a particular case; reliance on this suggestion for the subjugation of the federal judiciary to Congress is therefore off the mark. This often-repeated point is an important piece of evidence against the majoritarian conception of judging.

What is most interesting for our purposes is Publius's third point, which emphasizes the structural constraints on judicial overreaching notwithstanding life tenure: "Particular misconstructions and contraventions of the will of the legislature may now and then happen; but they can never be so extensive as to amount to an inconvenience, or in any sensible degree to affect the order of the political system."

This is so because the "general nature of the judicial power" is not intrinsically coercive but is, at its heart, a persuasive function; because, even if the judicial department had aggressive designs, it faces a "total incapacity to support its usurpations by force"; and because looming in the background is the power of instituting impeachments, which should dissuade judges from sustained and egregious departures from convention. Even if Publius tends to overestimate the efficacy of these structural constraints, it appears that the institution's design assumes that a judge's words are contingent upon the social support of others. The persuasive power of a court has "force" only insofar as its decrees elicit approval and cooperation.

As always, the truth lies somewhere in between the positions staked out by the pamphleteers on the nature of federal tribunals. The judicial power was neither meant to be as toothless as some of its proponents suggested nor as antidemocratic as its critics feared. Several principles can be pieced together from the historical record about the jurist's rhetorical freedom. First, the core of the judicial function consists of a power to "declare the sense of the law" and the power to "pronounce legislative acts void because [they are] contrary to the Constitution." "The interpretation of the laws," *Federalist 78* states, "is the proper and peculiar province of the courts."

Second, this interpretive discretion includes the authority to craft internal "rule[s] of construction . . . not enjoined upon the courts by legislative provision, but adopted by themselves." Independence encompasses some inherent authority to manage the citizens' presentations of law to the Judiciary, as well as the jurists' presentations to the people-at-large. Thus, there existed ample support for self-regulating precepts of eloquence.

Third, as this exchange reflected, the judicial function includes the capacity to resort to ordinary language in order to effectuate the pronouncements of law. This is as true when constitutional values are at stake as it is when more common interests obtain. Stressing the virtue of interactivity and the importance of judicial voice to the polity, courts are to act as "intermediate bod[ies]" to prevent "invasions . . . instigated by the major voice of the community."

Fourth, jurists are to keep in mind the "intention of the people" without "substitution of their pleasure to that of the legislative body." Its obligations with respect to the external community involve maintaining the symbolic function of law and utilizing the "integrity and moderation of the judiciary" to incentivize others to consider the interests of the Constitution. Publius writes that judicial review "not only serves to moderate the immediate mischiefs of those which may have been passed, but it operates as a check upon the legislative body in passing them; who, perceiving that obstacles to the success of iniquitous intention are to be expected from the scruples of the courts, are in a manner compelled, by the very motives of the injustice they meditate, to qualify their attempts." Once again, Publius focuses on the social significance of judicial involvement in the political process — namely that it may yield greater attentiveness to constitutional norms. The point itself can be generalized: raising the costs of unconstitutional behavior and making transgressors pay that cost can influence Americans' perception of the Constitution. More broadly, this cultural dimension of judging involves tending to the law's appearances and protecting the public sense of justice against the corrosive feelings of "distrust and distress" — perceptions with which the Framers were uniquely concerned.

To sum up: the early years of our political tradition were characterized by warring descriptions of judging; the first, an interactive and constructive ideal, was eventually overtaken by the second notion of the court as a "bulwark" against the designs of overheated majorities (a fever initially seen as most likely to afflict the Legislature). As this simplistic, enforcement-based conception periodically obscured the facilitative one, influential persons convinced themselves that restraining juridic power to impede the legislative will ought to be the central concern of constitutionalism.[17] But the speed with which this misdiagnosis colored prevailing views of the Supreme Court — which, in turn, accelerated an entrenchment of Antifederalist rhetoric — did not make its description of judging within a constitutional democracy any more accurate. Nor did it obliterate the older facilitative tradition.

Apprehending the Judiciary's cultural responsibilities as historically authorized aligns with the ideal of civic republicanism generally and the Framers' specific, though scattered, references to the importance of cultivating respect for constitutional limits. Especially illuminating is James Madison's conversion from an early opponent of the idea of a Bill of Rights to its principal drafter. Coming out of the Constitutional Convention, he thought the formal articulation of specific rights unnecessary, as the people themselves would not stand for derogation from the rights they deemed essential; the entire enterprise seemed inconsistent with the idea of "popular rights." Madison would later refer to his own handiwork as "neither improper nor altogether useless" and as "those safe, if not necessary, and those politic if not obligatory amendments,"[18] sowing confusion as to his actual position.

It is tempting to mistake Madison's support for the Bill of Rights for a cynical calculation, as no more than an effort to head off calls for another convention or the opportunity to amend the draft Constitution during ratification debates. While Madison's political acumen surely pointed him in a new direction, there is ample evidence that he reevaluated his position in principled terms after the public outcry for a Bill of Rights. Rather than agree wholeheartedly with the most enthusiastic supporters of either strategy, he gravitated toward a middle position consistent with his republican principles: text can be useful in debate.

On October 17, 1788, Madison wrote to his friend and mentor, Thomas Jefferson, to report on political developments stateside. His account of the controversy over a Bill of Rights reflected an exposition of his initial reactions, as well as his mature thinking on the matter. Madison began by stressing his principled support for a Bill of Rights: "My own opinion has always been in favor of a bill of rights; provided it be so framed as not to imply powers not meant to be included in the enumeration." He then articulated four separate reasons for why he has "never thought the omission a material defect": first, he thought "the rights in question are reserved by the manner in which the federal powers are granted." That is to say, the precise wording of the Constitution necessarily excludes powers not expressly delegated by the people; a Bill of Rights would be redundant. Second, he feared that a "positive declaration of some of the most essential rights" would engender debate over how broadly or narrowly to describe the rights, and this discussion would inevitably provoke a fight over specific applications of rights. To illustrate the point, Madison pointed to concerns raised in New England that a prohibition on religious tests "opened a door for Jews Turks and infidels." Madison therefore saw danger to the entire project if the desire for articulation engaged more particular sectional and cultural differences. He worried that certain rights — such as "rights of Conscience" — would suffer "if submitted to public definition" rather than defined by "an assumed power." Third, Madison believed, consistent with his theory of divided government, that separation would promote liberty: a "limited powers of the federal Government" combined with "the jealousy of the subordinate Governments" afford a functional kind of "security" not seen in other forms of government. Fourth, Madison was not sanguine about the effectiveness of "parchment barriers" in holding back an aroused citizenry — "experience proves the inefficacy of a bill of rights on those occasions when its controul is most needed."[19]

Any one of these reasons alone might have been reason enough to forget about a Bill of Rights. At this point, Madison could have recommended that the Framers bow to what others described as "the loud clamors against the plan of the convention, on this score" and asserted that either political exigencies or respect for popular opinion justified indulging others' desire for a Bill of Rights.[20] Instead, Madison backed away from the hard-line position advocated by Hamilton that the textual commitment of rights was not merely "impracticable" but also "dangerous." Instead, he gave a principled ground for "recommend[ing] the precaution": doing so may spur the process of political acculturation. First, by committing certain rights to writing, however imperfectly, the Framers would be declaring "political truths" in a "solemn manner" such that they might "become incorporated with the national sentiment." If this were so, the act of writing could influence debates in later generations, and, more important, "counteract the impulses of interest and passion" — traits that would otherwise erode respect for constitutionalism. Second, while he believed the primary threat of oppression arose not from "usurped acts of the Government" but from "interested majorities," the inscriptive act could play some role in helping the people to check themselves. In anticipation of appeals to depart from established rights-favoring practices, Madison argued, "a bill of rights will be a good ground for an appeal to the sense of the community." That is to say, in resisting a potential "subversion of liberty," the existence of text could serve a discursive function. As Madison would later clarify in a speech to Congress proposing the amendments, the act of inscription may "have a tendency to impress some degree of respect for them, to establish the public opinion in their favor, and rouse the attention of the whole community, it may be one mean to controul the majority from those acts to which they might be otherwise inclined."

In short, Madison foresaw, albeit in somewhat rudimentary form, that an emerging constitutional culture would interact with, and occasionally have to overcome, individual preferences and majoritarian valuations. Neither the fact that rights were committed to text nor the dutiful implementation of the drafters' intention was critical; rather, each was subordinate to any function that writing might have on the collective attitudes of the citizenry. In other words, Madison believed that text is one part of a people's vocabulary.

This reading is confirmed by Madison's summation in his letter to Jefferson, which again deemphasizes the importance of text and makes the case for strategic ambiguity where passions might be strongest: "I am inclined to think that absolute restrictions in cases that are doubtful, or where emergencies may overrule them, ought to be avoided. The restrictions however strongly marked on paper will never be regarded when opposed to the decided sense of the public; and after repeated violations in extraordinary cases, they will lose even their ordinary efficacy."

Madison issued an additional warning against text-bound approaches to constitutionalism: the strategy of anticipating all social contexts in a single selection of words may very well be counterproductive when social reality intrudes. Maintaining a degree of contestability to the text would preserve principle without unduly inhibiting the need for strong government. In his reflection upon the function for a Bill of Rights within a large republic, Madison certainly felt that text had a role to play, but he left little doubt that social sentiment — the realm of mutual expectations, beliefs, and respect — would be the key to achieving durable commitments. Hamilton, too, wished ordinary people engaged in the debate to put text into perspective: "whatever fine declarations may be inserted in any constitution respecting it, must altogether depend on public opinion, and on the general spirit of the people and of the government" as the "only solid basis of all our rights."

Jefferson Versus Madison: On the Revitalization of Text

That the unruly nature of self-rule and the order-imposing force of law must be mediated rather than resolved is reflected in a truly rich exchange of letters between Madison and Thomas Jefferson during the ratification period. All too often, one man's views have been treated as emblematic of the new order, while the other's perspective has been dismissed. Far less frequently has each man's letters been treated as if they revealed essential truths about the experiment upon which Americans had embarked.

Author of the Declaration of Independence and a fierce defender of local democracy, Jefferson was the lyricist of the American Revolution. Among his contemporaries, he came the closest to grasping that the law, as both a social instrument and a source of collective aspirations, must be calibrated to the needs and practices of presently constituted peoples. Writing to Madison from Paris on September 6, 1789, Jefferson proposed to take up the question of "[w]hether one generation of men has a right to bind another," which he situated "among the fundamental principles of every government." His answer: "The earth belongs always to the living generation"; "the dead have neither powers nor rights over it."[21]

Above all, Jefferson prized the unquenchable need for law's renewal: "The tree of liberty," he was fond of saying, "must be refreshed from time to time with the blood of patriots and tyrants." On another occasion, he observed that "a little rebellion now and then was a good thing." In his letter to Madison, Jefferson channeled his lifelong concern for political vitality into a specific problem he had witnessed time and time again: how crushing debt and calcified law can paralyze a nation and prevent it from realizing a prosperous future.[22]

Jefferson's ideas were not without precedent. To break up extreme concentrations of wealth, prevent overcultivation of the land, and stimulate communal bonds, ancient Jewish law provided for the cancellation of outstanding debts every seven years and the redistribution of land on the year of the Jubilee (every fifty years). The teachings of Jesus of Nazareth are thought to recall this ancient tradition of debt forgiveness (the Lord's Prayer in original transcription read "forgive us our debts" rather than "trespasses").[23]

What Jefferson called for was nothing less than a secular Jubilee. Working from actuarial tables predicting the average life span, he reasoned that "19 years is the term beyond which neither the representatives of a nation nor even the whole nation itself assembled, can validly extend a debt." Jefferson's startling conclusion: "Every constitution, then, and every law, naturally expires at the end of 19 years."

The insurmountable difficulty with Jefferson's debt relief proposal specifically and his audacious theory of generational separation generally lay in their
implementation. Does this proposal not make government "too mutable"?
What authority would govern during the interregnum between political regimes? In gentle but firm tones, Madison took his mentor to task on these
points, but in substance they were devastating to his proposal for automatic
termination. In place of a sunset provision in the Constitution, Madison suggested that Jefferson's concerns might be addressed through an ameliorative
principle that would caution "the living generation from imposing unjust or
unnecessary burdens on their successors."[24]

Madison may have demolished the notion of generational separation as
poorly conceived, but he did not disturb Jefferson's basic observation that "no
society can make a perpetual constitution, or even a perpetual law." Sensing
that the initial moment of creation could not be the end of political time,
Jefferson grasped the need for renewal of law that Madison denied through
silence. By contrast, Madison, who sacralized the moment of creation, nevertheless appreciated the need for stability in the law that Jefferson found
chafing. Each, accordingly, was able to present only a partial solution to the
conundrum of law's revitalization: Jefferson advocated a regular return to a
preconstitutional state; Madison placed his faith in adherence to the formal
mechanisms sketched by the founding document—"a system which we wish
to last for ages."[25]

Because it would subject all economic transactions to the same sunset provision, Jefferson's jubilee would grant some individuals a windfall, while damaging others' economic interest, and these costs would be borne disproportion-
ately by some members of society. After the first generation of transactions, and
assuming perfect information, most citizens would learn to modify their behavior to contract only for short-term services or otherwise to account for the
sunset provision. If these made up the full costs of renewing the people's faith in
the law, they might well be a price worth paying. But private debt is not the same
as political commitment, and here Jefferson's analogy began to break down.

Jefferson's mistake was to flirt with the antithesis of rhetorical freedom, a
state in which the individual feels unbound by past practices. Political freedom
comes from remaking the syntactic structures of liberty, not in (futilely) forc-
ing the citizenry to inscribe baseline commitments from scratch every few
seasons. The agency costs of rebuilding the public imagination are too high,
the risk of demoralization too great. Financial losses absorbed by a community are one thing; a precipitous decline in political faith is quite another.
Federalist 62 describes "the most deplorable effect of all" flowing from government that is "too mutable": "that diminution of attachment and reverence

which steals into the hearts of the people, towards a political system which betrays so many marks of infirmity, and disappoints so many of their flattering hopes. No government, any more than an individual, will long be respected without being truly respectable; nor be truly respectable, without possessing a certain portion of order and stability."[26]

Thus, despite his valuation of social sentiment, Madison would enshrine the initial moment of constitutional creativity as the primary source of legitimacy or "respect," however attenuated the relationship of the living to that event. Recapitulating Hobbes's theory of total alienation of sovereignty, Madison adhered to the fiction of the living's "implied consent" to be mastered by the dead hand of the past. He wrote of "improvements" made by the dead to the political order that "form a charge against the living who take the benefit of them," but little of the sovereignty of those who must live under such conditions to accept, modify, or reject what an earlier generation believed essential. Reducing constitutionalism to probate, Madison seized on a motivating principle: executing the "will of the dead."

There is a deeper problem still, shared by the two accounts: their acceptance of the people as a static body in time. Locked within such a paradigm, to prefer the living (present > past) is to break faith with our ancestors and court lawlessness, but to honor the dead (past > present) is to subjugate the interests of the living to the whims of those whose political advantage is gained through sheer happenstance. This is the fruitless conversation that has bedeviled constitutionalism almost from the start.

Escape from this logical dead-end comes from treating constitutionalism as a series of overlapping constructions of text maintained according to the demands of eloquence and reason. A more satisfying answer may be found by recasting these thinkers' own differences: Jefferson as the defender of cultural vitality rather than permanent revolution, Madison as the proponent of institutional management rather than moment-based constitutionalism.

Because both men underestimated the revolutionary possibilities within existing cultural and institutional processes, it could be said that a mature system of legal vernacular and political belief does justice to Jefferson's much maligned insight that "the earth belongs in usufruct to the living." More so than his protégé, Jefferson saw that the living's connections to the communities of the past and the future are not equivalent. The living must justify their actions with "ages and millions yet unborn" in mind;[27] yet they are, and must remain, revisable forecasts. A people's actual obligations run forward in time, even as its common language joins past achievements and present beliefs in a seamless whole.

Although generations are not the only social unit that can produce cultural change, Jefferson's defense of revolution focuses on generational distinctive-ness. As a social unit, a generation is larger than a faction (which is "united and actuated by some common impulse of passion, or of interest") but smaller than a society.[28] A generation has no clearly identifiable beginning or end point beyond the birth and death of its members. Hence, Jefferson's attempt to reach mathematical certainty as to the extent of generational influence on the law is somewhat distracting. Yet, his observation that constitutions have life cycles outside of legal text remains valuable.

At the same time, envisioning a coordinating function for the judiciary in the process of linguistic transformation honors Madison's incisive comments about the need for predictability in the law. Through the lens of cross-generational alliances, complexity is the touchstone: one coalition gains in-stitutional support for its most pressing concerns, just as another is on the cusp of wresting away the mechanisms of control over another area of social life. In locating revolution in the syntactic structure of constitutionalism, the precepts of eloquence have harnessed its essence. But, unlike the Jacobins, with whom Jefferson was so taken, governing language has also saved revolution from itself. Filtered through the ornate apparatus designed by Madison, the pas-sionate outbursts and stylized petitions of the people can shape the meaning of canonical texts in peaceful and orderly fashion. If the people fervently believe in the need for a reimagination of the Constitution and are committed to the project, the tools are within their grasp.

We earlier considered and rejected the claim that the model of linguistic transformation renders the Constitution too mutable. Is it possible that a language-centered constitutionalism is actually too stable in that it can be overly manipulated by elites? According to this critique, the felicity of expres-sion displayed by a Louis Brandeis or a Martin Luther King is seen not as a positive quality to be emulated but as one that threatens to replace democracy with a tyranny of the forensically gifted. Why, such a skeptic asks, should one's liberty turn on one person's ability to articulate an argument more cogently than the next person?

This is a challenge that deserves to be confronted squarely. It would, in the first place, be an error to confuse the aesthetically pleasing with the persuasive or instructive. Style is merely one aspect of eloquence, and beauty can become an obstacle to efficient communication. It is not always the high-minded and literary that prevails; the unaffected and the earthy have been known to carry the day. While originality may win admirers among the learned, workmanlike reconfiguration of familiar language may be more comforting to a good many more Americans.

At all events, this line of attack proves too much. To object to rhetorical freedom because some citizens will prove themselves particularly adept at exercising it is not only to question whether the concept can be implemented but also to attack the premises of self-rule. While it is no doubt true that rhetorical skillfulness will vary among citizens, the same could be said about any number of advantages that one might enjoy in politics, from finances to professional connections to personal charisma, and the usual answer to such objections is that these disparities are reasons to care about the parameters within which politics is engaged but not reason enough to renounce the project of democracy. What can be said is that the precepts of eloquence can be taught, modeled, and replicated. Unlike many other kinds of disparities that might impair one's ability to participate in self-governance, it is possible to envision the amelioration of linguistic disadvantage.

In every public debate there is some gap between the able and the willing. Given that the natural advantages enjoyed by some in the law, as in politics, can never be eradicated, the answer is to refuse them status as exclusionary criteria. The truth is that the survival of democracy as ideal and practice has depended on equal parts grit and ingenuity, fortuity and timing. For all his investment in matters of political design, Madison cautioned that institutions are necessary but not sufficient conditions for self-governance: "The people who are authors of this blessing, must also be its guardians. Their eyes must be ever ready to mark, their voice to pronounce, and their arm to repel or repair aggressions on the authority of their constitutions."[29] Carving out a space for the commonplace and the abbreviated in democratic constitutionalism does not require endorsing the idea that the forensically gifted should rule. Instead, it entails acceptance of a more modest proposition: political liberty depends upon our own words.

Coda

Americans' encounters with the First Amendment have inscribed its terms upon their minds, not in a linear fashion but rather in a layered experience in which competing ideas and the methods for characterizing those ideas struggled for salience and priority. Study of this collaborative exercise revealed two imperatives: the imperative of the state to mythologize its existence and the imperative of ordinary citizens to find concrete meaning in their political heritage. To succeed, democratic constitutionalism must navigate the tensions between the search for communal attachments and the refinement of rules to live by. Ignoring the first risks the possibility that the people will lose sight of their civic identities. In such a world, private preferences dominate public debate and extinguish hope in mutuality. Forgetting the second invites natural advantages and disabilities to dictate who can influence governing ideals and what the terms of debate ought to be. The rule of law then disintegrates into rule by the strong.

In elaborating these tensions, *Eloquence and Reason* treated constitutionalism as a species of language acquisition. According to this account, constitutional language is a governing discourse employed by public officials temporarily authorized to speak for the state and citizens whose belief in the state is essential for its survival. In its technical as well as its popular elements, constitutional language negotiates, rather than resolves, the tension between the imperative to myth-make and the imperative to reason. Rhetoric is used instrumentally to address social problems. It is also deployed metaphorically to create and perpetuate coherent visions of political life. Despite the complicated nature of governing language, the more a citizen becomes proficient in its usage, the more likely it is that a nation's deeply held values can be realized.

In analyzing the continuities and discontinuities of popular First Amendment discourse, the book downplayed the comparative advantages that each actor might enjoy in debate over the Constitution. It is, of course, hard to ignore a president's capacity to rouse constituents by virtue of the trappings of the office or the activist's claim to know the authentic concerns of the persons in whose name action is taken. So, too, in the struggle over ruling ideals, the judge's construction of text benefits from expectations of the officeholder as fair-minded and neutral, as well as a lingering misapprehension that a juridic reading is the last word on a subject. These advantages do exist, and they enhance the efforts of those committed to exploiting the political pathways through which governing language is created. Yet, when actors invoke the Constitution, strong rhetorical consistencies can emerge, overcoming areas of presumed expertise and institutional politics.

Identification of a rhetorical convergence in the law describes the conditions under which effective public discourse can happen at a historical moment, as well as the active terminology in a people's lexicon. It does not impose a normative requirement to speak in those terms. There may be reasons for a party to search for congruence, just as there may be reasons to pursue rhetorical opposition, but these considerations have more to do with one's instrumental purposes in using language — that is, building alliances with others, or entrenching or destabilizing a regime — than with the legitimacy of the words chosen.

The Judiciary's role in this entire process remains a matter of some dispute. Two conceptions of judicial review emerged over time, one that is satisfied with intermittent efforts to reach enforceable outcomes and another that prioritizes the regularized mediation of cultural conflict. The first conception demands that judges read constitutional text by trying to discern the intentions of others and limits judicial review to the extent that force may be brought to bear to alter the behavior of others. The second accepts persuasion as the primary function of judicial authority and finds value in maintaining rhetorical engagement. For historical, cultural, and institutional reasons, this book endorsed the second model: adjudication as facilitation.

For those who are convinced that the facilitative tradition best balances the competing concerns entailed in judging, three general principles may be extracted from the model. First, because the tension between the two imperatives is greatest when it comes to describing the constitutional process, a jurist must err on the side of transparency. To ensure that nonjudicial actors appreciate how to make courts socially accountable, it is essential that judges portray the system in pluralistic and interactive terms rather than rely upon clichés about judicial authority. The very idea of the Constitution as a cultural product implies that there has been, and ought to remain, a healthy disagreement about the methodologies, goals, and valuations that together generate constitutional meaning. Therefore, it is important that an adjudicator describe the legal process in ways that elucidate rather than obscure these differences.

It is now possible to take the next logical step: because privileging one set of traditions necessarily excludes other plausible possibilities, one should eschew legal rules organized around single principles or an overly small set of substantive concepts from which there can be little deviation. Respect for pluralism in constitutional knowledge is not an excuse to avoid making hard choices when confronting social disputes; what it demands is sensitivity to the social foundations of the law in determining how tradition should be brought to bear on a problem. Once choices are made, the precepts of eloquence require those choices to be justified and communicated effectively.

Second, the facilitative tradition endorses a presumption in favor of judicial participation. It has become all too common to speak of courts "intervening" in a social dispute as if they had no business being there in the first place; the Supreme Court itself has occasionally encouraged such thinking. But it is a strange and tenuous idea to be perpetuating, nonetheless. To conceive of the judicial function in this manner is to adopt the fiercest criticisms of judicial review — the very objections presumably rejected by the Founding generation when it ratified the Constitution. Such a position contradicts the text of the Constitution, which admits of no qualifications to judicial power except those approved by Congress.

Not only does the presumption of judicial participation better accord with original political designs; it also makes sense from the perspective of ensuring that law is grounded in the sentiments of the people. Even though a construction of text is never the last word, a judge brings expertise, knowledge, and a historically situated perspective in determining how to synthesize governing traditions and which discursive trends to validate. For those concerned about the domination of lawmaking by courts, reactions to judicial readings of law are not only inevitable but also must be taken into account. For those who have lost faith in the power of courts to dictate broad social change, this book suggested another reason for preferring engagement rather than abdication. Judicial participation cultivates a democratic ethos, just as it adds to the people's existing political vocabulary. Thus, even though a court by itself cannot bend others to its will, a decision maker can craft rulings with an eye toward empowering others better situated to translate constitutional text into action.

A third lesson to be drawn from the creation and dissolution of linguistic regimes is that rules suited for one historical moment — even as they relate to a single subject matter — might not be optimal at a later point in time. In fact, blind adherence to outmoded protocols may prove counterproductive. This is not a matter simply of refining the law so that it is more logical but also of avoiding obsolescence and ensuring social grounding for text. When context changes sufficiently to call into question certain methods of conceptualizing the stakes of a dispute, preferred rhetorical strategies, too, must be adjusted.

From these three principles, a more robust normative theory can be elaborated. Yet, doing so will require a more extended account of the social factors that tend to influence decision makers and a commitment to certain substantive principles for the evaluation of such considerations. To reach some preliminary insights in this vein, the book drew from Americans' experience with the First Amendment. If there is an idea that should animate further investigations of the American languages of power, it is this: the habits of citizens shape the parameters of discussion but do not determine the outcome. Rhetorical freedom means that all people, after all, can have something meaningful to say about the Constitution if they use the proper form. The precepts of eloquence encourage virtuous citizens to employ active constitutional terms to reach accord rather than to rely merely on advantages in station, background, or affiliation. And it is the temporary convergences, these moments of sustained, ritualized, and occasionally acute intercourses, that reveal the most about how the constitutional system operates.

Notes

Chapter One. Freedom as a Matter of Faith

1. For an account of antebellum debates over the scope of the First Amendment, see Michael Kent Curtis, *Free Speech, The People's Darling Privilege: Struggles for Freedom of Expression in American History* (Durham, NC: Duke University Press, 2000). For a taste of the range of modern disputes over the scope of the First Amendment, see Steven H. Shiffrin, *Dissent, Injustice and the Meanings of America* (Princeton, NJ: Princeton University Press, 1999); Robert C. Post, *Constitutional Domains: Democracy, Community, Management* (Cambridge, MA: Harvard University Press, 1995). Thomas Curry presents a useful account of early religious ideas that influenced the writing of the First Amendment. Thomas J. Curry, *The First Freedoms: Church and State in America to the Passage of the First Amendment* (Oxford, UK: Oxford University Press, 1986).

2. Austin proposed that law be understood as a command from a sovereign, backed by a sanction, that is habitually obeyed. John Austin, *Providence of Jurisprudence Determined* (Cambridge, UK: Cambridge University Press, 1995), 12–16.

3. Kent Greenawalt, *Fighting Words: Individuals, Communities, and Liberties of Speech* (Princeton, NJ: Princeton University Press, 2000), 3. Reflecting the lopsidedness of political support for expressive liberty, six in ten Americans can correctly identify the textual source of the right to free expression; no other right can be placed by more than two in ten. *State of the First Amendment 2004 Survey*, available at www.firstamendment center.org/sofa—reports/index.aspx. Among those who favor neutral rules of governance, Herbert Wechsler's work can be considered influential. Herbert Wechsler, "Toward Neutral Principles of Constitutional Law," *Harvard Law Review* 73 (1959): 1.

4. Not only does legal culture tolerate a wide array of state and federal jurisdictions to regulate First Amendment rights, but substantive legal rules can explicitly provide for governance according to the local norms of "contemporary communities," as it does in the area of sexually explicit speech. *Jenkins v. Georgia*, 418 U.S. 153 (1974) (rejecting "national standard" approach to obscenity). For a detailed view of the competing schools of First Amendment interpretation, see William Van Alstyne, "A Graphic View of the Free Speech Clause," *California Law Review* (1982): 107.

5. Zechariah Chafee, *Free Speech in the United States* (Cambridge, MA: Harvard University Press, 1941), 97–100. For accounts of constitutional development that stress political contest and disjunctions, see Ken I. Kersch, *Constructing Civil Liberties: Discontinuities in the Development of American Constitutional Law* (Cambridge, UK: Cambridge University Press, 2004); Geoffrey R. Stone, *Perilous Times: Free Speech in Wartime From the Sedition Act of 1748 to the War on Terrorism* (New York: Norton, 2004).

6. Paul W. Kahn, *The Reign of Law: Marbury v. Madison and the Construction of America* (New Haven: Yale University Press, 1997).

7. Michel Foucault, *The Order of Things: An Archaeology of the Human Sciences* (New York: Vintage, 1973), 87.

8. Michel Foucault, *The Archaeology of Knowledge and the Discourse on Language* (New York: Pantheon, 1972), 215–37.

9. Robert Nozick, *Anarchy, State, and Utopia* (New York: Basic Books, 1974), 149, 320. Nozick envisions a libertarian and laissez-faire supercommunity, which could tolerate subcommunities with more robust conceptions of social bonds.

10. John Rawls, *A Theory of Justice* (Cambridge, MA: Belknap Press, 1999), 14–15. In the original position, "no one knows his place in society, his class position or social status; nor does he know his fortune in the distribution of natural assets and abilities, his intelligence and strength, and the like. Nor, again, does anyone know his conception of the good." At the same time, individuals are permitted to be aware of "political affairs and the principles of economic theory; they know the basis of social organization and the laws of human psychology." Ibid. at 118–19. Sandel points out that Rawls's conception of the self as antecedent to the community, and rights as constitutive rather than a possession, denies "intersubjective" forms of understanding. Consequently, he laments both the conceptual incoherence and the "moral fragility of the deontological self" envisioned by Rawlsian justice. Michael J. Sandel, *Liberalism and the Limits of Justice* (New York: Cambridge University Press, 2d ed., 2006), 55–57, 60–66, 178.

11. *Declaration of Independence* (1776); *The Federalist* Nos. 10, 14 (James Madison). On the peculiar blend of Christian theology and Enlightenment theories of civil governance that contributed to the intellectual ferment of the revolutionary era, see Gordon S. Wood, *The Creation of the American Republic, 1776–1787* (New York: Norton, 1969), 91–126.

12. Nozick, *Anarchy, State, and Utopia*, at 50. In discussing this rights-privileging perspective, Nozick argues that "[t]reating us with respect by respecting our rights, [the minimal state] allows us, individually or with whom we choose, to choose our life and to realize our ends and our conception of ourselves, insofar as we can, aided by the voluntary cooperation of other individuals possessing the same dignity." See ibid., at 334. It is no answer to defend prepolitical theories on the ground that they are concerned with the

macrostructure of civil society and not its particularities, for each presents more than a descriptive account of self-governance, extrapolating guidelines from hypothetical origins for the solution of practical problems. These principles may promise thick notions of justice, as in the case of Rawls, or present a thin theory of the state, as in the case of Nozick, but they all lash the people to the mast so that they might resist their worst instincts in meeting the challenges of practical governance. For Nozick, the destructive impulse to be guarded against is the state's incessant drive to redistribute social goods, the enemy of the "inviolate individual's" capacity to "strive for a meaningful life." For Rawls, the danger presented by social cooperation is that the least will be mistreated by those who are comparatively well off and that over time the material gap will grow.

13. Methodologically, the study follows Geertz, who espouses a perspective toward cultural inquiry that treats man as "an animal suspended in webs of signification that he himself has spun." Clifford Geertz, "Thick Description: Toward an Interpretive Theory of Culture," in *The Interpretation of Cultures* (New York: Basic Books, 1973), 5; see also Clifford Geertz, *Local Knowledge: Further Essays in Interpretive Anthropology* (New York: Basic Books, 1983). A cultural analysis such as this one can, for the most part, exist alongside a philosophical one that advocates institutional development of a particular tradition. See Frederick Schauer, *Free Speech: A Philosophical Inquiry* (Cambridge, UK: Cambridge University Press, 1982); C. Edwin Baker, *Human Liberty and Freedom of Speech* (Oxford, UK: Oxford University Press, 2001).

14. H. Jefferson Powell, *A Community Built on Words* (Chicago: University of Chicago Press, 2002). See also H. Jefferson Powell, *Languages of Power: A Source Book of Early American Constititutional History* (Durham, NC: Carolina Academic Press, 1991). An influential excavation of the discontinuities in the neo-Roman theory of the free state can be found in Quentin Skinner, *Liberty Before Liberalism* (New York: Cambridge University Press, 1998).

15. Clifford Geertz, "Thick Description: Toward an Interpretive Theory of Culture," at 3, 17.

16. Jed Rubenfeld, *Freedom and Time: A Theory of Constitutional Self-Government* (New Haven: Yale University Press, 2001), 7.

17. The Privileges and Immunities Clause of the Fourteenth Amendment is a prime example of the waning of discursive habits. Hobbled soon after its enactment in *The Slaughterhouse Cases*, 16 Wall. 36 (1873), it has never regained its footing in the popular imagination. Freedom of expression was frequently referred to as a "privilege" of citizenship, but that formulation has seemed increasingly archaic.

18. This is the case of *Davis v. Commonwealth of Massachusetts*, 167 U.S. 43 (1897), which quotes from Holmes's opinion for the Supreme Judicial Court, *Commonwealth v. Davis*, 39 N.E. 113 (Mass. 1895).

19. In *Lochner v. New York*, the U.S. Supreme Court ruled that a worker safety law that proscribed the maximum number of hours a baker may work per day and week transgressed "the general right of an individual to be free in his person and in his power to contract in relation to his own labor." 198 U.S. 45, 58 (1905).

20. *Hague v. Committee for Industrial Organization*, 307 U.S. 496, 515 (1939); see also *Schneider v. State of New Jersey*, 308 U.S. 147, 151 (1939) ("the streets are natural and proper places for the dissemination of information and opinion").

21. As James Madison explained, "The federal and State governments are in fact but different agents and trustees of the people, constituted with different powers, and designed for different purposes." *The Federalist* No. 46.

22. The *Hague* Court achieves this major doctrinal shift without expressly overruling *Davis*. It does so by distinguishing between contexts, suggesting that the earlier case involved a statute purporting to control all access to the site, whereas the law here targeted only expressive access. Steve Winter attributes the transformation of legal language to "widespread social changes in the background assumptions that shaped the contemporary conception of the park and its proper uses." Steven L. Winter, *A Clearing in the Forest: Law, Life, and Mind* (Chicago: University of Chicago Press, 2003), 266. Winter's otherwise enlightening presentation of the case neglects the role of politics in facilitating changes to the social milieu.

23. *Capitol Square Review and Advisory Board v. Pinette*, 515 U.S. 753 (1995) (citing phrase in support of right to erect Christmas display in front of courthouse); *Grayned v. City of Rockford*, 408 U.S. 104 (1972) (protecting demonstration in support of integration of high school faculty, staff, and extracurricular activities); *Shuttlesworth v. City of Birmingham*, 394 U.S. 147 (1969) (reversing conviction of Reverend Fred Shuttlesworth where permit regime was administered with intent to frustrate his ability to protest racial practices of city); *Saia v. People of New York*, 334 U.S. 558 (1948) (assessing antinoise ordinance).

24. The new country's iconography almost immediately reflected its revolutionary character. Inscribed on the reverse side of the Great Seal was the phrase "Novus Ordo Seclorum," or "A New Order of Centuries." Gaillard Hunt, *The History of the Seal of the United States* (Washington, DC: Government Printing Office, 1909), 41.

25. Gordon S. Wood, *Creation of the American Republic, 1776–1787* (New York: Norton, 1993), 362 (quoting Hichborn, *Oration, March 5, 1777*, in Niles, ed., *Principles*, 47).

26. H. Jefferson Powell, "Parchment Matters: A Meditation on the Constitution as Text," *Iowa Law Review* 71 (1986): 1427.

27. Compare *Patterson v. Colorado*, 205 U.S. 454 (1907) (opining that "'the main purpose of [the First Amendment] is to prevent all such previous restraints upon publications as had been practiced by other governments,' and they do not prevent the subsequent punishment of such as may be deemed contrary to the public welfare") with *Madsen v. Women's Health Center*, 512 U.S. 753 (1994) (permitting injunction as to speech but tailoring its scope); *Forsyth County v. Nationalist Movement*, 505 U.S. 123 (1992) (approving parade and demonstration licensing scheme).

28. According to Peter Medine, *The Arte of Rhetorique* went through eight printings and three different publishers. Sir Thomas Wilson, *The Art of Rhetoric*, Peter E. Medine ed. (University Park: Pennsylvania State University Press, 1994), 8–9.

29. John Brigham, *Constitutional Language: An Interpretation of Judicial Decision* (Westport, CT: Greenwood Press, 1978); Philip Bobbitt, *Constitutional Interpretation* (Oxford, UK: Blackwell, 1991).

30. Keith Whittington, *Constitutional Construction: Divided Powers and Constitutional Meaning* (Cambridge, MA: Harvard University Press, 1999). Whittington envisions five levels of constitutional debate, each characterized by a different relationship to

the sources of law, the degree of settlement of a problem, the role expectations of a particular actor, and the degree of creativity that is permissible. For Whittington, these forms are policymaking, interpretation, construction, creation, and revolution.

31. An example of this methodology can be found in Robert Cover's study of natural law idiom in antislavery discourse, albeit "confined to residual and interstitial" usage. Robert M. Cover, *Justice Accused: Antislavery and the Judicial Process* (New Haven: Yale University Press, 1975), 125. Cover sets out to discover the true zone of rhetorical discretion available to a judge who took his judicial obligation as seriously as his moral imperative, caught "between the demands of role and the voice of conscience." Ibid., at 6.

32. Thomas I. Emerson, *The System of Freedom of Expression* (New York: Random House, 1970), 3.

33. Alexander Meiklejohn, *Free Speech and Its Relation to Self-Government* (New York: Harper and Bros., 1948), 18.

34. Ibid., at 26; John Hart Ely, *Democracy and Distrust: A Theory of Judicial Review* (Cambridge, MA: Harvard University Press, 1980), 105.

35. The orientation associated with this tool is known among legal experts as "strict scrutiny," a term of art that metaphorically conveys the jurist's task as requiring "exacting" analysis.

36. H. L. A. Hart, *The Concept of Law* (Oxford, UK: Oxford University Press 1997), 81.

37. Frederick Schauer, "The Exceptionalist First Amendment," in *American Exceptionalism and Human Rights*, Michael Ignatieff ed. (Princeton, NJ: Princeton University Press, 2005). According to this subconstitutional principle, judges and policymakers are supposed to refrain from valuing one kind of expression over another. But the principle itself collides with other tendencies, including the ingrained practice of favoring political expression and the willingness to tolerate suppression of traditionally unprotected forms of speech.

38. *New York Times Company v. United States*, 403 U.S. 713, 714 (1971).

39. Justice Douglas's separate concurrence echoes this relationship between expansive liberty and the perfectability of the democratic process by emphasizing that the inverse is also true: "secrecy in government . . . perpetuat[es] bureaucratic errors." Ibid., at 724.

40. Meicklejohn, *Free Speech*, at 27.

41. *Chaplinsky v. New Hampshire*, 315 U.S. 568, 571–72 (1942); see also *Roth v. United States*, 354 U.S. 476, 484 (1957) ("But implicit in the history of the First Amendment is the rejection of obscenity as utterly without redeeming social importance").

42. Max Black, *The Labyrinth of Language* (New York: Praeger, 1968), 5.

43. *Virginia v. Black*, 538 U.S. 343 (2004) (upholding statute that banned the burning of a cross with "an intent to intimidate a person or group of persons"); *Wisconsin v. Mitchell*, 508 U.S. 476 (1993) (ruling that sentencing enhancement for selecting a crime victim on the basis of race is consistent with free speech guarantees).

Chapter Two. Metaphor and Community

1. *Abrams v. United States*, 250 U.S. 616, 630 (1919) (Holmes, J., dissenting); *Frohwerk v. United States*, 249 U.S. 204, 209 (1919).

2. Jeremy Bentham, *Works* I:V: 235 (1843), 92.

3. Steven L. Winter, *A Clearing in the Forest: Law, Life and Mind* (Chicago: University of Chicago Press, 2001), 68.

4. Aristotle, *The Art of Rhetoric*, H. C. Lawson-Tancred tr. (London: Penguin, 1991), 235. For an analysis of the emotive quality of metaphor, see Northrop Frye, *Myth and Metaphor: Selected Essays, 1974–1988*, Robert D. Denham ed. (Charlottesville: University Press of Virginia, 1990).

5. George Lakoff and Mark Johnson, *Metaphors We Live By* (Chicago: University of Chicago Press, 2003), 11.

6. Ibid., at 115–19; George Lakoff, *Women, Fire & Dangerous Things: What Categories Reveal About the Mind* (Chicago: University of Chicago Press, 1987), 284–85; M. J. Reddy, "The Conduit Metaphor: A Case of Frame Conflict in Our Language About Language," in *Metaphor and Thought*, A. Ortony ed. (Cambridge, UK: Cambridge University Press, 1979), 164–201. See also Jack Balkin, *Cultural Software: A Theory of Ideology* (New Haven: Yale University Press, 2002); Winter, *A Clearing in the Forest.*

7. So many publicly valued rights and objects have been characterized as "grand bulwarks of liberty," from the right to trial by jury, *Neder v. United States*, 527 U.S. 1, 30 (1999), to the notion of the free press, *McConnell v. Federal Election Commission*, 540 U.S. 93, 286 (2003), to the Great Writ, *Hamdi v. Rumsfeld*, 542 U.S. 507, 557 (2004) (Scalia, J., dissenting). Even the whole of the Bill of Rights has been described in this way. *United States v. Havens*, 446 U.S. 620, 634 (1980).

The genesis of fire rhetoric in free speech discourse can be traced to the World War I decisions, though related formulations appeared in ordinary language before then. *Gitlow v. New York*, 268 U.S. 652 (1925) ("A single revolutionary spark may kindle a fire that, smouldering for a time, may burst into a sweeping and destructive conflagration"); see also *Frohwerk v. United States*, 249 U.S. 204, 209 (1919) ("the circulation of the paper was in quarters where a little breath would be enough to kindle a flame").

8. *Romer v. Evans*, 517 U.S. 620, 652 (1996) (Scalia, J., dissenting). *Lawrence v. Texas*, 539 U.S. 558, 602 (2003) (Scalia, J., dissenting).

9. See, e.g., Akhil Reed Amar, "Attainder and Amendment 2: *Romer*'s Rightness," *Michigan Law Review* 95 (1996): 203, 228 (characterizing Scalia's *Romer* dissent as "derisive"); "Taking the Initiative," *New Republic*, June 10, 1996, at 8 (calling Scalia's dissent "spiteful").

10. Benjamin N. Cardozo, *The Nature of the Judicial Process* (New Haven: Yale University Press, 1921), 45. It has become de rigueur for the media to describe the latest social controversy as a "culture war"; in a country where conflict is common and virtually every social question becomes a legal one, the terminology threatens to expand beyond any sensible utility. See, e.g., Linda Greenhouse, "Gay Rights Laws Can't Be Banned, High Court Rules," *New York Times*, May 21, 1996, at 1. Process conservatives find the culture war imagery appealing because it reinforces general notions of judicial neutrality; social conservatives find it attractive for their agenda items, on which they believe they can prevail in a system of pure majoritarian politics. The "culture war" metaphor occludes the fact that the social contest over the citizenship rights of sexual minorities involves many different coalitions and agendas. Jack Balkin has provided an excellent discussion of the weaknesses of Scalia's perspective—namely that every fight over social

status is a cultural conflict, and the principle of equality occasionally requires courts to choose a side in such contests. See Jack M. Balkin, "The Constitution of Status," *Yale Law Journal* 106 (1997): 2313. Bruce Ackerman's appellation for the rights-privileging intellectual tradition: "rights foundationalism." Bruce Ackerman, "Constitutional Politics/Constitutional Law," *Yale Law Journal* 99 (1989): 453, 465–69.

11. It is not only the case that constitutional language cheats time; it also needs time so that it might flourish. Political foundings often defer a set of significant social questions in the name of cohesion and settlement in the short run. It is not merely the act of putting off hard questions that breaks a gridlock and sets the conditions for self-governance. It is also the recognition that cultural conditions may later be more amenable to the resolution of intractable disputes. Deferral of conflict buys time for the maturation of political views, allows participants to gain familiarity with rhetorical forms, and even permits more effective modalities to be discovered through trial and error.

12. *The Federalist* No. 2 (Jay); *The Federalist* Nos. 10, 40 (Madison). The starting point of John Hart Ely's magisterial *Democracy and Distrust* is that the Constitution is "overwhelmingly concerned with . . . process writ large." John Hart Ely, *Democracy and Distrust: A Theory of Judicial Review* (Cambridge, MA: Harvard University Press, 1980), 87.

13. Plato, *The Republic*, Raymond Larson tr. (Arlington Heights, IL: Crofts, 1979), Book 2, 377b–378e, at 49–50.

14. Ibid., Book 3, 415a–d, at 84–85.

15. Ibid., Book 4, 430, at 97. Speaking nonliterally about political myth-making, Socrates says, "you know when dyers want to dye wool purple they select from all the possible colors wool that is naturally white, give it a preliminary treatment to make the color take, and only then dye it. Things dyed like that are permanent, and even detergent can't wash out the dye." Ibid., at Book 4, 429d–e, at 96–97. On equality and virtue, see ibid., Book 3, 423, at 90. For an extended discussion of Plato's understanding of social roles and specialization in the ideal state, see ibid., Book 2, 370b–c, at 41–42. Plato, who apparently found metaphors and models useful as second-best devices for achieving truth, uses the term *eikon* to refer to "illustration," "image," "comparison," and "metaphor"; he uses *paradeigma* to refer to the existence of a "model." See E. E. Pender, "Plato on Metaphors and Models," *Metaphor, Allegory, and the Classical Tradition*, G. R. Boys-Stones ed. (Oxford, UK: Oxford University Press, 2003), 55.

16. Sir Thomas Wilson, *The Arte of Rhetorique* (1553), Book III.

17. Benedict Anderson, *Imagined Communities: Reflections on the Origin and Spread of Nationalism* (London: Verso, 1983).

18. Ibid., at 6.

19. Philip Bobbitt creates a typology of six constitutional arguments: textual, structural, historical, doctrinal, ethical, and prudential. Philip Bobbitt, *Constitutional Interpretation* (Oxford, UK: Basil Blackwell, 1991), 12–13, 22.

20. The Supreme Court initially ruled in favor of the school board in *Minersville School District v. Gobitis*, 310 U.S. 586 (1940), before reversing course in *West Virginia State Board of Education v. Barnette*, 319 U.S. 624, 642 (1943). I explore the way in which presidential rhetoric altered the social context for legal language in Chapter 5. For repetitions of this phrase in later interpretive outcomes, see *Texas v. Johnson*, 491 U.S. 397,

415 (1989); *Wallace v. Jaffree*, 472 U.S. 38, 55 (1985); *Board of Education v. Pico*, 457 U.S. 853, 870 (1982); *Branti v. Finkel*, 445 U.S. 507, 513 n.9 (1980); *Elrod v. Burns*, 427 U.S. 347, 356 (1976).

21. *Texas v. Johnson*, 491 U.S. 397, 418 (1989).

22. Ibid., at 437–39 (Stevens, J., dissenting).

23. Ibid., at 420. See also *United States v. Eichman*, 496 U.S. 310, 319 (1990) ("Punishing desecration of the flag dilutes the very freedom that makes this emblem so revered, and worth revering.").

24. Texas *v. Johnson*, 491 U.S. at 418.

25. Ibid., at 419–20.

26. *The Federalist* No. 14 (Madison). For the First Amendment as "bedrock" see *Texas v. Johnson*, 491 U.S. at 414; for the First Amendment as the "lifeblood" of democracy, see *Federal Election Commission v. Colorado Republican Federal Campaign Committee*, 533 U.S. 431, 466 (2001). For the notion of dissent described as "an article of faith," see *Paris Adult Theater v. Slaton*, 413 U.S. 49, 73 (1973) (Douglas, J., dissenting); *Gibson v. Florida Legislative Investigation Committee*, 372 U.S. 539, 570 (1963) (Douglas, J., concurring).

27. John Locke, *An Essay Concerning Human Understanding*, Alexander Campbell Fraser compl. (New York: Dover, 1959), Volume II, Book III, Ch. 1, at 3–6; Book III, Ch. 10, at 142–43, 146.

28. See generally Lakoff and Johnson, *Metaphors We Live By*, at 115–19; Albert N. Katz, "Figurative Language and Thought: A Review," in *Figurative Language and Thought*, Albert N. Katz et al. eds. (New York: Oxford University Press, 1988), 7–13. As Larry Solan argues, "[t]he fact that much of our knowledge of language can be attributed to our biological endowment . . . accounts for the relative ease and speed with which we acquire this knowledge." Lawrence M. Solan, *The Language of Judges* (Chicago: University of Chicago Press, 1993), 17; see also Howard Gardner and Ellen Winner, "The Development of Metaphoric Competence: Implications for Humanistic Disciplines," in *On Metaphor*, Sheldon Sacks ed. (Chicago: University of Chicago Press, 1978), 121, 130–34 (discussing findings of study showing that some children create metaphors at "an astonishingly high level," though children later pass through a literal stage of language usage); Donna R. Pawlowski et al., "Effects of Metaphors on Children's Comprehension and Perception of Print Advertisements," *Journal of Advertising* 27:2 (1998): 83–98 (finding that metaphors can improve a child's understanding and interest in a topic, and in some children, aid the ability to "recall" the presentation itself).

29. Mark Johnson, *The Body in the Mind: The Bodily Basis of Meaning, Imagination and Reason* (Chicago: University of Chicago Press, 1987).

30. 352 U.S. 380, 383 (1957).

31. *International Salt Company v. United States*, 332 U.S. 392, 403 (1947) (Frankfurter, J., dissenting in part). See generally Robert L. Tsai, "Fire, Metaphor, and Constitutional Myth-Making," *Georgetown Law Journal* 93 (2004): 181.

32. See, e.g., "Vermont House Votes Down Call for Flag-Burning Amendment," *New York Times*, February 14, 1995, at 1995 WLNR 3773090 (statement of state attorney general in opposing the measure).

33. Ernst Cassirer, *Language and Myth*, Susanne K. Langer tr. (New York: Dover, 1953),

85 (quoting Friedrich Wilehlm von Schelling). For Ricouer, "metaphorical meaning does not merely consist of a semantic clash but of the *new* predicative meaning which emerges from the collapse of the literal meaning, that is, from the collapse of the meaning which obtains if we rely only on the common or usual lexical values of our words. The metaphor is not the enigma but the solution of the enigma." Paul Ricouer, "The Metaphorical Process as Cognition, Imagination, and Feeling," in *On Metaphor*, Sacks ed., at 141, 144.

34. Ted Cohen, "Metaphor and the Cultivation of Intimacy," in *On Metaphor*, Sacks ed. at 1, 6.

35. Louis Michael Seidman, *Our Unsettled Constitution* (New Haven: Yale University Press, 2001); Cass R. Sunstein, *The Partial Constitution* (Cambridge, MA: Harvard University Press, 1999); Bruce Ackerman, *We the People: Foundations*, Vol. 1 (Cambridge, MA: Harvard University Press, 1991).

36. See generally Robert L. Tsai, "Democracy's Handmaid," *Boston University Law Review* 86 (2006): 1 (analyzing figurative discourse of founding politics).

37. Sabine Maasen and Peter Weingart, *Metaphors and the Dynamics of Knowledge* (London: Routledge, 2000), 3–4 (describing metaphor as a "messenger of meaning" and analyzing the ease with which it circulates).

38. *Reno v. American Civil Liberties Union*, 521 U.S. 844, 882 (1997).

39. See, e.g., John Schwartz and Joan Biskupic, "Supreme Court Rejects Curbs on Online Speech," *Washington Post*, June 27, 1997, A1; John Aloysius Farrell, " 'Decency' Law for the Internet Is Struck Down," *Boston Globe*, June 27, 1997, at A1; "Justices Rule Against Help for Suicides; Internet Porn Curb Loses Test," *Chicago Tribune*, June 26, 1997, at 1; "Internet Smut," *AP Online*, June 27, 1997; Editorial, *Richmond Times-Dispatch*, June 27, 1997, at A18; "Case Summary for *Reno v. ACLU*," *First Amendment Topics*, at http://www.firstamendmentcenter.org/faclibrary (identifying this passage as "quotable").

40. A number of thinkers have theorized about how to maximize the empowerment of social or political minorities; others have focused on the importance of multiplying institutional variety so as to promote a range of public policies. Will Kymlicka, *Multicultural Citizenship: A Liberal Theory of Minority Rights* (Oxford, UK: Clarendon Press, 1995); Heather K. Gerken, "Second Order Diversity," *Harvard Law Review* 118 (2005): 1099; Heather K. Gerken, "Dissenting by Deciding," *Stanford Law Review* 58 (2005): 1745; Richard C. Schragger, "Cities as Constitutional Actors: The Case of Same-Sex Marriage," *Journal of Law and Politics* 21 (2005): 147; Robert Schapiro, "Polyphonic Federalism: State Constitutions in the Federal Courts," *California Law Review* 87 (1999): 1409.

41. See Victor Turner, *The Anthropology of Performance* (New York: PAJ Books, 1988), 34; Victor Turner, *Drama, Fields, and Metaphors* (Ithaca, NY: Cornell University Press, 1974), 38. Turner's functionalist approach to ritual presumes, though not without some criticism, that a return to normalcy is desirable. On legal performatives, see J. M. Balkin and Sanford Levinson, "Law as Performance," in *Law and Literature*, Michael Freeman and Andrew D. E. Lewis eds. (Oxford, UK: Oxford University Press, 1999); Sanford Levinson and J. M. Balkin, "Law, Music, and Other Performing Arts," *University of Pennsylvania Law Review* 139 (1991): 1597; Robert A. Ferguson, "The Judicial Opinion as Literary Genre," *Yale Journal of Law and Humanities* 2 (1990): 201.

42. 268 U.S. 652, 669 (1925).

43. Ibid. at 654–55.

44. Roger C. Schank and Robert P. Abelson, *Scripts, Plans, Goals, and Understanding* (Hillsdale, NJ: Erlbaum, 1977), 41.

45. While Schank and Abelson call these language structures "scripts," Lakoff prefers "scenarios" or "gestalts." See Schank and Abelson, *Scripts, Plans, Goals, and Understanding,* at 41; Lakoff, *Women, Fire, & Dangerous Things,* at 284–85. See also Anthony G. Amsterdam and Jerome Bruner, *Minding the Law* (Cambridge, MA: Harvard University Press, 2000), 45.

46. *Reno v. American Civil Liberties Union,* 521 U.S. at 852, 885.

47. See, e.g., Justice Kennedy's discussion of why *Bowers v. Hardwick* should be overruled, *Lawrence v. Texas,* 539 U.S. 558, 575 (2003) ("The foundations of *Bowers* have sustained serious erosion"), as well as the *Casey* plurality's analysis of why *Roe v. Wade* should not be cast aside, *Planned Parenthood v. Casey,* 505 U.S. 833, 857 (1992) ("No evolution of legal principle has left *Roe*'s doctrinal footings weaker").

48. See Deborah Hellman, "The Importance of Appearing Principled," 37 *Arizona Law Review* (1995): 1107; Richard H. Fallon, Jr., "Stare Decisis and the Constitution: An Essay on Constitutional Methodology," *New York University Law Review* 76 (2001): 570, 588; Henry P. Monaghan, "Stare Decisis and Constitutional Adjudication," *Columbia Law Review* 88 (1988): 723, 749–53.

49. *Stanley v. Georgia,* 394 U.S. 557, 568 (1969).

50. *Roth v. United States* and *Alberts v. California,* 354 U.S. 476 (1957).

51. The ruling had the effect of short-circuiting the regulatory regime. It left intact the state's authority to regulate distribution and marketing of obscenity but disabled the state from targeting demand. If regulating possession amounted to mind control, then why should that constitutional interest not flower into a reasonable right to acquire such materials? Conversely, if state officials have any interest in regulating obscenity, they ought to have effective means at their disposal. It is safe to say that the High Court's interpretive move — along with its cumbersome tinkering with the *Roth-Miller* test during this entire period — severely undermined the principled bases for obscenity law. The question then becomes: is the remainder of obscenity law a relic of a bygone era, or is *Stanley* the isolated island in a regulatory sea?

52. In *Roth v. United States* and *Alberts v. California,* 354 U.S. 476 (1957), which began to set out a more rigorous test for obscenity, Justice Harlan would have preferred a rule that reviewed federal regulations of obscenity with greater skepticism than state regulations. Viewing obscenity law as violative of the principle of content neutrality, Justices Douglas and Black favored allowing obscenity free rein so long as it was not "brigaded with illegal action." See also *Ginzburg v. United States,* 383 U.S. 463 (1966) (fractured rationales); *A Book Named "John Cleland's Memoirs of a Woman of Pleasure" v. Attorney General of Massachusetts,* 383 U.S. 413 (1966) (same); *Smith v. California,* 361 U.S. 147 (1959) (same).

53. 394 U.S. at 565. This quotable conception of law was recycled in *Planned Parenthood of Southeastern Pennsylvania v. Casey,* 505 U.S. 833, 915 (1992) (Stevens, J., concurring in part and dissenting in part).

54. 394 U.S. at 565.

55. Witness Justice Brennan's charge that regulation of adult theaters amounted to

"state-ordered regimentation of our minds." *Paris Adult Theater I v. Slaton*, 413 U.S. 49, 110 (1973) (Brennan, J., dissenting).

56. 354 U.S. 476 (1957); see *Miller v. California*, 413 U.S. 15 (1973).

57. *Roth*, 354 U.S. at 488.

58. See *Paris Adult Theater I v. Slaton*, 413 U.S. 49, 88 (1973) (Brennan, J., dissenting); *California v. LaRue*, 409 U.S. 109, 138 (1972) (Marshall, J., dissenting); *Stanley*, 394 U.S. at 563; *Manual Enterprises, Inc. v. Day*, 370 U.S. 478, 491 (1962); *Smith v. California*, 361 U.S. 147, 155 (1959).

59. As the Court explained in *Casey*, "It is a promise of the Constitution that there is a realm of personal liberty which the government may not enter." 505 U.S. 833, 847 (1992). See also *Boy Scouts of America v. Dale*, 530 U.S. 640, 648–49 (2000); *California Democratic Party v. Jones*, 530 U.S. 567, 592 n.3 (2000); *Federal Communications Commission v. Women Voters of California*, 468 U.S. 364, 379 (1984); *United Steelworkers of America, AFL-CIO v. Sadlowski*, 457 U.S. 102, 128 (1982); *U.S. Postal Service v. Council of Greenburgh Civic Associations*, 453 U.S. 114, 144 (1981); *Village of Schaumburg v. Citizens for a Better Environment*, 444 U.S. 620, 633 (1980); *Hynes v. Mayor and Council of Borough of Oradell*, 425 U.S. 610, 617 (1976); *Erznoznik v. City of Jacksonville*, 422 U.S. 205, 218 (1975); *Presbyterian Church of United States v. Mary Elizabeth Blue Hull Memorial*, 393 U.S. 440, 448 (1969); *Kingsley International Pictures Corporation v. Regents of the University of State of New York*, 360 U.S. 684, 699 (1959); *Kedroff v. St. Nicholas Cathedral of Russian Orthodox Church of North America*, 344 U.S. 94, 120 (1952); *Thomas v. Collins*, 323 U.S. 516, 541 (1945).

Chapter Three. Linguistic Transformation

1. To Kalven, "the story of the development of the law up to *Brandenburg* lies close to the heart of the American free speech tradition." Harry Kalven, Jr., *A Worthy Tradition: Freedom of Speech in America*, Jamie Kalven ed. (New York: Harper and Row, 1988), 16, 125, 227. Most casebooks start with the rulings of the Supreme Court during the First World War and proceed chronologically, thereby reinforcing a sense of progress through judicial enlightenment. Obviously, the rights codified in the American constitution have an ancient pedigree. It is also true that free speech controversies occurred outside of the courts before and after these canonical lawsuits. What the persistence of this narrative underscores is the close association of judicial review with the First Amendment.

2. *Brandenburg v. Ohio*, 395 U.S. 444, 446–449 (1969).

3. Kalven, *A Worthy Tradition*, at 234. Owen Fiss calls *Brandenburg* "one of the blessings of our liberty." *Liberalism Divided: Freedom of Speech and the Many Uses of State Power* (Boulder, CO: Westview Press, 1996), 13. The decision has been raised to ward off efforts to regulate everything from flag burning to virtual child pornography to tobacco advertising. See *Hurley v. Irish-American Gay, Lesbian, Bisexual Group of Boston*, 515 U.S. 557, 574 (1995); see also *Ashcroft v. Free Speech Coalition*, 535 U.S. 234, 236 (2002); *Lorillard Tobacco Company v. Reilly*, 533 U.S. 525, 579 (2001); *Boy Scouts of America v. Dale*, 530 U.S. 640, 660 (2000) ("The First Amendment protects expression, be it of the popular variety or not," citing *Brandenburg*); *Texas v. Johnson*, 491 U.S. 397, 418 (1989).

4. As Justice Douglas argued, "I see no place in the regime of the First Amendment for

any 'clear and present danger' test, whether strict and tight as some would make it, or free-wheeling as the Court in *Dennis* rephrased it." *Brandenburg,* 395 U.S. at 454.

5. *DeJonge v. Oregon,* 299 U.S. 353 (1937).

6. See generally Haig Bosmajian, *Metaphor and Reason in Judicial Opinions* (Carbondale, IL: Southern Illinois University Press, 1992), 197; Robert L. Tsai, "Fire, Metaphor, and Constitutional Myth-Making," *Georgetown Law Journal* 93 (2004): 181; L. A. Powe, Jr., "Searching for the False Shout of Fire," *Constitutional Commentary* 19 (2002): 345.

7. *Schenck v. United States,* 249 U.S. 47 (1919); *Frohwerk v. United States,* 249 U.S. 204 (1919).

8. *Dennis v. United States,* 341 U.S. 494, 511 (1951).

9. *Beauharnais v. Illinois,* 343 U.S. 250, 258–59 (1952).

10. Victor Turner, *Dramas, Fields, and Metaphors* (Ithaca, NY: Cornell University Press, 1974), 52.

11. *Thiel v. Southern Pacific Company,* 327 U.S. 217, 234 (1946) (Frankfurter, J., dissenting); *International Salt Company v. United States,* 332 U.S. 392, 403 (1947) (Frankfurter, J., dissenting); *American Communications Association v. Douds,* 339 U.S. 382, 419 (1950) (Frankfurter, J., concurring); *Butler v. Michigan,* 352 U.S. 380, 383 (1957).

12. See, e.g., *Lorillard Tobacco Company v. Reilly,* 533 U.S. 525, 581 (2001); *Sable Communications v. Federal Communications Commission,* 492 U.S. 115, 127 (1989); *Moore v. City of East Cleveland,* 431 U.S. 494, 521 (1977).

13. *R.A.V. v. City of St. Paul,* 505 U.S. 377, 396 (1992).

14. For a provocative critique of *R.A.V. v. City of St. Paul,* see Judith Butler, *Excitable Speech: A Politics of the Performative* (New York: Routledge, 1997).

15. Justice Holmes's articulation appeared in his *Abrams* dissent, 250 U.S. 616, 630 (1919).

16. *Lamont v. Postmaster General,* 381 U.S. 301, 308 (1965).

17. On the pattern involving the classroom-as-marketplace, see *Rosenberger v. Rector and Visitors of the University of Virginia,* 515 U.S. 819, 850 (1995); *Widmar v. Vincent,* 454 U.S. 263, 274 n.5 (1981); *Healy v. James,* 408 U.S. 169, 180 (1972). For the Internet-as-marketplace, see *Reno v. American Civil Liberties Union,* 521 U.S. 844, 885 (1997). On the use of the legal saying as a generalized warning, see *Virginia v. Hicks,* 539 U.S. 113, 119 (2003). For a taste of the "neutrality" version, see *Federal Communications Commission v. Pacifica Foundation,* 438 U.S. 726, 745 (1978).

18. *Tinker v. Des Moines Independent Community School District,* 393 U.S. 503 (1969).

19. *Abrams v. United States,* 250 U.S. 616, 630 (Holmes, J., dissenting).

20. See, e.g., *Perry Education Association v. Perry Local Educators' Association,* 460 U.S. 37, 71 (1983) (Brennan, J., dissenting).

21. *First National Bank of Boston v. Bellotti,* 435 U.S. 765, 809–10 (1978) (Brennan, J., dissenting); see also *McConnell v. Federal Election Commission,* 540 U.S. 93, 265 (2003) (Scalia, J., concurring in part and dissenting in part); see the same decision also at 336 (Kennedy, J., concurring in part and dissenting in part). For examples of the disfavored strategy of resisting the market gestalt entirely, see *Columbia Broadcasting System, Inc., v. Democratic National Committee,* 412 U.S. 94, 199 (1973) (Brennan, J.,

dissenting) (decrying broadcasters who are bent upon "absolute exclusion of virtually all of our citizens from the most effective 'marketplace of ideas' ever devised"). Public broadcasting is one medium that has resisted the laissez-faire approach. See *Federal Communications Commission v. Pacifica Foundation*, 438 U.S. 726, 772 (1978) (Brennan, J., dissenting) (disagreeing with ban on "indecent" monologue and favoring a "marketplace unsullied by the censor's hand").

22. *McCreary v. American Civil Liberties Union of Kentucky*, 545 U.S. 844, 883 (2005) (O'Connor, J., concurring).

23. *United States v. National Treasury Employees Union*, 513 U.S. 454, 491 (1995) (Rehnquist, J., dissenting) (arguing that ban on government employees' receipt of honoraria did not burden First Amendment); *Randall v. Sorell*, 126 S. Ct. 2479, 2510 (2006) (Stevens, J., dissenting); see also *Time v. Hill*, 385 U.S. 374, 407 (1967) (Harlan, J., concurring in part) ("we cannot avoid recognizing that we have entered an area where the 'marketplace of ideas' does not function and where conclusions premised on the existence of that exchange are apt to be suspect").

24. *Philadelphia Newspapers, Inc. v. Hepps*, 475 U.S. 767, 782 (1986) (Stevens, J., dissenting) (libel); *44 Liquormart, Inc. v. Rhode Island*, 517 U.S. 484, 496 (1996) (commercial speech). On the "uninhibited marketplace of ideas," see *Virginia v. Hicks*, 539 U.S. 113, 119 (2003); *CBS, Inc. v. Federal Communications Commission*, 453 U.S. 367, 395 (1981); *Red Lion Broadcasting Company v. Federal Communications Commission*, 395 U.S. 367, 390 (1969).

25. *Texas v. Johnson*, 491 U.S. 397, 418 (1989); *Tinker v. Des Moines Independent School District*, 393 U.S. 503, 512 (1969); *Thomas v. Collins*, 323 U.S. 516, 537 (1945).

26. *Texas v. Johnson*, 491 U.S. at 437 (Stevens, J., dissenting).

27. *United States v. Eichman*, 496 U.S. 319, 323 (1990) (Stevens, J., dissenting).

28. For a critical take on these developments, see Jed Rubenfeld, "The First Amendment's Purpose," *Stanford Law Review* 53 (2001): 767. For a generally laudatory perspective, see Eugene Volokh, "Why *Buckley v. Valeo* Is Basically Right," *Arizona State Law Journal* 34 (2002): 1095; Eugene Volokh, "What Speech Does 'Hostile Work Environment' Harassment Law Restrict?" *Georgetown Law Journal* 85 (1997): 627.

29. *Virginia State Board of Pharmacy v. Virginia Citizens Consumer Council*, 425 U.S. 748, 781 (1976) (Rehnquist, J., dissenting); see also *Bigelow v. Virginia*, 421 U.S. 809, 826 (1975).

30. *McDaniel v. Paty*, 435 U.S. 618 (1978).

31. *Rosenberger v. Rectors and Visitors of the University of Virginia*, 515 U.S. 819, 850 (1995). Justice O'Connor replicates this theme in her concurrence: "It is clear that the University has established a generally applicable program to encourage the free exchange of ideas by its students, an expressive marketplace that includes some 15 student publications with predictably divergent viewpoints." Ibid., at 848.

32. Bruce Ackerman, *We the People: Foundations*, Vol. 1 (Cambridge, MA: Belknap Press, 1991), 19. According to Ackerman, these are the only meaning-making events that have satisfied the conditions of signaling, proposal, deliberation, and codification. He treats events that fall short of these criteria as failed or inchoate revolutions. For those who deny the causal impact of FDR's court-packing plan and claim that intellectual traditions within the Court were already moving in this direction, see Barry Cushman,

Rethinking the New Deal Court: The Structure of a Constitutional Revolution (New York: Oxford University Press, 1998); G. Edward White, *The Constitution and the New Deal* (Cambridge, MA: Harvard University Press, 2000).

33. Article V of the Constitution provides in pertinent part: "The Congress, whenever two thirds of both Houses shall deem it necessary, shall propose Amendments to this Constitution, or, on the Application of the Legislatures of two thirds of the several States, shall call a Convention for proposing Amendments, which, in either Case, shall be valid to all Intents and Purposes, as Part of this Constitution, when ratified by the Legislatures of three fourths of the several States, or by Conventions in three fourths thereof, as one or the other Mode of Ratification may be proposed by the Congress."

34. Jim Pope's theory of republican moments expands upon Ackerman's self-styled "three-moment theory of constitutional creation." However, even Pope's approach, which encompasses the labor movement's achievements and failures, misses a number of significant developments in constitutional language. See James Gray Pope, "Labor's Constitution of Freedom," *Yale Law Journal* 106 (1997): 941; James Gray Pope, "Republican Moments: The Role of Direct Popular Power in the American Constitutional Order," *University of Pennsylvania Law Review* 139 (1990): 287

35. Richard A. Primus, *The American Language of Rights* (Cambridge, UK: Cambridge University Press, 1999), 177.

36. Benjamin N. Cardozo, *The Nature of the Judicial Process* (New Haven: Yale University Press, 1921), 17. "[T]he process of judging" itself "is a phase of a never ending movement." Benjamin N. Cardozo, *The Growth of the Law* (Westport, CT: Greenwood Press, 1973), 142.

37. Guido Calabresi, *A Common Law for the Age of Statutes* (Cambridge, MA: Harvard University Press, 1982). For a social science account arguing that "the language of the law seems to have a reality and motive force that shapes, to a large degree, the paths that the law enunciated by the Court takes," see Lee Epstein and Joseph F. Kobylka, *The Supreme Court and Legal Change: Abortion and the Death Penalty* (Chapel Hill: University of North Carolina Press, 1992), 310. As Epstein and Kobylka claim, "the path of the law is charted by conversations between lawyers (judges and advocates) conducted in a language and using a terminology fashioned and conveyed through a central shared experience (law school and participation in the legal profession)." Ibid. at 311. While the model of linguistic transformation shares some of these cultural premises, it treats language as more cross-situational and participatory than Epstein and Kobylka suggest.

38. Cardozo, *Growth of the Law*, at 1, 55. Cass Sustein's work on Burkean minimalism, which strives for a pragmatist reading of Burke, belongs in the incrementalist tradition, as does Dan Farber's and Suzanna Sherry's preference for "common law evolution." Cass R. Sunstein, "Burkean Minimalism," *Michigan Law Review* 105 (2006): 353; Daniel A. Farber and Suzanna Sherry, *Desperately Seeking Certainty: The Misguided Quest for Constitutional Foundations* (Chicago: University of Chicago Press, 2002), 152–58.

39. Cass R. Sunstein, *The Partial Constitution* (Cambridge, MA: Harvard University Press, 1993), 202–31. For other criticisms of the marketplace of ideas as a principled basis for organizing First Amendment principles, see Catharine MacKinnon, *Only Words* (1993); Kathleen M. Sullivan, "Free Speech and Unfree Markets," *UCLA Law Review* 42 (1995): 949; C. Edwin Baker, "Toward a General Theory of the First Amendment," *Iowa Law Review* 62 (1976): 1.

40. *Kunz v. New York*, 340 U.S 290, 302 (Jackson, J., dissenting).

41. Jean-Jacques Rousseau, "The Social Contract or Principles of Political Right," in *The Social Contract and Discourses* (Great Britain: Everyman, 1993), 180, 193. According to Rousseau, "the general will is, in each individual, a pure act of the understanding which reasons, when the passions are silent, about what a man can ask of his fellows and what his fellows have the right to ask of him." Rousseau, "The General Society of the Human Race," in ibid., at 174.

42. Rousseau, "The Social Contract," at 172. Legal language arranged to facilitate the aggregation of individual desires may simply embody "amour-propre" — socially induced forms of self-love — rather than the ethical considerations and shared identifications upon which self-governance depends. Distinguishing "amour-propre" from "amour de soi" (a more primitive form of self-regarding behavior rooted in human beings' need to satisfy basic bodily needs), Rousseau found this impulse to represent the greatest psychological threat to political community.

Chapter Four. Political Pathways

1. As Cover argued, "Because of the violence they command, judges characteristically do not create law, but kill it. Theirs is the jurispathic office. Confronting the luxuriant growth of a hundred legal traditions, they assert that *this one* is law and destroy or try to destroy the rest." Robert M. Cover, "Nomos and Narrative," *Harvard Law Review* 97 (1983): 4.

2. Harry Kalven, Jr., *The Negro and the First Amendment* (Columbus: Ohio State University Press, 1965), 67.

3. Robert A. Dahl, "Decision-Making in a Democracy: The Supreme Court as a National Policy-Maker," *Journal of Public Law* 6 (1957): 279, 285.

4. Dahl repeatedly speaks of a "national majority" but turns to indirect tests to discern the public will because of flaws in the capacity of polling and election returns to gauge policy preferences accurately. Ibid., at 284. In particular, Dahl focuses on the fact that laws pass both houses of Congress, assuming that a "lawmaking majority" is "equivalent to a national majority."

5. Those who favor a populist reading of Dahl include Neal Devins, "The Majoritarian Rehnquist Court?," *Law and Contemporary Problems* 67 (2004): 63; Richard Funston, "The Supreme Court and Critical Elections," *American Political Science Review* (1975): 795. Among those who prefer an elite reading of Dahl are Lee Epstein, Jack Knight, and Andrew D. Martin, "The Supreme Court as a Strategic National Policy Maker," *Emory Law Journal* (2001): 583; Jonathan D. Casper, "The Supreme Court and National Policy Making," *American Political Science Review* (1976): 50.

6. *Federal Election Commission v. Massachusetts Citizens for Life, Inc.*, 479 U.S. 238, 264 (1986) (quoting *Palko v. Connecticut*, 302 U.S. 319 (1937)).

7. *Brown v. Louisiana*, 383 U.S. 131, 142 (1966).

8. See *Lowell v. City of Griffin*, 303 U.S. 444 (1938) (invalidating ordinance banning distribution of circulars without a permit); *Saia v. New York*, 334 U.S. 558, 562 (1948) (on a religious speaker's ability to use a loudspeaker: "The police need not be given the power to deny a man the use of his radio in order to protect a neighbor against sleepless nights"); *Niemotko v. Maryland*, 340 U.S. 268 (1951) (protecting right of religious

speakers in park); *Feiner v. New York*, 340 U.S. 315 (1951) (rejecting First Amendment defense where speaker appeared to provoke discomfort and some level of disorder); *Chaplinsky v. New Hampshire*, 315 U.S. 568, 574 (1942).

9. Lester C. Olson, "Portraits in Praise of a People: A Rhetorical Analysis of Norman Rockwell's Icons in Franklin D. Roosevelt's 'Four Freedoms' Campaign," *Quarterly Journal of Speech* 69 (1983): 15–24.

10. *DeJonge v. Oregon*, 299 U.S. 353 (1937).

11. *Kunz v. New York*, 340 U.S. 290 (1951).

12. See generally Francesca Polletta, *Democracy Is an Endless Meeting: Democracy in American Social Movements* (Chicago: University of Chicago Press, 2002); David L. Chappell, *A Stone of Hope: Prophetic Religion and the Death of Jim Crow* (Chapel Hill: University of North Carolina Press, 2004); Taylor Branch, *Parting the Waters: America in the King Years, 1954–63* (New York: Simon and Schuster, 1988); Doug McAdam, *Freedom Summer* (New York: Oxford University Press, 1988).

13. *Garner v. Louisiana*, 368 U.S. 157 (1961). The decision spawned three concurring opinions. Justice Frankfurter wrote separately to emphasize that the state had not explicitly barred nonviolent activity in private shops. Justice Douglas favored a stronger alternative not taken: the state could not constitutionally assist private establishments in the perpetuation of racial segregation. Justice Harlan believed that the state law was unconstitutionally vague. His concurrence tried to draw a connection between street protest and soapbox oration based on its contribution to debate: "Such a demonstration . . . appeals to good sense and to 'the power of reason as applied through public discussion,' [and is] as much as, if not more than, a public oration delivered from a soapbox at a street corner."

14. *Edwards v. South Carolina*, 372 U.S. 229 (1963).

15. Gordon S. Wood, *Creation of the American Republic, 1776–1787* (New York: Norton, 1969), 310.

16. *Cox v. Louisiana*, 379 U.S. 536, 547 (1965); see also *Gregory v. City of Chicago*, 394 U.S. 111, 112 (1969) (reversing disorderly conduct convictions of protestors where marches were "peaceful and orderly").

17. *Brown v. Louisiana*, 383 U.S. 131 (1966). But see *Adderley v. Florida*, 385 U.S. 39 (1966) (affirming trespass convictions where protestors refused to leave property used strictly for nonpublic jail purposes).

18. *Brown v. Louisiana*, 383 U.S. at 168 (Black, J., dissenting); *Gregory*, 394 U.S. at 117 (Black, J., concurring). Although he does not explicate the thought fully, Kalven's play on words in describing the outcome in *Gregory* is a testament to the novelty and vitality of the citizen-assembly metaphor: "If the policeman is to be allowed to play the role of chairman at street corner meetings at all, he may only do so under a detailed set of *Robert's Rules of Orders* provided for him by the legislature." Kalven, *A Worthy Tradition*, at 104.

19. As the Court explained, "Participants in an orderly demonstration in a public place are not chargeable with the danger, unprovoked except by the fact of the constitutionally protected demonstration itself, that their critics might react with disorder or violence." *Brown v. Louisiana*, 383 U.S. 131, 133 n.1 (1966).

20. *National Association for the Advancement of Colored People v. Button*, 371 U.S.

415, 431 (1963); *Brotherhood of Railroad Trainmen v. Virginia ex rel. Virginia State Bar*, 377 U.S. 1, 7 (1964). Decisions relying on the political salience of an oration include *New York Times Company v. Sullivan*, 376 U.S. 254, 270 (1964); *Konigsberg v. State Bar of California*, 353 U.S. 252 (1957); *Sweezy v. New Hampshire*, 354 U.S. 234, 250 (1957). The ladder metaphor appears most dramatically in *National Association for the Advancement of Colored People v. Claiborne Hardware Company*, 458 U.S. 886, 913 (1982), which culminates the transformation of free speech language by effectively reversing the Supreme Court's prewar position on economic boycotts.

21. *Claiborne Hardware Company*, 458 U.S. at 907.

22. *People of the State of Illinois ex rel. McCollum v. Board of Education of District No. 71*, 333 U.S. 203, 211 (1948). For an originalist account of the Establishment Clause in which the commitment was "meant to depoliticize religion," see Leonard W. Levy, *Original Intent and the Framers' Constitution* (Chicago: Macmillan, 1988), 194.

23. *Abington School District v. Schempp*, 374 U.S. 203, 226 (1963).

24. See *McGowan v. Maryland*, 366 U.S. 420, 461 (1961) (stating that wall does not preclude clashes over context and that "[i]nnumerable civil regulations enforce conduct which harmonizes with religious canons."); *Zorach v. Clauson*, 343 U.S. 306, 314–15 (1952) (upholding release time program for religious studies because failure to accommodate such instruction would amount to "hostility to religion").

25. See brief of Amici Curiae National Catholic Educational Association Lutheran Education Association National Union of Christian Schools National Conference of Yeshiva Principals at 2, *Board of Education v. Allen*, 392 U.S. 236 (1968); Brief of Amici Curiae Protestants and Other Americans United for Separation of Church and State at 10, *Board of Education v. Allen*.

26. *Torasco v. Watkins*, 367 U.S. 488, 493–94 (1961).

27. *Lemon v. Kurtzman*, 403 U.S. 602, 614 (1971); *Committee for Public Education v. Nyquist*, 413 U.S. 756, 761 (1973).

28. *Walz v. Tax Commission of City of New York*, 397 U.S. 664, 676 (1970).

29. Paul Kengor, *God and Ronald Reagan: A Spiritual Life* (New York: ReganBooks, 2004), 164–69, 228–29, 236, 306. Reagan's acceptance speech at the Republican National Convention on July 17, 1980, has been described as "one of his most powerful public displays of religious faith." Ibid., at 154.

30. Brief for Amicus Curiae United States Supporting Petitioner, *Lynch v. Donnelly*, June 30, 1983; see also Brief of Amicus Curiae United States Supporting Petitioner, *County of Allegheny v. American Civil Liberties Union*, November 17, 1988 (attacking "simplistic" and "absolutist" framework that would demand "total separation"); Brief of Amicus Curiae United States, *Lee v. Weisman*, May 24, 1991 (decrying "sanitized separation" and urging Court to think of "[t]he Nation's tradition of acknowledging its religious heritage [] not as a series of discontinuous events at isolated institutions . . . but as a tapestry of civic culture"); Brief of Amicus Curiae Concerned Women for America in Support of Petitioners, *County of Allegheny v. American Civil Liberties Union* ("The focus of the constitutional era was not the eradication of religion from public life," to "sever government from religion," or to "show a callous indifference to religious groups").

31. Brief of Petitioner, *Lee v. Weisman*, May 24, 1991; Brief of Amicus Curiae Richard Collin Mangrum in Support of Respondents, *Board of Education of Westside Commu-*

nity Schools v. Mergens, October 23, 1989; Brief of Amicus Curiae United States Catholic Conference in Support of Respondents, *Board of Education of Westside Community Schools v. Mergens*, October 2, 1989. Michael McConnell writes that separationism would "more closely resemble[] freedom from religion . . . than freedom of religion." Michael W. McConnell, "Religious Freedom at a Crossroads," *University of Chicago Law Review* 59 (1992): 115.

32. Ronald Reagan, *Annual Convention of the National Association of Evangelicals*, Orlando, Florida, March 8, 1983.

33. Ronald Reagan, *Remarks and Question-and-Answer Session With Women Leaders of Christian Religious Organizations*, October 13, 1983; see also Ronald Reagan, *Remarks at a White House Ceremony in Observance of National Prayer Day*, May 10, 1982 ("I have never believed that the oft quoted amendment was supposed to protect us from religion. It was to protect religion from government tyranny."); Ronald Reagan, *Remarks and Question-and-Answer Session During an Administration Briefing for Editors From the Midwestern Region*, Chicago, Illinois, May 10, 1982 ("The first amendment is to protect not government from religion, but religion from government tyranny."); Ronald Reagan, *Remarks at Kansas State University, Alfred M. Landon Lecture Series on Public Issues*, September 9, 1982 ("But was the first amendment written to protect the American people from religion, or was it written to protect religion from government tyranny?").

34. Brief of Amicus Curiae Southern Center for Law and Ethics in Support of Respondents at 11–12, *Board of Education of Westside Community Schools v. Mergens*, 496 U.S. 226 (1990).

35. *Santa Fe Independent School District v. Doe*, 530 U.S. 290, 318 (2000) (Rehnquist, J., dissenting); *Good News Club v. Milford Central School District*, 533 U.S. 98, 118 (2001).

36. *McCreary County v. American Civil Liberties Union of Kentucky*, 125 S. Ct. 2722, 2757 (2005) (Scalia, J., dissenting); *Board of Education of Westside Community Schools v. Mergens*, 496 U.S. 226, 261 (1990) (Kennedy, J., concurring); *Mitchell v. Helms*, 530 U.S. 793, 827 (2000); *Rosenberger v. Rector and Visitors of the University of Virginia*, 515 U.S. 819, 845–46 (1995); *Church of Lukumi Babalu Aye v. City of Hialeah*, 508 U.S. 520, 534 (1993).

37. Justice O'Connor's first usage of the phrase "endorsement" occurred in *Lynch v. Donnelly*, 468 U.S. 668, 687–94 (1984) (O'Connor, J., concurring). In that initial effort, she used the phrase liberally in her re-description of the central purposes of the three-prong *Lemon* test (which had focused on the state's purpose, the effect of governmental action, and the possibility of entanglement). She then argued that the City of Pawtucket's display of a crèche amounted to state acknowledgment of religion's role in public life rather than "conveying government approval of particular religious beliefs."

38. See generally Christopher L. Eisgruber and Lawrence G. Sager, *Religious Freedom and the Constitution* (Cambridge, MA: Harvard University Press, 2007); Douglas Laycock, "Equal Access and Moments of Silence: The Equal Status of Religious Speech by Private Speakers," *Northwestern University Law Review* 81 (1986): 1 (advocating "neutrality" based reading of Religion Clauses); Michael W. McConnell, "Religious Freedom at a Crossroads," *University of Chicago Law Review* 59 (1992): 115 (advocating pluralist interpreta-

tion); Christopher L. Eisgruber and Lawrence G. Sager, "The Vulnerability of Conscience: The Constitutional Basis for Protecting Religious Conduct," *University of Chicago Law Review* 61 (1994): 1245 (positing "toleration" based theory of religious liberty).

39. Paul Kahn, *The Reign of Law: Marbury v. Madison and the Construction of America* (New Haven: Yale University Press, 1997).

40. For cases in which the High Court has found differential treatment of religion to be "viewpoint discrimination" against speech, see *Good News Club v. Milford Central School District*, 533 U.S. 98, 107 (2001); *Rosenberger v. Rector and Visitors of the University of Virginia*, 515 U.S. 819 (1995); *Lamb's Chapel v. Center Moriches Union Free School District*, 508 U.S. 384 (1993).

41. Richard Hofstadter claimed that "heated exaggeration, suspiciousness, and conspiratorial fantasy" have been ingrained features of the American mind. Richard Hofstadter, "The Paranoid Style in American Politics," *Harper's Magazine*, November (1964): 77–86. Liberalism generally (and rights strategies particularly) has been sustained not only by rational concerns but also by bouts of paranoia and fearfulness and by the enduring capacity of civic leaders to tap into this residual anxiety. For solitary references to the "importance of rebuilding the wall of separation between church and state," see *Capitol Square Review and Advisory Board v. Pinette*, 515 U.S. 753, 797 (1995) (Stevens, J., dissenting); *Lee v. Weisman*, 505 U.S. 577, 600–01 (1992) (Blackmun, J., concurring); *Mitchell v. Helms*, 530 U.S. 793, 873 (2000) (Souter, J., dissenting); *Marsh v. Chambers*, 463 U.S. 783, 802 (1983) (Brennan, J., dissenting).

42. Larry D. Kramer, *The People Themselves: Popular Constitutionalism and Judicial Review* (New York: Oxford University Press, 2004), 8; Larry D. Kramer, "The Supreme Court 2000 Term Foreword: We the Court," *Harvard Law Review* 115 (2001): 4. Kramer is not alone in turning toward the role of popular movements in creating constitutional meaning. See generally Jack Balkin and Sanford Levinson, "Understanding the Constitutional Revolution," *Virginia Law Review* 87 (2001): 1045; Reva Siegel, "She the People: The Nineteenth Amendment, Sex Equality, Federalism, and the Family," *Harvard Law Review* 115 (2002): 947; "Legislative Constitutionalism and Section Five Power: Policentric Interpretation of the Family and Medical Leave Act," *Yale Law Journal* 112 (2003): 1943.

43. Kramer ends his work by posing the question as a "choice between a system of judicial supremacy and one based on departmental or coordinate construction." Kramer, *The People Themselves*, at 252. Elsewhere, Kramer suggests that he favors the Justices "affirmatively surrender[ing] interpretive authority" over subject matter. Kramer, "We The Court," at 114. Does this mean that popular constitutionalism may take any number of forms? Perhaps, but Kramer himself does not so far delineate the outer boundaries of popular constitutionalism other than to note that judicial supremacy is its chief competitor.

Chapter Five. War and Syntax

1. Perhaps for these reasons, Ackerman subordinates the wartime interactions between the people and their leaders, and much that comes after the 1940s, to the towering achievements of the New Deal. Ackerman aims to recover the "meaning of the New Deal Revolution" from the tide of merely "formative" events such as "the war against Hitler,

the crusade against Communists." Bruce Ackerman, *We the People: Transformations*, Vol. 2 (Cambridge, MA: Belknap Press, 1998), 258. For treatments of the Reconstruction Amendments, see Garrett Epps, *Democracy Reborn: The Fourteenth Amendment and the Fight for Equal Rights in Post-Civil War America* (New York: Henry Holt, 2006); Daniel Farber, *Lincoln's Constitution* (Chicago: University of Chicago Press, 2003); Eric Foner, *Politics and Ideology in the Age of the Civil War* (New York: Oxford University Press, 1980); William E. Nelson, *The Fourteenth Amendment: From Political Principle to Judicial Doctrine* (Cambridge, MA: Harvard University Press, 1988). Hamilton expressed his view on the risk and scope of civil war in *The Federalist* No. 16.

2. Although Cardozo referred to the First Amendment as "the indispensable condition, of nearly every other form of freedom" in *Palko v. Connecticut*, 302 U.S. 319 (1937), the statement did not carry with it any presumption of unconstitutionality when laws affected such rights, and the case itself actually involved not a First Amendment matter but rather a claim of double jeopardy. Most other references suggesting that First Amendment controversies involved a special class of disputes did not command a majority until the shift in presidential rhetoric by FDR.

3. See generally Richard E. Neustadt, *Presidential Power and the Modern Presidents: The Politics of Leadership from Roosevelt to Reagan* (New York: Free Press, 1990); Stephen Skowronek, *The Politics Presidents Make: From John Adams to Bill Clinton* (Cambridge, MA: Belknap Press, 1997); Jeffrey K. Tulis, *The Rhetorical Presidency* (Princeton, NJ: Princeton University Press, 1987); Keith E. Whittington, *Constitutional Constructions: Divided Powers and Constitutional Meaning* (Cambridge, MA: Harvard University Press, 2001).

4. *Minersville School District v. Gobitis*, 310 U.S. 586 (1940); *West Virginia School Board v. Barnette*, 319 U.S. 624 (1943).

5. In the interim, Justice Stone, who dissented in *Gobitis*, became Chief; Jackson and Rutledge joined the Court. Although Frankfurter had been an early member of the Roosevelt administration, Jackson, who came to the Court directly from the administration as its Attorney General, arguably had a claim to know better the priorities of the administration regarding the European war and internationalism. Richard Friedman stresses the importance of the appointments process as "the chief generator of constitutional change" during his period. Richard D. Friedman, "A Rendezvous With Kreplach," *Green Bag 2d* 5 (2002): 453. Peter Irons, too, while claiming that few rulings "have ever provoked a violent reaction as the *Gobitis* decision," focuses on the personnel changes that transpired between the cases and finds nothing to shed light on Jackson's personal motivations for breaking from a "close friend and judicial ally." Irons depicts national political actors who faced this crisis in relatively passive terms, simply reminding citizens to "respect the Constitution." Peter H. Irons, *A People's History of the Supreme Court* (New York: Viking, 1999), 341–42. By contrast, and as an example of the external account, Morton Horwitz attributes the switch simply to the "wartime atmosphere" without discussing any particular mechanics of constitutional change. Morton J. Horwitz, *The Transformation of American Law, 1870–1960: The Crisis of Legal Orthodoxy* (New York: Oxford University Press, 1992), 252.

6. G. Edward White, "The First Amendment Comes of Age: The Emergence of Free Speech in Twentieth-Century America," *Michigan Law Review* 95 (1996): 299.

7. William E. Leuchtenburg, *Franklin D. Roosevelt and the New Deal, 1932–1940* (New York: Harper and Row, 1963), 299.

8. Gobitas was the spelling of the family name, but through a clerical error legal papers forever memorialized their name as "Gobitis."

9. Brief of Petitioners, *Minersville School District v. Gobitis*, April 6, 1940.

10. Brief of Respondents, *Minersville School District v. Gobitis*, April 12, 1940.

11. Franklin D. Roosevelt, *Annual Message to Congress*, January 3, 1940.

12. See James MacGregor Burns, *Roosevelt: The Lion and the Fox, 1882–1940* (San Diego: Harcourt, Brace, Jovanovich, 1956), 457.

13. Franklin D. Roosevelt, *Annual Message to Congress*, January 3, 1936; Franklin D. Roosevelt, *Annual Message to Congress*, January 4, 1939; Roosevelt, *Annual Message to Congress*, January 3, 1940.

14. Roosevelt first utilized this phrase in his audio address to the nation on December 29, 1940. In that speech, he described the global conflict, which the United States had not yet officially entered, as "a last-ditch war for the preservation of American independence." FDR argued: "Never before since Jamestown and Plymouth Rock has our American civilization been in such danger as now." Just three months before, Germany had joined an alliance with Italy and Japan. As FDR saw it, "The Nazi masters of Germany have made it clear that they intend not only to dominate all life and thought in their own country, but also to enslave the whole of Europe, and then to use the resources of Europe to dominate the rest of the world." In describing the aims and methods of totalitarianism, he stated: "The history of recent years proves that shootings and chains and the concentration camps are not simply the transient tools but the very altars of modern dictatorships. . . . The proposed 'new order' is the very opposite of a United States of Europe or a United States of Asia. It is not a government based upon the consent of the governed. . . . It is an unholy alliance of power and pelf to dominate and enslave the human race."

15. Franklin D. Roosevelt, *Third Inaugural Address*, January 20, 1941.

16. For a more thorough examination of the public statements and actions of executive branch officials eroding the Supreme Court's reading of the First Amendment, see Robert L. Tsai, "Reconsidering *Gobitis*: An Exercise in Presidential Leadership" (working paper on file with author); see also Mark Graber, "Counter-Stories: Maintaining and Expanding Civil Liberties in Wartime," in *The Constitution in Wartime: Beyond Alarmism and Complacency*, Mark Tushnet ed. (Durham, NC: Duke University Press, 2005), 95, 103–04.

17. *Jones v. City of Opelika*, 316 U.S. 584 (1942), vacated, 319 U.S. 103 (1943); see also *Murdock v. Commonwealth of Pennsylvania*, 319 U.S. 105 (1943).

18. *West Virginia State Board of Education v. Barnette*, 319 U.S. 624 (1943). Robert B. Westbrook, *Why We Fought: Forging American Obligations in World War II* (Washington, DC: Smithsonian Books, 2004), 62.

19. Brief of Appellees, *West Virginia Board of Education v. Barnette*, March 8, 1943, at 38, 75, 77. "Concurrently with the spread of totalitarianism," the students wrote, "various states of the Union passed laws requiring the compulsory flag salute in schools." Ibid., at 22.

20. E. J. Hobsbawm, *Nations and Nationalism Since 1780: Programme, Myth, Reality* (Cambridge, UK: Cambridge University Press, 1990), 85.

21. *Roth v. United States*, 354 U.S. 476, 484, 488 (1957).

22. Franklin D. Roosevelt, *Annual Address to Congress*, January 6, 1941. *Barnette*, 319 U.S. at 537–40.

23. *Barnette*, 319 U.S. at 647–60 (Frankfurter, J., dissenting).

24. W. H. Lawrence, "Civil Liberties Gain by the Flag Decision," *New York Times*, June 20, 1943, at E10.

25. Hannah Arendt, *The Origins of Totalitarianism* (San Diego: Harcourt, 1968), 325–36; Richard A. Primus, *The American Language of Rights* (Cambridge, UK: Cambridge University Press, 1999), 177.

26. Harry S. Truman, *Annual Message to the Congress on the State of the Union*, January 7, 1948.

27. Harry S. Truman, *State of the Union Address*, January 8, 1951.

28. Reagan made his intentions known at his First Inaugural: "It is time to check and reverse the growth of government, which shows signs of having grown beyond the consent of the governed." Ronald Reagan, *First Inaugural Address*, January 20, 1981. He also claimed that "the States created the Federal Government." For comparisons of presidential leadership, see William E. Leuchtenburg, *In the Shadow of FDR: From Harry Truman to George Bush* (Ithaca, NY: Cornell University Press, 1983); Skowronek, *The Politics Presidents Make*.

29. Ibid.

30. *United States v. Montalvo-Murillo*, 495 U.S. 711, 723 (1990) (Stevens, J., dissenting); *Terry v. Ohio*, 392 U.S. 1, 38 (1968) (Douglas, J., dissenting); *Russell v. United States*, 369 U.S. 749, 779 (1962) (Douglas, J., concurring).

31. Consider Justice Jackson's dissent in *Terminiello v. City of Chicago*: "Hitler summed up the strategy of the mass demonstration as used by both fascism and communism: 'We should not work in secret conventicles but in mighty mass demonstrations, and it is not by dagger and poison or pistol that the road can be cleared for the movement but by the conquest of the streets.'" 337 U.S. 1, 23–24 (1949).

32. *Stanley v. Georgia*, 394 U.S. 557, 560–65 (1969).

33. *Brandenburg v. Ohio*, 395 U.S. 444, 454–57 (1969).

34. *Tinker v. Des Moines Independent School District*, 393 U.S. 503, 508–11 (1969).

35. *Watchtower Bible and Tract Society of New York, Inc., v. Village of Stratton*, 536 U.S. 150 (2002).

36. *City of Erie v. Pap's A.M.*, 529 U.S. 277, 279–94 (2000).

37. *Young v. American Mini Theaters*, 427 U.S. 50, 61–71 (1976).

38. *Korematsu v. United States*, 323 U.S. 214, 214, 223, 240 (1944).

39. *Griswold v. Connecticut*, 381 U.S. 479 (1965). Much of Douglas's work is drawn from his dissent in the Supreme Court's earlier decision that a challenge to the anti-contraception law was not justiciable, though he toned down some of the stronger anti-Nazi rhetoric. *Poe v. Ullman*, 367 U.S. 497 (1961). There, he argued that "[t]he regime of a free society needs room for vast experimentation. . . . Yet to say that a legislature may do anything not within a specific guarantee of the Constitution may be as crippling to a free society as to allow it to override specific guarantees so long as what it does fails to shock the sensibilities of a majority of the Court." To Douglas, the law "is an invasion of the privacy that is implicit in a free society" because it "involves an inquiry into the relations between man and wife." In his most explicit reference to the legacy of the last war, he

quotes Robert L. Calhoun, professor at Yale Divinity School and author of "Democracy and Natural Law," *National Law Forum* 5 (1960): 31: "One of the earmarks of the totalitarian understanding of society is that it seeks to make all subcommunities — family, school, business, press, church — completely subject to control by the State. . . . In a democratic political order, this megatherian concept is expressly rejected as out of accord with the democratic understanding of social good, and with the actual make-up of the human community." Turning back to the Connecticut law, Douglas concluded: "The idea of allowing the State that leeway is congenial only to a totalitarian regime." 367 U.S. at 522.

40. *Lawrence v. Texas*, 539 U.S. 558, 562 (2003).

41. *Bowers v. Hardwick*, 478 U.S. 186 (1986).

42. Nelson Lund and John O. McGinnis have called *Lawrence v. Texas* "a paragon of the most anticonstitutional branch of constitutional law" and "a tissue of sophistries embroidered with a bit of sophomoric philosophizing." Nelson Lund and John O. McGinnis, "*Lawrence v. Texas* and Judicial Hubris," *Michigan Law Review* 102 (2004): 1555. Lino Graglia has argued that as an act of "judicial policymaking" the ruling "cannot in any sense be said to be a product of law," one that has "seemingly written libertarianism into the Constitution." Lino A. Graglia, "*Lawrence v. Texas*: Our Philosopher-Kings Adopt Libertarianism as Our Official National Philosophy and Reject Traditional Morality as a Basis for Law," *Ohio State Law Journal* 65 (2004): 1139.

Chapter Six. Adjudication as Facilitation

1. Lawrence Lessig, "Fidelity in Translation," *Texas Law Review* 71 (1993): 1165, 1173, 1209; see also William Michael Treanor, "The Original Understanding of the Takings Clause and the Political Process," *Columbia Law Review* 95 (1995): 782.

2. Larry Sager helpfully describes and critiques what he calls the "agency model" of constitutionalism. Lawrence G. Sager, *Justice in Plainclothes: A Theory of American Constitutional Practice* (New Haven: Yale University Press, 2004), 26, 30–31.

3. Robert H. Bork, *The Tempting of America* (New York: The Free Press, 1990), 151–53; John Hart Ely, *Democracy and Distrust: A Theory of Judicial Review* (Cambridge, MA: Harvard University Press, 1980), 73, 87, 116.

4. Bork, *The Tempting of America*, at 138.

5. Robert C. Post, *Constitutional Domains: Democracy, Community, Management* (Cambridge, MA: Harvard University Press, 1995), 48. Michael Dorf has usefully focused the question of constitutional design on the basic task of promoting "deep collaboration." Although he sets up the initial problem as one of legal indeterminacy, his perspective "invite[s] consideration of the institutional structures best suited to treating ambiguous legal texts as invitations to practical problem solving, constrained by commitments to popular sovereignty as well as to rights." Michael C. Dorf, "Legal Indeterminacy and Institutional Design," *New York University Law Review* 78 (2003): 875.

6. Robert A. Burt, *Constitution in Conflict* (Cambridge, MA: Belknap Press, 1992), 29. Prominent expositions of the backlash thesis as it relates to the struggle over racial justice can be found in Michael J. Klarman, *From Jim Crow to Civil Rights: The Supreme Court and the Struggle for Racial Equality* (New York: Oxford University Press, 2004);

Gerald N. Rosenberg, *The Hollow Hope: Can Courts Bring About Social Change?* (Chicago: University of Chicago Press, 1993).

7. Burt, ibid., at 358, 373.

8. *Isaiah* 2:1–4.

9. *Joel* 4:10.

10. Joseph Campbell, *The Power of Myth* (New York: Anchor Books, 1991), 107. According to Martha Nussbaum: "The literary imagination is a part of public rationality" that counteracts "refusals to imagine one another with empathy and compassion." She advocates "poetic judging," urging decision makers "to think of people's lives in the novelist's way." Martha C. Nussbaum, *Poetic Justice: The Literary Imagination and Public Life* (Boston, MA: Beacon Press, 1995), xvi–xvii, 99.

11. Bruce Ackerman, *We the People: Transformations*, Vol. 2 (Cambridge, MA: Belknap Press, 1998), 376.

12. *The Federalist* No. 16 (Hamilton). For an arresting account of how Americans have actually received the Constitution as a cultural object, see Michael Kammen, *A Machine That Would Go of Itself: The Constitution in American Culture* (New York: Knopf, 1986).

13. *The Federalist* No. 78 (Hamilton).

14. Jack N. Rakove, *Original Meanings: Politics and Ideas in the Making of the Constitution* (New York: Vintage Books, 1996), 187.

15. "Brutus XI," January 31, 1788, in *The Debate on the Constitution: Federalist and Antifederalist Speeches, Articles, and Letters During the Struggle Over Ratification, part 2: January to August 1788* (New York: Library of America, 1993), 129.

16. *The Federalist* No. 81 (Hamilton).

17. For a fascinating account of Americans' obsession with the countermajoritarian difficulty, see Barry Friedman, "The Birth of an Academic Obsession: The History of the Countermajoritarian Difficulty, Part Five," *Yale Law Journal* 112 (2002): 153; Barry Friedman, "The History of the Countermajoritarian Difficulty, Part One: The Road to Judicial Supremacy," *New York University Law Review* 73 (1998): 333.

18. James Madison, "Speech in Congress Proposing Constitutional Amendments," June 8, 1789, in *James Madison: Writings, 1772–1836* (New York: Library of America, 1999), 437–52; Letter from James Madison to John G. Jackson, Dec. 27, 1821 in *The Writings of James Madison*, Vol. IX, Gaillard Hunt ed. (New York: G. P. Putnam's Sons, 1910), 70, 75.

19. Letter from James Madison to Thomas Jefferson, October 17, 1788, in *James Madison: Writings, 1772–1836* (New York: Library of America, 1999), 418–23.

20. *The Federalist* No. 84 (Hamilton).

21. For a thoughtful exposition of Jefferson's intellectual contributions, see Stuart Gerry Brown, "The Mind of Thomas Jefferson," *Ethics* 73:2 (1963), 79.

22. Some historians have surmised that Jefferson's own struggles with debt caused him to have special insight into the psychological dimensions of debt management. Joseph Ellis, *American Sphinx: The Character of Thomas Jefferson* (New York: Knopf, 1997), 114.

23. The Jewish tradition is full of generational themes: after the Israelites' escape from Egypt, they are forced to wander for forty years — sufficient time for the generation born

and acculturated in captivity to die out — before they are permitted to enter the Promised Land. See generally *Exodus* 16:32–36; *Numbers* 33:1–44.

24. Letter from James Madison to Thomas Jefferson, February 4, 1790, in *James Madison: Writings, 1772–1836* (New York: Library of America, 1999), 473–77.

25. James Madison, "Speech in the Federalist Convention on Senate," June 26, 1787, in *James Madison: Writings, 1772–1836* (New York: Library of America, 1999), 110–11.

26. *The Federalist* No. 62 (Hamilton or Madison).

27. Richard Henry Lee of Virginia described the Constitution in these terms. "Letters from the Federal Farmer," in *The Complete Anti-Federalist*, 7 vols., Herbert J. Storing ed. (Chicago, 1981), 2: 249.

28. I rely here on Madison's own definition of a faction, which comprises either a minority or a majority of citizens so organized. *The Federalist* No. 10.

29. James Madison, "Government of the United States," *National Gazette*, February 6, 1792, in *James Madison: Writings, 1772–1836* (New York: Library of America, 1999), 508–09. Simeon Baldwin of Connecticut was part of this chorus: "The best system of government cannot insure freedom, riches, and national respect, without the vigilance, the industry and the virtuous exertions of the people." "Simeon Baldwin's Oration at New Haven, July 4, 1788," in *The Debate on the Constitution: Federalist and Anti-federalist Speeches, Articles, and Letters During the Struggle Over Ratification, Part 2: January to August 1788* (New York: Library of America, 1993), 514, 524.

Index